# HUNGRY

# ALSO BY DR. ROBIN L. SMITH

*Lies at the Altar: The Truth About Great Marriages*

*Inspirational Vitamins: A Guide to Personal Empowerment*

# HUNGRY

The Truth About Being Full

## DR. ROBIN L. SMITH

**HAY HOUSE, INC.**

Carlsbad, California • New York City
London • Sydney • Johannesburg
Vancouver • Hong Kong • New Delhi

*Published and distributed in the United States by:* Hay House, Inc.: www.hayhouse
.com® • *Published and distributed in Australia by:* Hay House Australia Pty. Ltd.:
www.hayhouse.com.au • *Published and distributed in the United Kingdom by:*
Hay House UK, Ltd.: www.hayhouse.co.uk • *Published and distributed in the
Republic of South Africa by:* Hay House SA (Pty), Ltd.: www.hayhouse.co.za •
*Distributed in Canada by:* Raincoast: www.raincoast.com • *Published in India
by:* Hay House Publishers India: www.hayhouse.co.in

*Cover and Interior design:* Tricia Breidenthal

**Library of Congress Cataloging-in-Publication Data**

Smith, Robin L.
Hungry : the truth about being full / Robin L. Smith. — 1st ed.
    p. cm.
ISBN 978-1-4019-4002-7 (hbk. : alk. paper) 1. Smith, Robin L.
2. Self-acceptance. 3. Self-realization. 4. Self-acceptance — Religious aspects —
Christianity. 5. Self-realization — Religious aspects — Christianity. I. Title.
    BF575.S37S65 2013
    158.1—dc23

                              2012036094

**Hardcover ISBN: 978-1-4019-4003-4**
**Digital ISBN: 978-1-4019-4004-1**

16 15 14 13    6 5 4 3
1st edition, February 2013
3rd edition, March 2013

Printed in the United States of America

## THIS BOOK IS DEDICATED TO

### *Dr. Warren E. Smith & Rosa Lee Smith*
*Daddy and Mommy, for giving me roots of love and
compassion, resilience, abundance, wisdom, generosity,
humor, and integrity and wings to fly with gentle grace
and fierceness into a life that I can truly call my own.*

### *Sandra E. Scott-Waller*
*For a friendship whose beauty reflects the glories of creation,
whose depth mirrors the endless floor of the ocean, and whose
breath expands across the galaxies of time and eternity.*

### *Kallan Noel Smith*
*My beloved Kalle—who healed my broken heart
with the indestructible gift of unconditional love and
invited me to love again the stranger who was myself.*

# CONTENTS

———————

# INVITATION

*"The most terrifying thing is to accept oneself completely."*

CARL JUNG

I'm being born as I give birth.

That's what writing *Hungry* felt like: childbirth, where the baby was breech. Writing this book was one of the most difficult and necessary assignments of my life. It turned my whole life and self upside down. I felt as though I was in a never-ending at-risk pregnancy, and I didn't know how to deliver a healthy *Hungry*. I had to fight to know, listen to, trust, and honor my voice. It was a brutal fight *to get my voice into the room* so that I could break a toxic cycle of silence—my tendency to inflate and trust the value of others' voices over my own.

Birthing *Hungry* severed the cord of invisibility and annihilation that had been strangling my life. There were those who told me that *Hungry* needed to be tamed and toned down, which created deep internal conflict and confusion. I didn't know whose voice to listen to or whose voice was *right*. I despaired to the point of thinking each voice knew more than I did; that they could discern God's voice better than I could. This had been the story of my life: always expected to be like someone else, to use someone else's language, to write a book the way someone else thought I should. All the while ignoring what my inner voice was saying to me. Making *Hungry* my own baptized me. It forced me to reclaim my true identity and authentic voice. To honor my truth.

I could not have imagined the journey I would take as I wrote this book. I traveled to destinations as close as hidden self-loathing, and even closer, like the discovery of the self-love that reclaimed me once and for all. I once heard actress Debra Winger refer to life as a "mortality sandwich," full of joys and sorrows, ups and downs, successes and failures, tragedies and triumphs, answers that leave us with many more questions, life and death . . . immortality and mortality, beginnings and endings. That is what much of this writing process has involved for me.

*Hungry* is about awakening and becoming conscious about our thoughts, feelings, and actions. It's not about the hunger for food, but the craving to reclaim and embrace our true identity. It's not about making a plan or signing up for a program to change our lives or relationships. It is about signing up to be a witness to our own lives and journeys. *Hungry* is about awakening to the pangs of our longings; about finding ways to be kind and compassionate to parts of ourselves that we dislike, dishonor, or which bring us shame. There are no lofty goals to achieve or high hurdles to jump over. *Hungry* is not about getting rid of our hunger—it's about embracing it. Telling the truth, at least to ourselves, about what we deeply long for, want, and need.

This is not a traditional self-help book, promising a quick or instant fix and then letting us down in the end. It's better: Rather than showing us how to fix what's broken, *Hungry* is about the birthright of our wholeness and the triumph of our humanity. It's my belief that true and transforming "self-help" is birthed from peeking in on how others have found their way through tough and turbulent times—and then seeing which parts of someone else's path speak to us.

Unlike many other professionals—psychologists, ministers, and healers—who seldom let the world *see* them, I recognize and embrace my faults, my humanness. Unfortunately, there is still an enormous amount of shame placed on the healer/expert for needing help. But we all need help. The power of the wounded healer is that the best healers, the most effective healers, are first in touch with their own woundedness and are therefore better able and equipped to help others on the path of feeling, facing, healing, living, and thriving. I proudly own the ups and downs of my own life, and I rejoice in my own healing. I wish for nothing more than for my experiences—and my imperfections—to remain with you as inspiration for your own healing. I hope that by opening a window into my own life, you will find some new insight into yours.

Taking this journey may be rough and rocky at times. But it's the beginning of creating a new life that is worthy of you. A life that is your own. The message written across the sky—and on every page of this book—is that "you are worthy, and it's okay to be you."

Being hungry is not an illness; it is not something to be cured or healed. Instead, it is something to be cared for, addressed, and attended to. This book is about stepping into your own story at whatever act you find yourself. It's about listening, watching, tasting, and learning from the wisdom within and without.

In this day of having instant access to the lives of others, we have often forgotten the necessity of having access to our own lives, feelings, and worlds. *Hungry* is inviting us to become voyeurs into our raw, real, and rough journeys with hunger as we uncover, discover, and find our way back to our real selves.

I hope that each word, in some small or large way, will whisper and sometimes even shout at you to *come home*, back to your truest self, with great compassion, empathy, and rugged grace.

There is an African tribe that at night whispers in their children's ears, "Be who you are." *Hungry* is the cry of every living soul, pleading with you to *be who you are!*

*Section I*

# HUNGRY

# CHAPTER 1

# Dying to Be
# Me and Hungry
# to Be Free

———•———

*"As the deer panteth after the water brooks,
so panteth my soul after thee, O God."*

PSALM 42:1

For so much of my life, I was *dying to be me and hungry to be free*. Even though I looked alive and vital, the hourglass measuring the aliveness of my soul was swiftly draining to the bottom. I was losing my battle to be myself. I was in my prime. My career was taking off; I was surrounded by loving friends and family. Yet it felt like time was running out.

I had always thought that by the time I was in my 40s, life would be good—maybe even great. I assumed that most of the kinks would have been ironed out to some degree. But from where

I stood, I wasn't 40-something and fabulous. On the outside, maybe. But inside I was 40-something and falling, faking, and failing. If I added one more "F" to the list, I would be a goner.

My chance to embrace joy fully—and to satisfy my deep hunger to be *me*—was quickly coming to a close. I had worked diligently to make my dreams come true, so that I would be what I considered successful and established by age 40. I finished high school at age 16 and went directly to college, graduating early at the age of 20. I then went on to seminary, completed my master's degree, and got married one week after graduation. Soon thereafter I entered my doctoral program and established my private practice.

When I was 27, my beloved father got sick and died unexpectedly. With his death went life as I knew it. By 28, I was separated from my husband. I was financially, spiritually, emotionally, and physically broken, yet I continued to grow my private practice and even entered the media world. I weathered each storm and moved forward; still counting on life stabilizing and turning around by the time I reached 40. Little did I know! While I exceeded my professional goals and aspirations by that age, the ship of my life— of my happiness, satisfaction, and authenticity—could still sink. And sink it did.

When I was younger, I had been an accomplished sprinter. But nothing had prepared me for the race I entered in my 40s—the race for my life, my voice, and my identity. If something didn't change soon, I was going to wither and fade away. I had checked off the items on my "to accomplish" list thinking that once I got to the end of the list I would be able to breathe with ease. To my surprise, the more checkmarks I accumulated, the faster the rest of my life began to plummet. It was like an inverted statistical relationship: The bigger things got in my professional world, the less access I had to my true identity. Even as I was ascending into the stratosphere where dreams come true, I was also descending into hell's kitchen. I endured failed love relationships, broken commitments, unmet expectations, disappointments, and betrayals. And all the while the media industry reminded me that I was nothing more than window dressing, soon to be replaced with a newer mannequin.

In 2010, when I was involved in a very serious automobile accident, I had no idea that the worst was yet to come: my bank account was depleted, my assets were wiped out, I had to apply to various hardship assistance programs, my home was burglarized, my beloved dog, Kalle, became very ill and it looked like she wouldn't recover, and a rainstorm flooded and destroyed the lower level of my home. I felt like I couldn't go on.

Later that year I received a promising call. I was offered a professional opportunity, which on the surface seemed like my saving grace. After eight months, however, I was given the news, "We don't want you." Penniless, spiritless, stripped, and dead, I added to my horrors the knowledge that I was being told, "You are not what we want." How could my story end this way?

There were two wake-up calls that came in quick succession. The first was the diagnosis of a fatal dis-ease. (Not the kind you might think, but deadly nonetheless.) The next was a rumbling in my belly, a discovery of the kind of hunger that food could not satiate. Let me tell you about both of them.

## DIAGNOSIS: DYING TO BE ME

I finally gave myself permission to stop running and to listen to myself. Well, that's not exactly true. I got stopped in my tracks. I didn't have the presence of mind or the courage to stop myself, so like any good parent who loves their child, I had been stopped by a force that loved me even when I didn't know how to love myself. I call that loving force *God*.

I was never physically spanked as a child, but life has a way of disciplining its children who don't, can't, or won't listen. At that moment it was like a loving parent had pulled me aside and ordered me into "time-out," a period to breathe, reflect, and recalibrate. This was not a vacation, but time for me to really get to know myself.

During this time, I remember receiving two direct messages from God. The first, I wrote on a yellow Post-it—which I still carry in my wallet. It says, "I'm not in 'time-out' because I was bad or naughty, but because I wouldn't slow down." The second message came when I finally collapsed and could barely get out of bed for any reason. I wondered what was wrong with me, whether I was sick, overly exhausted, or depressed. All I heard was, "Robin, you're on bed rest." All of my systems had to be shut down while I was dismantled emotionally and physically. Even my spiritual life as I had known it had to go on hiatus until I healed from the inside out. I was scared to death! So much needed to be done, including completing this book and making a living again, so I wouldn't lose more than I'd already lost. But I was paralyzed. It felt like rigor mortis had set in and taken up permanent residence.

Had I listened sooner—paid attention to the signs, to the flaming fire-engine-red flags—might my butt not be so sore, my heart not so scarred, my soul more rested? I'll never know, because I hadn't listened before. But I was listening now.

What I heard was a diagnosis. It did not come from a doctor, or any external source. It came from within. And it was terminal.

"I am dying to be me."

For months I had been searching. I literally roamed—through my house, the woods, the community, the supermarket, the streets, and the co-op. I drove around aimless, feeling lost. The journaling that had for years offered comfort became alien to me. I searched books and billboards, hungry for answers and peace. I wandered and wondered, perplexed as to why my world had fallen apart. I wondered if my life was going to end on this harsh note—broken, bitter, and shattered.

"Oh my God," I kept saying over and over to myself. "Oh my God."

(Not "Oh my goodness," mind you. The goddess of goodness could not handle this one.)

Like a mantra, I kept repeating it. "I'm dying to be me. I'm dying to be me." But unlike the fatal diagnosis it was, it felt somehow . . . good. It was like I had been reunited with a long-lost

friend or relative, who knew me as well
knew myself. I had no desire to run away
fatal blow of information. Somewhere, I had a str
ic relief, as if all the running, hiding, maneuvering,
dodgeball with my soul's hunger, my deeper feelings, w
I was *glad*. I had been *apprehended* by the loving hands of Go
was forbidden to go on one more day pretending. Pretending that
I wasn't dying to be me.

The prognosis wasn't good. Something needed to change in
a real way. It wasn't that I needed to do anything drastic, but I
had to do something *real*, something that would get to the root of
my pain and suffering. I had already spent years doing one kind
of extreme makeover transformation after another. There was the
motel in the Arizona desert—my own form of inpatient hospital-
ization. There were the years of intensive therapy, delving into
every self-help book and spiritual retreat experience I could find. I
planned a gathering with some of my closest friends who flew in
to Philadelphia from around the country to be midwives to each
other. We engaged in a process of trying to give birth to and embrace our true selves, with the help of my therapist/wisdom guru.

Somehow I knew that facing myself in these ways would be a
dangerous journey. But what I also knew was that continuing to
run from and neglect my true self was even more dangerous, destructive, and draining. I no longer wanted to live a life that was
not mine, a life that would come and go, a life in which I would
have lived and died as a slave. I would not live and die asleep,
choosing fantasy over the richness of God's abundant love and
presence.

I had no idea that my answer and healing was not to be found
in *doing*. I did not know that another session with a spiritual guru
couldn't touch what I was hungry for. I didn't understand that my
healing was in stopping, coming to a halt, rather than searching
for another fix. Instead, each time I thought, *This is the fix . . . this
will do it*. Only to discover weeks, months, or years later that I was
just as trapped as ever. I now understood the harder truth. If you
want to be free, you have to pay the piper.

as—if not better than—I
nge and euphor-
from this potentially
and playing
ss over.
I

But I had no idea what
One day at home, while
n the storage room for a
.bled onto more than I was
ound. Twenty years of bleed-
ent colors of ink highlighted
began as a simple task became
ger for real love and acceptance,
eality that I was "dying to be me."
: meltdown. I found myself going
, of journals as the tears flowed from
n, as if I was crying over the death of
my dear... I was. It was *me* who had died. I could
hardly bear to ... year after year, I had been living and
recording the same ni... .marish reality—my own death by starvation. Starvation for emotional and relational nourishment. I sat
on Kalle's soft aqua bed and cried my heart out. So *this* is what
had been wrong with me all these years. I had *always* been *dying
to be me.*

Once I put myself back together I thought, *Okay, I am dying to
be me. Now what should I do?* What was the treatment for people
like me? I knew that I couldn't be the only case; somehow I knew
this "illness" was far from rare. In fact, once I heard of it I knew in-
tuitively that "dying to be me" is the leading cause of death in the
world. Physical, emotional, spiritual, financial, and sexual death.
It's the creator of masks that suffocates our true life force. I started
to see incidents in the national and international news. I observed
how it runs in families, how it's even found in houses of faith.

There is a Hasidic tale of a rabbi who was asked which questions we might have to answer in the afterlife. Of all the deep
questions that any person could be asked, he replied, there was
only one that really mattered. It wasn't "Rabbi, why weren't you
Moses?" It was much simpler and closer to the bone of truth. The
question would be, "Rabbi, why weren't you *you*?"

My own case of "dying to be me" was so severe that if I were Catholic, I would have been given Last Rites. I was already having my deathbed come-to-Jesus moment. My wake-up call.

It took several years. I needed to write my next book, and was feeling pressure that it had to go number one like *Lies at the Altar*. Every idea sounded good at first, only to shatter into a million tiny pieces. My heart and hopes seemed to shatter at the same time. I had publishers and agents wanting my next big seller to flow from within, but the machine I used to be—the one that could crank out creative magic—was stalled. I wondered when I was going to be found out. I had told my best friend and those closest to me about my dis-ease, but I don't think they believed that things were as bad for me as they were.

"Maybe my season is over," I thought. "Maybe my life as I knew it has ended and I just can't accept reality." This was not the life that I planned for, nor the life I worked tirelessly to build.

Even though I had come to accept my diagnosis, still I was emotionally constipated and spiritually anemic. I was in a corner and there seemed no way out of my misery but through. I was working a little, but not enough to support myself. I was living off of my savings, which were quickly becoming as anemic as me. I was off on the inside and I couldn't find my center. There was something else I needed to know ___ I didn't know what it was. I needed to find a treatment for ___ " And it had to happen fast, because time was r___ for my life.

## I'M HUNGRY

I had just finished shoot___ to be a real disappointmen___ return on my investment l___ in my body and every pa___ fried. Overcooked in the ___

I remember vividly t___ time, the hunger was r___

weekend, I felt absolutely insatiable. Nothing I ate, no matter how good it tasted, was satisfying. I always wanted more. I was famished, and food and eating were on my mind constantly. It was so not like me. I love to eat good food, and some would even call me a foodie, but this was different. I was *obsessed* with food. If I wasn't eating, I was thinking about what I would eat at my next meal, or what tasty snack might electrify my taste buds. I went to my favorite market several times during the weekend, and I also visited a few specialty food shops that I love. I was searching the shelves for something that would gratify my appetite. I love to cook, and I'm really good at it. I thought maybe if I cooked "this" or "that," maybe if I ate "this" or "that," I would be satisfied. Perhaps I'd make my secret luscious marinated grilled swordfish with fresh grilled veggies and a fabulous mixed greens salad with fresh berries and nuts. Or maybe I needed comfort food, and should make my delicious macaroni and cheese dish that I can't go to a family gathering without. Could it be that my body was crying out for something spicy—pan-seared salmon with fresh pressed garlic and lime juice squeezed straight from a ripe green lime? Maybe my homemade cornbread stuffing would quench and quiet my untamed hunger.

I was searching for what I could eat that would satisfy my demanding taste buds. Nothing hit the spot, and my desperation was elevating with each empty bite. *Was my body craving salt or sugar?,* I wondered. Had I developed a mineral deficiency that was making me ravenous? Something felt off. My body was begging for more, but more of *what*? I had no idea. Nothing I ate came even close to touching my hunger.

I was scheduled to attend a birthday party on Sunday afternoon, and as I begrudgingly got in my car and pulled out of my ge, I was already thinking about what food might be awaiting e. I was like an addict looking for my next fix of drugs or ly for me it was food. This was not the well-manicured aged *me*.

issahickon Avenue in Philadelphia, the wind-to clear the rain. My mood was quiet and surrendered. A few minutes into my drive, it hit me, and I said out loud, "I'm hungry!" The words flowed out of my mouth like living water, and as my ears heard the truth with clarity and precision, I knew something had shifted. I pulled my car over to the side of the road, opened the notes section of my phone, and typed in all-caps: I'M HUNGRY.

I didn't know at that moment that my life was about to change forever, but I did know that something big had just happened. I hadn't yet put together that this was the missing piece of my puzzle—and the second half of my diagnosis. That knowing I was hungry would help me solve the ongoing mystery of *dying to be me*.

The rest of the way to the birthday party I went through a litany of what I was truly hungry for in my life:

I'm *hungry* for real love—not crumbs I try to call a meal.

I'm *hungry* for relationships where respect is the cornerstone of the connection.

I'm *hungry* to be in relationships that don't require me to dim my bright light in order to be offered a seat at the table.

I'm *hungry* to have my gifts and talents truly appreciated by those I work with.

I'm *hungry* to not need to dumb myself down so that others feel smart.

I'm *hungry* to be beautiful and sexy and not a Barbie doll for a man.

I'm *hungry* to have a partner who doesn't feel like a predator.

I'm *hungry* for passion and great sex that is worthy of my mind, body, and spirit.

I'm *hungry* to not have to play small when my spirit and dreams are big.

I'm *hungry* to be brave and not let fear drive my life. I'm hungry for an undivided self, soul, life, love, and relationship.

I'm *hungry* to know I am loved and am irrevocably a child of God.

I'm *hungry* to be me.

Enraptured by my revelation, I prayed, "God, your child is *hungry*. I want more. I want the real thing, not fake, not airbrushed, not a wannabe. I'm hungry for a real life and a real *me*."

That was my turning point. I love to share it, because it speaks truth to the lie that insatiable hunger should be hidden or disguised—that it is shameful, inappropriate, or a sign of weakness.

I began to notice with fresh eyes the gnawing discomfort of the people I encountered at speaking engagements, at parties, on planes, or street corners. I felt such empathy for their pain. I tuned into their hunger—the shame, the loss of self and identity, the feeling of not being enough, the inner brutalization going on in their lives. I could see that they were terrified of speaking their own difficult truths—like people at a party who, when asked how they're doing, respond, "Great, great." Or those at church who have the pat answer, "I'm blessed and highly favored." There is no permission to say, "I'm blessed—and I feel like mess." I always think those family holiday letters, the ones giving people the update on all that is good in life, do such a disservice. There is no voice given to the tender difficulties and the raw places that life demands we face. All the faking does nothing but make us more and more hungry, force-feeding illusions that only a photoshop program can create. Lies, pretending, and hiding make us even hungrier—and, ultimately, send us into a condition of starvation.

I watched people accepting without question the big lie: In order to be worthwhile, we have to get with the program and let other people define our value. We have to fill our plates with delicacies that someone else chooses for us, and not complain if they aren't to our liking. And we have to look perfect while doing it! What an impossible and soul-draining burden.

## REJECTING THE FAKE

In 2006, when I wrote *Lies at the Altar: The Truth About Great Marriages*, I was beginning to explore the corrosive power of lies—those we tell ourselves and each other. I knew that the carefully created romantic façade was destroying solid marriages, and that love and trust could not thrive where truth was not allowed. I knew that it was a dicey proposition to write about real love in committed relationships without selling the "love cocktail" as the obtainable goal. But it is the wearing off of the love cocktail that uncovers and unmasks our deepest longings and hungers for more than what we are settling for. The love cocktail makes real love seem boring and dead, when the opposite is true. Fantasy is great for a moment, but it's not sustainable and all it does is create an insatiable hunger that nothing and no one can satisfy.

Yet, when I began to talk about building truth into the marriage preparation period, many people responded with sheer terror. At book signings women would whisper to me, "If he knew this about me . . . " Men in passing let me know that they would rather die than allow a woman to get close to their vulnerability, where she might play the blame-shame game. People were aghast when I said they couldn't just bury their truths and expect to live happily ever after. On the premarriage frontier, the lies and the hiding were huge. This was also the case for the many couples in long-term relationships and marriages where the couple would be multimillionaires had they purchased stock in the Krazy Glue they used to hold their relationships together. Many couples had become prisoners to their own lies, to their shame, to their ego-driven hunger for image over the real thing. In this society, it's not hard to understand why so many people are choosing superficiality over substance. Why celebrating a silver or golden anniversary has nothing to do with joy and connection, but is often a big celebration with elaborate masks where no can tell anymore what is a mask and what is real. We've become too skilled for our own good at "wearing the mask that grins and lies."

So much is fake: fake breasts, fake hair, fake teeth with the fake smile to go along with the fake happiness, fake intimacy, fake investments. Fake, fake, fake. In our obsession with reality television, we ignore the fact that very little of what we call reality TV is even remotely real. The same is true for our lives.

That same dynamic is at the heart of this book. The message I want to get across is a breakthrough for those who have hidden their hunger and desires for so long they don't even know what's real anymore. I speak from the heart, because I, too, denied my hunger and was ashamed of it. Now with each day, I live more in the freedom of truth. I fully embrace when I am hungry and do my best to attend to my needs. What I'm not doing anymore is pretending to be full when I am starving to death. Living in the truth saves, restores, and renews my life daily, and I want to pass that gift on.

# CHAPTER 2

# HUNGRY FOR MY SELF

*"And the day came when the risk to remain tight in a bud was more painful than the risk it took to blossom."*

COMMONLY ATTRIBUTED TO ANAÏS NIN

One day I was cleaning out a closet and I came across a small box I had received as a gift. I opened it curiously, not remembering what was inside or who had given it to me. Nestled on a bed of white tissue was a plaque bearing a large gold star trimmed in black. Below was the inscription, A STAR IS BORN, with a glistening card that read YOU'RE A STAR. I shrugged and began to toss it in the trash, and then I stopped, staring at it. I was struck by a sudden and intense thought: *Who is the person who had once received this as a gift?* I didn't identify with her at all. But suddenly I remembered exactly what it was about . . . something I thought I *had* to be.

Years earlier, when I had the privilege and honor to work regularly as an on-air psychologist, many people thought I was a star.

This fed a longtime fantasy of mine: the hunger to be successful and known. I had no idea that the success I wanted had to do with becoming my true self, the person I was meant to be at my core. At the time I thought I had to be someone else. I clearly remember brainstorming my brand and status with a friend and mentor who called me "Star." Together we were excited and celebrated the future that we hoped would be mine. "You've made it!" gushed another friend, after I had been given one of the greatest media opportunities of my professional life, which spilled over into my personal life. That break led to several years of amazing experiences working in TV and radio. I had been given a generous opportunity that was validating to my spirit and opened doors to an international platform. I will be forever grateful for this and the many blessings provided and used by God to help direct me to my true path.

One of the biggest gifts I gained from this experience was what in the music industry they call "blowing up": making it big, becoming a celebrity. This soothed my insecurities, but it also led me to create a façade that eventually blew up in my face.

When the other shoe dropped, it was harsh. It was painful. It was as if my life had been set ablaze. So much fell apart, yet the process greatly gifted me with what was true, what remained, what the fire could not destroy. I had been so *hot* and in demand that I was on 14 planes in 13 days going from keynote to keynote, appearance to appearance, in and outside of the United States. Then one day I looked up, and my calendar was empty. What had I done wrong? I had the same affirming message, the same warm personality, the same "Dr. Robin believes in you" spirit, but no one wanted me. How had my oh-so-hot status become my cooling board—the slab a dead person lies on?

Luckily my cooling board ultimately became my springboard, launching me toward my true identity and the life that was mine to live. Out of the ashes and rubble of my life, I was born anew. I came to know, feel, and taste the luscious flavor of a hunger for myself, the hunger to live my life full-time—not as a part-time lover of myself. Since that time, even if others reject me

or are unfaithful, I have a clear convicti
betray myself.

But back before the disaster, I was w
took to live my dream. A local newspaper
ing that I had been "anointed" by someoi
cessful and esteemed. While it was intoxic
the seductive power of seeing that in print.
a religious significance in its affirmation.
long for—to be chosen, to be admired, to bc applauded? Because
I did not know who I was or was meant to be, I was willing to go
through any makeover necessary for my anointment to take hold.
Public performance requires that people look like more than they
really are. It's like playing dress-up when I was a little girl, using
my mother's clothes and makeup. I felt the fun and thrill all over
again. I was willing to do what I needed to shine . . . to stand out . . .
to be visible . . . to be exceptional.

Today, when I have my hair and makeup done to appear publi-
cally, I am reminded that the "everyday me" is considered *not good
enough*. But back then, the more the beast of "glam" was fed, the
further I pulled away from myself. Today when I look at pictures
of myself then, I don't even recognize myself. I was like a living
Barbie: bendable, breakable, plastic.

I thought that I had to sell a different self. In the process, I put
myself up for sale.

I imagine that many who watched me on television or listened
to me on the radio wondered, "Is she for real?" I played the part I
was given beautifully. But deep down I was so scared of not being
special that I did what I knew how to do and had always done: I
worked overtime to adapt and please.

I was battling desperately to maintain a fragment of my essential self, and finding it almost impossible to do in that unwavering
spotlight. Later, when I was asked to do a pilot for a daytime TV
show, the producers said, "We want you to dress like Mrs. Obama."
That was a bit perplexing, but I said, "Okay," and thought, *Whatever that means. She is beautiful, brilliant and has a style all her own,
but here I am being asked yet again to be someone else. If you hired me,*

*t wanting me to be me?* I brought to rehearsal a pink sleeve-
dress that I thought looked great.

"No," they said. "Mrs. Obama wears yellow."

I explained, "Yellow looks terrible on me. My skin tone is different than hers."

They just stared at me, while I experienced what could only be
described as being out of body. A line popped into my head from
the poet David Whyte: "The soul would rather fail at its own life
than succeed at someone else's."

My soul was dying to be me and I was beginning to know it.

My experiences being feted in the media were exhilarating.
I had more offers to speak, preach, and teach around the world.
But did they really want *me,* the real me, the me who was dying to
be *me?* Being in demand with television executives can make you
feel so special—until you're not. Not surprisingly, my moment in
the spotlight was fleeting. And while it lasted, it was only partially
real. I was conscious of being asked to make a choice: be *me* or
be accepted by *them*. For a time I wavered. It was an old habit of
mine—dressing up the dead reality to look alive. Maybe I could
pull it off one more time. But my soul was exhausted from fear.
The dis-ease to please had taken its toll. I had finally had enough,
and I couldn't make it work. I ran out of gas and could no longer
find meaning in living a life that was not my own.

Baskin-Robbins has a flavor of the month, and there is a lot
of hoopla around promoting that flavor. But after a few weeks it
is discontinued and replaced by a new flavor of the month. What
happens to all those discontinued flavors? They just disappear. I
myself was starting to feel like last month's flavor.

I had a new question: "When your self is externally referenced,
what happens when the reference is taken away?"

In my case I experienced great loss and felt a sense of emptiness. The darkness pressed in on me, challenging my optimism
and good nature. The world seemed to be conspiring against me.
A series of brutal events followed, as if to cement my status as a
hopeless case. I was running on empty, and life furthered my hunger by piling on losses.

I wasn't angry with God or life, or with anyone. I felt dead, and dead people can't feel anything.

The Universe was trying to get my attention, and it seemed to be working overtime in every area of my life. As I surveyed the inner and outer wreckage, the questions pounded at me with the force of a tsunami:

If the worst happens, if the mask is stripped off, who am I?

Am I still a self?

Am I still worthy?

Can I exist and matter to myself if I don't exist and matter to others?

Those questions became the signposts on the journey I was meant to travel. I was often limping and crying along the way, but this journey saved my life. This journey *gave me* my life. I found that when all the glorious masks and protective helmets were pulled away, I was hungry—ravenous even—for *myself*. I came to see that the events that felt so unfair, harsh, and cruel were necessary for the painful birth of the self for which I had been longing and craving.

As hard as it was, not a day goes by when I wake up wanting to go back to the woman I was before, a prisoner who did not own her own identity.

I came to understand that I could anoint *myself*, literally and figuratively. Or, more importantly, I could be anointed—not for any accomplishments or achievements, but as a child of God. I could be anointed for *being me full-time*, not part-time but all the time, for better or worse. I could make a vow to be faithful to myself. To love, honor, and cherish myself, in sickness or in health, for richer or poorer, until death. What a grand revelation!

In my book, *Lies at the Altar*, I acknowledged Ms. Oprah Winfrey for "being the bridge that brought me back to myself." Seven years later, I look at those words and realize that they were truer than I could have imagined at the time. Back then I meant that she significantly contributed to launching me professionally in a way that I could only have dreamed. I had just ended a very destructive relationship, and working for Oprah helped me save my home. It allowed me to get back on my feet and breathe without fear and trembling. Her affirmation, encouragement, and endorsement not only allowed *Lies at the Altar* to make it to the market, but made it the instant commercial success it was. So when I gave her that acknowledgment, I was thanking her for the way she supported my career.

But my soul knew better. The opportunities Oprah gave me provided the arena—and the motivation—to find my true self. It was through the recognition I got from working on her show that my image was "blown up"—which had been my dream. But my image was not me. It was merely my persona, with all my masks and nuances. The Barbie doll I created to please the world. It is only now that I really understand everything that happened—and how it had to happen, in order for me to become free.

Today, I unashamedly understand and embrace that I was simply dying to be me. Over time "Barbie" woke up, spoke up, and grew up!

The pope anoints babies, and the masses who beg for the blessing of his touch. Celebrities can anoint their favorite clothing designers, trainers, or hairdressers. But can people anoint themselves and each other? And if so, what would that look like? I had to ask myself what it truly means to be anointed. Could I anoint myself? Can spouses and partners, families and friends, bless and anoint one another? And what about a stranger? Can someone unknown anoint a fellow traveler?

In ancient religious traditions, someone was anointed by a holy appointed person—a person who was sanctioned to anoint others. This is still the case in many places throughout the world. As a child growing up, I had the great privilege of attending different Protestant churches of various denominations. My family went from a black Baptist church in our neighborhood, to a Presbyterian church in West Philadelphia, to a Church of God where more of my formative (and fun) time was spent. At this last stop, God seemed to be less uptight. Play and fun were encouraged, all while learning spiritual lessons. I attended a Quaker school for ten

years of my life and enjoyed the rich tradition of the Quaker Meeting for all of those years. (I still love going to Quaker Meetings. I always meet myself there, being invited to slow down, breathe, listen, and just "be" instead of "do.") My early days were also enriched by going to synagogue with many of my Jewish friends, who would in turn come to Sunday school or church with me.

I was always a seeker, wide open to new and ancient ways of experiencing God, Love, and Truth. For me, those three words are all one. In college, I took classes in world religions and tasted the richness of how others hungered to know, touch, and embrace the divine. I studied Buddhism, Islam, Hinduism, Taoism, and other traditions that have less name recognition. In all of them, there is an understanding that being anointed is part of taking back our lost or stolen identity.

The idea of "anointing" is most often used in reference to clergy or leadership anointing a follower. It's not necessarily kosher for an average John Doe to affirm and bless life and its value. Be that as it may, each person must figure out for himself how to receive the blessing that sends the message that each life counts—and to figure out how to have worth and value even if society, lovers, and employers kick us to the curb. Self- and other-anointing is essential on this human journey. Ultimately, each life is anointed and seen as special and of value simply because *we are here*. That's all: We are here, and not by any choice or decision of our own.

I have been anointed by clergy, family, friends, and strangers, and I have many times anointed myself. I have been anointed and have anointed others. I have been reminded of my virtue, value, and worth. I have been the memory for others when they couldn't find their own. One definition of anointed means "to rub, daub, or touch the head with ointment"; another says, "People and things are anointed to symbolize the introduction of a sacramental or divine influence, a holy emanation, spirit, power, or God. It can also be seen as a spiritual mode of ridding persons and things of dangerous influences." We hunger to be who we were born to be. We hunger to have people in our lives who desire our freedom and emancipation from the slavery of trying to be someone other

than who we are. We hunger to love the skin we're in, and to wear clothing that fits our values and beliefs. We hunger for what's real. It is challenging to reconnect with who we were before life, family, racism, sexism, ageism, faith and religious bigotry, poverty, and classism beat the living life out of us. If we don't have a real self, we have nothing. We may seem to have it all—expensive and fancy houses or cars; mannequin-looking spouses; all the Wall Street, Microsoft, or megachurch money in the world—but we are still poor beggars hungering for a real self, the most valuable commodity on the global market.

There is a gospel song that says, "Sometimes you have to encourage yourself." There have been times in my life—often in the darkest hours, where fear was breathing down my neck and doubt whispered ever-so-loudly, "Robin, you won't make it . . . "—in those times I have had to anoint and encourage myself. Maybe I couldn't get to my best friends, maybe my mentors weren't available, maybe my therapist was away on vacation, my pastor might have been occupied at the hospital bedside of someone dying, and maybe my significant other couldn't help me because he was caught up trying to save and restore his own life.

I was left having to depend on myself. To speak life, worth, value, affirmation, acceptance, comfort, and love to myself. In those moments, I could only count on God and me—and our anointing.

## THE SACRED QUEST FOR SELF

I embarked on a quest, suspecting that this wasn't just my struggle. Everywhere I looked people were hungry, starving to death. The truth is we are all craving to be who we were born to be, and our souls are crying, "I'm dying to be me." People gorge themselves with something, but still feel desperate and insatiable. We are starving ourselves of our true natures, hoping to find salvation in invisibility and compliance. Everyone is trying to fit in, wearing someone else's ideas of acceptability. Going along to get along. We are in an image-obsessed world where terms like

craving, insatiable, and starving are pathologized due to their association with weight. We are missing the real point. Weight is a demonized scapegoat for other social dis-eases. When weight is an issue, it is a symptom of the soul's hunger and our refusal to hear its cry. We are fixated on weight and don't seem to care about the soul. We have gym memberships, but what about a gym for the soul? The soul is starving and demands to be heard. Much of our suffering is about hunger.

What is hunger? It's a deep longing and a need to be truly known, accepted, respected, loved, valued, seen, and heard by the self and others. When hunger is neglected, ignored, denied, shamed, blamed, or misunderstood it makes us even hungrier. Actually, we become ravenous and feel insatiable. The more we deny our hunger pains, the stronger our cravings become, leading us to act out destructively—because hungry people do desperate things. This desperation might be manifested in overachieving, underachieving, depression, false elation, seeking power, becoming powerless, being a victim, being a victimizer, or having emotional and/or sexual affairs. Hunger has many faces, but one way or another it demands to be fed. As my mother used to say, "If it doesn't come out in the wash, it will come out in the rinse." Hunger unattended is a tormenter. It destroys our ability to live with joy, peace, and well-being and to love ourselves and others. But hunger *listened to* is an amazing teacher and guide.

Hunger is a constant. We hear the rumblings of hunger pains everywhere. I was on an emotional and spiritual starvation diet for most of my life. I didn't know it. I hadn't a clue. I was trying to compensate. The thing is, I wasn't really aware of it until the pains and the growling in my heart got too loud to ignore. I kept thinking I was imagining things, that I should be full and content. Which was ridiculous and impossible given how few of my relationships were sustaining and supporting me. It was as if I'd been invited to a five-star restaurant and was served only water. I suffered, watching others dine—and then wondered why my stomach was so empty. I was *that* unplugged from my true needs. I was afraid to feel what I felt and to know what I knew. I knew if

I owned my starvation, I wasn't going to be able to stay on the "go along to get along" train. I didn't know what was going to happen, but I knew I had to pull the emergency stop cord immediately. I wanted off and I wanted off *now*. I needed an up-close and personal, fresh, and honest encounter with my needs and desires, and with reality. As I look back on those years, it is frightening. I am amazed that I survived.

## THE STOLEN SELF

Hunger comes with being human. When we are ashamed of our hunger to get our needs met, it is comparable to being ashamed of our humanity. As I listened carefully to myself and others, I heard apology after apology for being hungry and human. Hunger is a huge part of being fully and unapologetically human. Hunger comes with the territory; it's our divine birthright and needs no explanation or apology.

My youngest niece just had her first baby. She and her husband are elated, as is our entire family. There were a few tender touch-and-go moments, but all is wonderfully well. Their baby—my fifth grandniece—was born in a high-tech, state-of-the-art new hospital.

Being in the hospital with all those babies had me thinking: what if there was a mix-up? As if coming out of the womb wasn't traumatic enough, now you've been given the wrong nametag and you're taken home and raised by the wrong family. It's not as impossible as any parent would hope. And for the child it's the ultimate nightmare—to find that you have been living someone else's life. But many of us live a spiritual form of identity theft, having our original selves stolen before we could choose for ourselves. We've been forced to live an identity that is not our own.

When we don't know who we are, we're set up to get involved in dead relationships, dead-end jobs, and joyless days. There is no life force flowing when we are living a life that is not true to who we are.

Recently, I gave an address to a women's conference in Washington, D.C. I spoke about identity theft, beginning with my own. Like many groups that invite me to speak, this one mostly knew of me from my television and radio persona. When I arrived, everyone was very polite, but somewhat formal—as if they were speaking to a celebrity, not a real person. Only I knew that we were about to get close to the bone of truth, to share a real emotional experience. And that's what happened. By the time I left, we all had tears in our eyes. Why? Because we had come to the banquet hungering for much more than the well-catered meal. We all arrived hungry for a glimpse of our real selves, and I opened up that possibility for us.

Taking off the mask was so releasing and such a relief. "How heavy that mask of falseness is," I told them. "How troubling to have to constantly decide which mask to put on every day—which person to be when you are afraid to risk being yourself. You have a choice in every moment of every day to let your God-given and God-loved face and soul shine through—and not to be like a part-time lover who cheats on you and whispers sweet nothings in your ear. You are hungry to be seen, hungry to be special, hungry to be you." Wearing the mask is bad enough; even worse is *thinking the mask is the real you.* Forgetting that, underneath the mask, *you* are suffocating and crying out to be set free. We choose our masks based on our audience. How crazy it feels to answer your doorbell expecting a family member, only to learn that it's a friend who you feel judged by when you're not dressed to the nines. You open the window, saying, "Just a minute, I'm just getting out of the shower" when actually, you are fully clothed—just not in something you feel is "good enough" to wear for your "friend." What that moment calls for is to feel secure enough to be yourself.

My mother is old school. She's 90 years old, still elegant and regal, smart and proud, supportive and stately. She has always been beautiful, but in her family, she was made to feel like the "smart one." My aunt, who is 92, was made to feel like the "beautiful one." Both of these smart, beautiful, capable, and competent women were stripped of parts of their identities and have spent most of their lives trying to compensate for parts of themselves that they thought were not there. They couldn't see themselves clearly and fully because of the messages of others. Hate is a strong word, but my mother hates when I share stories about our family that are less than glamorous and flattering. She, like the rest of us, carries shame for her hunger and for the hunger of her children, grandchildren, and extended family. At times my mother and my father, without meaning to, shamed our hunger because of the shame they carried about their own.

It is glorious to give and receive, to embrace and accept that we are all hungry and that being hungry is part of being human. The equation for me is: HUMAN = HUNGRY and HUNGRY = HUMAN. There is no way around the fact that all of creation is hungry. Human beings seem to be the only corner of creation that apologizes for what is natural, organic, and part of the plan. We seem to want to be anything and everything except who and what we *are*.

## THE STARVING SOUL

Denying being hungry is living in the desert of deprivation. It's similar to the delirium that happens when a person has not had ample food or water. They start seeing mirages that reflect the balm of a gentle breeze, the soothing taste of an ice-cold drink, and the fragrant cornucopia of a lavish spread. But none of it is real. Perhaps the starving person dies imagining that all the plenty in the world is at hand. But she dies nonetheless.

Starvation is the result of living with the false nourishment of half-truths and lies, rather than the real nourishment of compassion and truth. At first, the falsehoods may feel exhilarating and filling, but their empty calories will eventually take their toll. It is important to separate fact from fiction and truth from lies or misinformation. For example:

**Fiction: Always putting others
first is the best way to live.**

**Truth: It is costly to ignore and deny yourself.**

All relationships require give and take. It's how we get along in the world. But there's a difference between compromising and collapsing. No one has the right to ask you to sacrifice yourself—to abort yourself—to accommodate their preferences and practices. You have to figure out what's negotiable and non-negotiable. I struggled with this for most of my life until a wise counselor said to me, "It's okay to have preferences." What a great revelation that was! Looking back I could see that I'd been fighting for my integrity all along. I remember going with my mother to register for plates before my wedding. I loved a particular set—they were black. The following conversation ensued:

Mother: "Robin, you cannot register for black plates."
Me: "Why not?"
Mother: "It's not done."
Me: "But I like them."

This type of circular discussion was common for us. My mother thought it was in poor taste to register black plates.

Being a pleaser is denying you have a self. It's giving yourself over to another's needs without taking care of your own. There is a difference between being generous and living to please. The truth is that giving can leave a person feeling ripped off. Giving without boundaries makes a victim of the giver, and can create a boiling pot of resentment. Making your life about pleasing others doesn't elevate you or give the recipient of your desperate largesse anything of value.

**Fiction: If you reveal your real self, you'll be rejected.**

**Truth: If you're encouraged to be someone other than your real self, that is rejection.**

Experience can be a cruel teacher if the lesson you learn from childhood is that the real you is unacceptable. It usually begins in small ways: "Don't say that." "Don't eat that." "Don't wear that." "Don't *want* that." "You did what?" "Fix your face." The messages can even feel benevolent. Parents say, "I'm doing this for your own good." But the visceral feeling is shame—shame that you're not good enough.

Shame is at the heart of hiding and denying hunger—a deep fear that you are so fundamentally unlovable that no one will want you if they knew the real you. A man I know died of suicide after he lost his money in the stock market—an extreme example, but it gets to the heart of this tragic and sad story. I can think of nothing sadder than a person who believes their very essence is unacceptable and unworthy of living unless they are always successful and "on top."

Living behind a mask may make things comfortable in the short term, but do you really want friends, lovers, and even colleagues to like and appreciate you for the mask? Or do you hunger to be accepted for your real self, warts and all? The arid life behind the mask chokes off breath and free will. A woman I know tells the story of her grandfather, who was raised in a religious Roman Catholic family. But for most of his adult life he snuck into Quaker Meetings. In his heart, he defined himself as a Quaker—all the while pretending to be a Catholic to keep peace in the family. Only after his death was the truth revealed. His freedom to be himself happened in death. My heart went out to him when I heard his story. I imagined his closed world, his unacceptable secret, and how lonely it must have been for him to keep his true nature locked away. His story represents the fear we all have to be ourselves. Sneaking to Quaker Meetings for worship was a brave step . . . at least he was trying to honor his hunger pains.

I often hear people proclaiming, "I want to be loved for the real me." In reality, however, they worry that the price of authenticity will be too high. The truth is, there is no higher price than the one paid for living a life that is a lie.

**Fiction: You can be happy living
someone else's life and values.**

**Truth: You need to know your
own script in order to live it.**

What are your true dreams? Do you know? The saddest thing in the world is to live from someone else's script and never take the opportunity to figure out what you really want. It's another form of identity theft—but this time the theft is made with your full permission. You hand yourself over willingly, signing your name in another's handwriting.

### Fiction: Being needy is being greedy.

### Truth: Every human being has legitimate needs that deserve to be met.

This being "needy" has become something associated with the plague of weakness, instead of as a divine birthright that comes with our certificate of authentication. If Cabbage Patch Kids come with birth certificates, surely human beings can ask for validation of their identity, worth, value, and rights. Being human and having needs is about being healthy, whole, and free. There's a typical put-down that occurs in unequal relationships. If the less powerful person expresses desires, he or she is accused of being "too needy." The accusation feels like a slap in the face. It hurts to be shamed and blamed for having basic needs and vulnerabilities that have every right to exist!

### Fiction: You are nobody without a mate, money, looks, fame—or any other external measure of success.

### Truth: You are sufficient and whole from birth.

You can't have a fulfilling relationship unless you bring your unique and blessed self to the table. Dependency, attachment, and fear are not love. They can get in the way of love and connection. They are defenses learned to manage scary feelings.

One of my patients told me the story of riding in a car with her mother shortly before her wedding. She was happy and relieved that she had found love, and she turned to her mother and said fervently, "I'm so excited about getting married. I'll never be lonely again."

Her mother looked at her and replied, "You are so nuts!"

My patient was flabbergasted. She hadn't expected that response, and she didn't understand what her mother meant. Later, she learned the truth for herself that her expectation of security wasn't written into the marriage contract. And her belief that she would never be lonely again wasn't written into the contract, either.

I have heard so many times, especially from women, that their lives are incomplete without a partner. (Men feel this way, too, but are often too ashamed to admit it.) Having a partnership forged in love and mutual respect is a wonderful thing, and we all want that. But remarkably, many people believe that this state is achieved by a magical ceremony that instantly confers bliss. No wonder there's so much disappointment and divorce!

The key to being a full partner is that state called self-esteem—literally, esteem for yourself. Self-esteem is the first step to building a healthy life. No external or materialistic possession can define you. You are more than what you do, where you work, how much money you make or lose, what you look like. You are a soul, a being, a person who longs to be loved, accepted, and known.

**Fiction: If you can't fix it, don't feel it.**

**Truth: Pretending to be okay won't make you okay.**

"Don't cry over spilled milk." This was a directive I learned growing up. If I could not change the situation, what was the point of feeling bad about it? I learned to bury my feelings, which only made my hunger worse. I have since discovered that what we don't face has dominion over us. Our denial of pain does not make it evaporate. It's like the goldfish that grows to fit the size of its bowl or pond. The bigger the hunger, the bigger the bowl of denial required to house and store it.

## FACING AND EMBRACING HUNGER

In talking with friends and family, people I know well, and absolute strangers, I've discovered that hunger holds endless questions for all of us. Do we accept conditions in our relationships that make us feel diminished, uncomfortable, or downright miserable? Are we afraid to say the words "I need"—thinking we'll be rejected, abandoned, shamed, or sent away? Are we anxious about sharing our true feelings? Do we feel we don't have a right to ask for what we want? Do we feel that honesty causes suffering? Do we find our relationships to be hard work? Do we live in fear that people will discover the real us and judge us negatively? Is our vow to love, honor, and cherish ourselves as important as the vows we make to others?

The challenge—and invitation—in every moment is to live through our own eyes. To say, "Will the real me please show up and stand up?" There is a quote that says, "When death finds you, may it find you alive." I have shared this many times as I go around the world speaking, inviting people to step out of their caves of shame and fear, to take a risk on love when aloneness feels much safer, to speak truth to others but begin the journey of speaking it to ourselves first, and to find a safe tribe of people to build a loving community where we can grow, fall down, make mistakes, and have the grace and support to try again. One step at a time is how we make this journey, one question at a time is how we move forward or decide that turning around is a wiser bet. Quieting the outer world so that the inner world can speak to us and give us sight and insight is the place to begin. We can begin this journey right at the place we find ourselves in this moment, in this space, happy or depressed, with money or on the verge of bankruptcy, sick or well . . . we can begin right here and right now, right where we are.

# CHAPTER 3

# IDENTITY THEFT— HAS ANYONE SEEN ROBIN?

*"I pray to the rain . . . /Return the remnants of my identity/
Bathe me in self-discovered knowledge . . . "*

SANDRA MARIA ESTEVES

There is a story that spoke very deeply to me about a speech once given by David Whyte during his transition from business-man to full-time poet. At a meeting, he asked the participants, "Has anyone seen David?" To me, this question showed a true search for personal identity.

As the story goes, this question occurred to David because he had been feeling scattered and discombobulated. He felt frenzied, lost, and disjointed, both in his external world and inside him-self. While everyone at the meeting laughed at his "joke," it was anything but a joke to him. "David" was the name he answered to, but he did not know who that person was. What he *did* know was that the life he had been living was not his own. That question awakened his sleeping giant. It alerted him to the fact that he had been living a life other than his own; that he'd been living outside of himself and his own authentic skin. He became acutely aware that being a poet was the only life he could live. He had been called to be a *poet* of all things, in a world that is much more impressed with high-level business executives.

I recently decided to open a conference with the same question: "Has anyone seen Robin?" The audience chuckled while looking at me inquisitively, wondering what was coming next. I have a reputation for being humorous, so people never quite know where my story is going.

I shared with this convention-center audience that from birth, most of us, if not *all* of us, suffer from some form of "identity theft" I spoke of in the previous chapter. Of course, we're not talking about the kind involving the theft of your social security number, credit card, bank account, driver's license, and passport information. This is a much more serious invasion of privacy: the stealing of your true identity as a unique, one-of-a-kind human being.

My own identity theft made me feel like I was wearing someone else's life and calling it my own. Over and over again, something felt *off*, but I couldn't pinpoint what it was. I just knew that my "clothes" were dragging along the road of life. My thoughts, feelings, beliefs, fears, tears, longings, and hunger felt either too big or too small, too loose or too tight, too black or too white, too conservative or too liberal. I would get a glimpse of who I thought I was and then she would quickly vanish. I remember passing a mirror in my house as I was swiftly moving from one room to the next. I caught someone peeping at me out of the corner of my eye and it startled me. I thought, *Whoa, who is that?* Well, it was *me*. Looking a bit harried, for sure. But something about her was different. My eyes looked different. Their warm sea color had not changed, nor the bags underneath that I've had since I was a little girl. *What* had *changed?*, I wondered. I stopped and looked deeply into the reflection of the familiar stranger in the mirror and knew instantly what was different. The fear was gone. As long as I can remember, without knowing it, I have carried a certain fear with me about being accepted, good enough, and truly loved and cherished. I have enough sad and troubling stories to fill a book on how this fear shaped my life over many years. The prospect that it was gone amazed me. I didn't know if it was gone for good, but I knew that who I saw looking back at me was who I *really* was. It wasn't a particularly good hair day and I had no makeup on, but I knew that "stranger who was myself." I had been looking for her, missing her and needing her to show up for years to help me claim and reclaim my life, self, and soul. And now she was finally standing before me.

There had been sightings of me—times when I could feel, see, touch, and taste my true colors. Times when I allowed myself to look outside the box in the gray areas, when I had dared to color outside of the lines while searching for the bits and pieces of me. I wanted and needed to be free to create a patchwork of mismatched patterns; the quilt that represented my life and made room for the pondering of my soul. But there seemed little room. I had been squeezed out of my own life. I felt like an orange whose juice and nutrients has been offered to satisfy and nourish others, leaving no life for itself. How could there be no room for me in my own life?

When I share my identity theft story and the long and painful journey "home" to myself—to reclaiming my life, voice, and the true essence of my soul—it seems to speak deeply to what many others are struggling with daily. People feel they are living lives, dreaming dreams, thinking thoughts, believing, grieving, loving, hating, feeling in ways that just don't fit. It doesn't fit because people have been living with the "paperwork" from someone else's life and thinking it was their own. The question, "When was the last sighting of the real me?" is one to ask not once or twice in our lifetime, but once or twice a day. "When was my real voice heard last—if ever? Has it been days, months, or years since anyone has seen or heard from the real me?" These questions need to walk with us daily. They sing to me, and sometimes haunt me. But they always invite me to show up as the real me, the only me, the true me.

Has anyone seen Robin? The tragic answer for years was "no." Only a few very trusted friends saw her. Even I rarely dared to look at her; most of the time I was scared and in hiding. Thank God, things have changed. Actually, not "things." *I* changed—and then my relationship to people and things changed.

I realized that the one person I couldn't live my life without was me. I gratefully see myself whether others choose to see me, want to see me, or are willing to see me. I hear and honor my voice when it makes me fit in like a smooth pair of cashmere gloves or stick out like a sore and inflamed thumb. A very close friend shared with me an experience she had on a chanting retreat. It was easy for the group to chant together, because the unique sound of each voice was drowned out by the others. But when practicing in a room alone, where there was only one voice to hear—her own— she felt awkward, self-conscious, embarrassed, and insecure. It was a wonderful experience to chant to music, or to the sound of other people's voices in unison with her own, but to learn to love and embrace the sound of her own voice was a huge challenge. The other people at the retreat felt similarly. They, too, felt discomfort, maybe even disdain, for the sound of their own voices—all while finding comfort and beauty in others'.

Isn't that common, that we would prefer to hide our voices inside the voice of another, to take refuge there? My friend's story reminded me of how separated we become from the sound of our own voices, what a distant stranger our own voice is and what a long journey home it is to love not only the sound of our voice, but the liberating truth that only our own voice holds. The process of getting to *know and love again the stranger who is yourself* with compassion is key to embracing self-love, self-power, self-knowledge, and self-understanding as we reclaim what first belonged to each individual life and soul.

In writing this book I fought tooth and nail with myself and others to make sure my voice was authentically in the pages. Even my beloved and devoted mother was worried and afraid that telling the truth and having my real voice in *Hungry* would damage my hard-earned and highly regarded reputation and *good* name. She feared that my image as one of the best of the best psychologists, preachers, and media on-air therapists would be tarnished and that my future might be harmed. I was quiet during our conversation as she tiptoed around how terrified she was for me. She had just finished reading the manuscript and said, "Robin, it's brilliant. I didn't think you could top *Lies at the Altar,* but I think you just did." But I know her so well. There was a hesitancy that followed her exuberant joy. I broke the silence of our small talk and asked, "Mommy, what is it?" She looked at me with trepidation. Out came a muddy river of fear and worry. I said, "Mommy, I get it and understand that in a world where some can be cruel and will beat down people who are already down that you would be worried for me. But the Bible says, 'The Truth will set you free,' and I am going with that promise and hope that others will be set free because I had the courage to tell the truth. I did what I was *called* to do by God and the rest is in God's hands and not mine."

This fight for my voice was a constant struggle for me, but one day, as I stood in a puddle of tears in my kitchen with a literary deadline breathing down my neck, my best friend said to me, "Robin, it will be okay, it will be fine. You will be fine and *Hungry* will be great. When you 'get your voice in the room' the story will flow." How in the world did I think I could I write a book about being hungry for a real life and identity and be missing in action myself?

Has anyone seen you?

Do you know your true self and voice?

What made you go into hiding?

Do you miss the real you?

## The "Painful P's"

The "Painful P's" that were required of me by the industry I was trying to navigate and succeed in are the same strangulating standards that are demanded of all women:

- Proving
- Promoting Self
- Poised
- Plastic
- Pageantry
- Private
- Prim
- Proper
- Pleasing
- Pushing
- Pulling
- Pressing
- Perfection

This is how little girls are groomed; these "Painful P's" are part of what strips us of our true identities. We spend the rest of our lives trying to grapple with this noose around the neck of our self-worth.

These P's lead to a painful unattainable hunger for perfectionism and poverty of the soul. Notice where they are showing up in your life today.

## THE RUNAWAY BRIDE

In the movie *Runaway Bride* starring Julia Roberts and Richard Gere, Julia Roberts's character is suffering from a severe case of identity theft. At one point she says that she likes her eggs cooked the same way her fiancé does. When her fiancé changes, so does the style of eggs that she claims as her favorite. I was like that character for many years! Not regarding eggs, but my preference of clothing. The length of my dress or skirt and its style depended on which man I was married to, dating, or intimately related to at any given time. Although it's tragic, my best friend and I are now able to laugh that over the last 25 years I wore dresses that either made me look like a prude or a video girl who was scantily dressed. I was lost and always trying to please, trying to do and be what was acceptable for *this* man, in *this* situation, for *this* moment in time. I had a style and flair of my own which I liked, but I didn't trust it or myself. I wasn't big enough to myself to trust my own barometer. As in other areas of my life, it has been a long journey home to myself in terms of what I wear. What helped me find my voice in this area was a seasoned and accomplished clothing stylist who asked me, "Dr. Robin, give me three words that describe who you are and what you want to communicate in your clothing." I have thanked her many times for popping the big question. *Dr. Robin, who are you? Who are you really? And how do you want to communicate that to yourself, your audience, and the world?*

## LOST AND FOUND

When I was a child there was a Lost and Found corner at my school where stray mittens or sneakers—separated from their matches, having fallen from backpacks while their owners were running to catch the bus—were to be placed. In 2012, what ends up in a school Lost and Found might look quite different. There are probably cell phones and iPods nestled amongst those lonely gloves. But while times may have changed for the Lost and Found, what hasn't changed is how many *people* are lost, how many of us are trying to find ourselves without a clue where to start. The "mission impossible" operation of tracking down the real you and the real me—with all of our original identity paperwork—is certainly the biggest assignment of our lives. It may even be the real reason we are here: to become who we are, not who someone says we should be.

I, for one, had been looking for myself for years. I looked for myself in success and in failure, in love relationships that worked and those that were great disappointments and full of heartache. I searched high and looked low in work and play. This effort felt like a war within and without . . . it was absolutely exhausting.

I was like a hungry lion searching for food. But the only food that could satisfy required me to regain, and bathe in, my true identity. This was my birthright: to be who I was born to be. It was the only thing that I couldn't fail at. I often pass on this piece of wisdom: we are sure to fail at living someone else's life, even if we outwardly give the appearance of having great success. I didn't need a fancy pedigree; I just needed to be me, all of me.

I felt more and more desperate as the mission seemed to be failing. I thought many times about calling off the search-and-rescue effort, but it felt too painful. I couldn't leave myself like a victim in a hit-and-run accident. The accident is traumatic enough, but what makes it unbearable is when the responsible party runs away from the scene of the crime, leaving the victim injured and alone. I couldn't continue to abandon myself. It was killing me and making me nothing but hungry, hurt, and heartbroken. I had to break this awful cycle of leaving myself high and dry. There seemed like no better time than my present moment of sheer agony to see if there was some way to live my life differently.

In 2008 I did a big overhaul on my home, inside and out. I did it with the exciting plan to sell my current house and buy my dream home. I lived in an amazing home, but one cold February morning I got a call from my Realtor, who said, "Robin, I have a house you have to see." When I walked in I *knew* this was the home where I wanted to live, love, work, play, write, create, grow old, and die. It was going to be a huge undertaking, but it felt as right as any of the biggest commitments I had ever made in my life. I was so excited about this opportunity because it far exceeded my dreams. At the time my heart was aching from a long-term, going-nowhere, so-called love relationship that was anything but loving. It was a crazy-making and crazy-feeling time for me. On the one hand, one of the best things in life was on my plate, the possibility of buying and living in my dream home. On the other hand, my heart was breaking. My home was being prepared for sale, with contractors everywhere from sunup to sundown. Each day after the workers would leave, I would bring out my two trusty buckets. Each was filled with scalding hot water, one hot and soapy and the other clear. I would use these to clean up the leftover dust and dirt from that day's labor. The workers did a great job cleaning up before they would leave, but my dog, Kalle, and I needed a "Mr. Clean" floor so we could walk barefoot, stretch out, and feel some sense of comfort and control. It felt like our home had been taken over by very competent Martians; they invaded our home by day, and lived on some other planet by night. Kalle was gracious even as this uproar interrupted our quiet, serene way of life. As long as we were together and she had her three square meals (plus many snacks and treats), she didn't really care.

One day Kalle was stretched out on the floor with her long glorious black body just outside the door to the music room. She was resting, while I was on my hands and knees cleaning. I had an Aretha Franklin CD playing in the background, and could hear her angelic voice singing, "God Will Take Care of You." With each dip into the bucket of hot water, and with each stroke of my arm, the tears rolled down my face, dropping onto my beautiful mahogany and walnut floors. I remember saying to Kalle, "I guess I don't need the bucket of water, I can just use my tears to clean the floors." In that moment, her big orange-brown eyes seemed to beckon me to lie down with her and rest from my labor. So I did. We laid face-to-face, nose-to-nose, looking into each other's eyes. My tears flowed like a river as Aretha rocked both of us to peace, if not to sleep. It was amazing how my hardwood floors felt soft and safe, holding us as Aretha reminded me that, "Yes, Robin, God will take care of Kalle and you. . . ."

I now understand more fully what was really going on. I was hoping to move with Kalle into a new home and build a new life, but something was missing. While Kalle filled—and healed—a huge hole in my heart, I wanted to share my life with a loving partner. I simply had not been able to attract this into my life since I'd lost my partner and lover in 1994. It has taken almost 20 years since to begin to turn my ship in the direction of living a life that is worthy of me and honors my hunger. Today, so many years later, if I cry when I hear Aretha sing that song, it's out of gratitude. I am no longer in an emotional pit of hell trying to find the air-conditioner switch. I wanted to take a crack at *living to be me* instead of *dying to be me*.

I saw that my lifelong goal of making peace with "just getting through" was way off track. It was certainly not the goal that God, the Universe, or anyone else who loved me would desire for me. I deserve so much more.

There is a line from the movie *Out of Africa* that speaks to me each time I see it. Robert Redford's character says, "I don't want to get to the end and find out that I'm at the end of someone else's life." I felt like if I didn't make a U-turn, I was headed in that direction.

A friend and a father in the ministry, the Rev. Dr. Otis Moss, Jr., shared with me his tender and brilliant understanding of what it means to make a "U-turn in life." We were talking about how I ended up in seminary in 1984. I had no plan to go to seminary. I was driving on City Line Avenue, a breath outside of Philadelphia, when I passed a seminary. I noticed it and made a U-turn in the middle of the street. That was dangerous in and of itself, but what would have been even more dangerous was if I *hadn't* made that U-turn. Had I not, I would have bypassed a very important part of my identity and destiny.

As Pastor Moss told me, a U-turn can be a sign of repentance. To *repent* is to turn and go in another direction. What did I need to repent for, what had I done wrong? The answer was nothing. Repentance doesn't necessarily mean you've done anything wrong. It only means you're ready to head in a different direction.

I don't know that Pastor Moss will ever know just how much his definition of making a U-turn changed my life. It is such a gift to be able to make a U-turn when I've passed my emotional, relational, spiritual, physical, financial, or sexual exit. He taught me in the way that all good teachers, parents, and leaders pass on an important message—with ease and grace. I never forget to tell myself, "Robin, it's okay to turn around if you've passed your rightful exit." I wish I had made more U-turns in my life or, better yet, I wish that I hadn't driven past myself for so many years. But "better late than never" is really true.

I've learned, and am still learning each day, that when I don't know what to do, it is often better to do nothing until I can listen for clear direction from within—and trustworthy people from the outside. There is the tendency to confuse busyness and activity with clarity and truth. Busyness without meaning and purpose is a breeding ground for hunger and a lot of unhelpful acting out. There have been many times when I didn't know what to do and believe me, I tried almost everything. I could certainly write a book on what *not* to do when you don't know what to do! It's like going grocery shopping when you're hungry or clothes shopping when you're depressed. We come home with lots of stuff we don't need, isn't good for us, and that we can't afford.

Years ago, I spent several days with one of the best therapists in the country, trying to "find myself." Actually, I was trying to *heal* myself. I stayed at a small, totally unpretentious, not-even-on-the-map motel deep in the desert. I now know this was a form of self-hospitalization. At the time I was teaching a class that I couldn't miss, so I flew out west, rented a car, drove hours to the middle of nowhere (and I mean *nowhere*), stayed for several days—spending many hours a day with this wise healer—and then took two connecting red-eye flights back to Philadelphia to be in my classroom by 7:00 A.M. Thursday morning. While the flights were grueling, what I faced over those few days made the travel feel like a piece of cake. I spent those days in the process of finding and re-claiming myself. Putting that much attention on the search-and-rescue effort was worth it, regardless of how much effort it took to get there. And yet there was still more excavation I would need to do. But after that journey I was determined. I was going to find myself, dead or alive.

## THANKSGIVING DAY

My mother wanted me to be born on Thanksgiving Day. She and my father were so grateful to have a child, having waited almost 11 years after the birth of my twin siblings. She felt there would be no better day than Thanksgiving for me to arrive. She asked the doctors to induce her and they were willing because I was due any day—actually, any moment. But my father was wiser. He said, "No, let her come when she is ready." Mommy and I have spoken of her wish many times, and all these years later, the thought of a Thanksgiving birth still remains a grand and glorious idea to her. What she still doesn't understand is that I wasn't born to make her happy (or sad, for that matter). I was born to be me. So from before I was born—and this is not unique to me at all—there was an agenda for my life that had little to do with me becoming who I was born to be. It had much more to do with fulfilling someone else's prescription; to meet *their* needs, desires, and hunger.

I'm grateful that I was wanted by my parents, but I'm very thankful that I wasn't born on Thanksgiving Day.

It is so scary to be lost, but it is even scarier to be lost and not know it. To think we are on the right track, in the right place, and at our destination—only to discover that we were sitting in the wrong theater, waiting for the wrong movie to begin, in the wrong city, in a country that is not our own, surrounded by strangers. (Or worse, enemies disguised as trusted friends.) That was me. When I woke up and realized that I was lost, my ship was way out in the middle of a choppy, unfamiliar ocean. There was no boat, no paddles or oars, no people that I recognized, no cell phone coverage, no distress kit to set off fireworks in hopes of alerting someone that I was lost and needed to be rescued. There were people, lots of them, floating around me in their own boats, and they, too, looked lost and scared. There were others who were in full drag, seasick like the rest of us but pretending as though everything was fine. If they were hitting the wall of "dying to be me," they planned to sink and die in full costume, masks still firmly in place as their heads bobbed up and down atop the choppy sea of lost selves. Clearly, the end was near for some. You could see they had given up, their life force washed away by pain, but they were still wearing plastic smiles. Clichés of "fake it till you make it" and "it's more important to look good than to feel good" have stolen many an identity. As the death of the self is hovering, with each pounding heartbeat feeling like the last, when fear is the only thing gripping your hand—a frozen smile threatens to steal even that last opportunity to be real.

What I was hungry for and desperately needed was a "self." My true self, which I took seriously even when other people blew me off and dismissed me. I was hungry to never again prostitute, ignore, or sell myself short—sell myself at all, for that matter. I wanted a "self" that would still shine brightly even if I became a castaway or was voted off the island. I was no longer willing to harm and mistreat myself, or mirror the dismissal and mistreatment of others. I was ready for the hunger for my "self" to get fed.

It has been a long journey *home* to myself, one that at times has felt endless. I begged, borrowed, and tried to steal back my identity from all the people and places where it had been taken or given away. Now I was finally ready to honestly answer the question, "Has anyone seen Robin?" I could, with a humble and open heart, offer a resounding "Yes." I was beginning to understand that I had to feed myself healthy emotional and spiritual food, that I was responsible for my own diet—for the nourishment of my mind, relationships, body, and spirit. That my life and my joy were my full-time job. And that it was up to *me* to report for active duty, to reclaim and bathe in my true and liberated identity.

# CHAPTER 4

# EMOTIONAL ANOREXIA

—————◆—————

*"He who conceals his disease cannot expect to be cured."*
ETHIOPIAN PROVERB

Last year I gave a keynote speech at a fundraiser for victims of domestic violence. As I stood at the podium and looked out into the crowd of beautifully dressed, well-to-do women, I imagined the tenor of my remarks would surprise them. They expected me to speak about others, not them; about victims, not their peers. But instead I told them, "This is an admirable cause, and I know you care very much about the women you are here to support. But I want to take a few moments to speak about the hidden abuse that is in this room. I know for a fact that in every gathering of women, no matter how successful or well-off they are, there's a form of self-abuse going on that is very prevalent. That self-abuse involves denying that you have needs. Denying that you have longings. Denying that you want something more than what you have right now. The expensive clothing in the customized closet in the super-sized, gated house; the pool and very impressive cars and well-manicured grounds—all of that medicates your hunger, but it doesn't fill it. Our souls aren't for sale, even if we are. You may live the perfect picture, but it may be that you're afraid to acknowledge what you're really feeling beneath the façade. You may have great abundance, but are left feeling empty."

I told them that I had watched for a while as they came into the room and greeted each other. I observed their greetings: Their shining, flawless smiles, their air kisses. In fairness to them, I acknowledged my own privilege, which allowed me to drive to this event in one of those fancy-type cars, accompanied by my best friend who met me there in hers. I owned that I looked exactly like them in my Prada dress, Blahnik shoes, and crystal diamond drop earrings. "Now, I'm sure not everyone in this room has had a fantastic year," I said, knowing this was most definitely true. "How many people came into this room today and went through a dialogue similar to this:

*How are you?*
*Great.*
*How are the kids?*
*Fantastic.*
*Everything good?*
*Yes. Never better.*

"Instead of this standard dialogue, did any of you respond, 'Well, it's been a tough year . . . the kids are struggling with their new school . . . Bill's company has been laying people off, and we're scared about what this all means . . . also, we started couples therapy six months ago, so let's just say the jury is still out.'"

As I spoke I could see them shifting around in their seats, sitting up in surprise, thinking, *Okay, what do I do with this? Do I keep my plastic smile right now as she's saying it? Do I try to relax and breathe into this? What do I do in this moment, where the truth has shown up unexpectedly? And can I sit with these unsettled feelings, or do I need to make sure that my inner Botox stays intact so that no one can see? Oh God, I hope I don't look as nervous as I feel.*

Finally, I said, "You know, there's a lot of financial wealth in this room. Your wills are probably intact, and they lay out who's going to get what. But what are you *willing* to your children regarding the issues of their hunger and their failures? How have you taught them to react when their lives don't turn out the way they'd hoped? Can you bequeath them something now—leave them a legacy—that will release them from shame, especially the shame of hunger? To not feel ashamed of their humanity? Because that's so much of what we're afraid of. That the more somebody sees our humanity, the more in danger we feel. What would it mean for you to will your children an image of you as a mother who is open to them being full? Open to their holes and wholeness and your own holes and wholeness?"

As I finished, a great silence came over the room. I saw the perfectly put-together women wiping away tears and bowing their heads, obviously moved. When I left the stage, one of the organizers touched my arm. I turned and saw tears spilling down her cheeks. She apologized for her emotion, saying, "I'm sorry. I wasn't expecting that."

I smiled at her warmly. "Don't apologize. This moment is worthy of our tears." And my own eyes misted, mirroring the truth that we were all sisters in the same struggle—the struggle to be kind to ourselves as we bump up against our fragile and resilient humanity.

I went into the ladies' room, and when I was standing at the sink a woman came up to me, hesitantly. She thanked me for my remarks, but I could tell she had more to say. I waited her out. Finally, she said, in a barely audible voice, almost a whisper, "Thank you for acknowledging that there could be someone in this room who is a victim of domestic violence, too, because I am that woman, and I know there are others like me here today. It's a painful and shameful secret we are all dying and trying to keep. And you know, we have lots of money and a house here, one in the Hamptons, and a flat in Europe. Last summer, I was beaten so badly at our European beachfront oasis that I had to take my children to spend the night in a hotel room for our safety."

I was immediately sympathetic to her, but as I began to speak she waved a hand stopping me. "What I really wanted to comment on was what you said about a will and a legacy we would leave our children," she said in a trembling voice. "We have a 26-year marriage with lots of money and lots of assets. But when you talked about what I'm giving my children, what I'm going to be passing on to them other than all this physical abuse and violence and this Kodak moment that was never real, I realized that I desperately want to leave them something healthy and real now before I'm dead or killed. I want to leave them something that will tell them that their hunger isn't bad. That my hunger was not bad. That I tried to keep our family together. That I'm not a horrible person or a weak person because I desired and tried to keep our family together."

Before I could respond, she slipped out the door and was gone. I would never know the rest of her story, but perhaps I had opened up a small sliver of light that would grow larger and brighter. Like many of the women in the room that night, she was starving but ashamed of her hunger—as if she didn't deserve a meal and a life. As if she could live without sustenance, safety, and love. Reflecting on it later, I realized that she might not take that bite for her own sake, but might do it for her children. It was a start. We all have to begin honoring our hunger somewhere.

## STARVING FOR ACCEPTANCE

My heart aches as I observe the starving souls around me. I feel their need and their despair. I see the longing beneath the carefully constructed masks. Denise, a 38-year-old junior partner in a law firm, sat in my office, describing herself as fat, lazy, and unhappy. She shared with me what I considered a harsh, derogatory nickname, telling me, "This is what my close friends and family, and even a few trusted co-workers at the firm call me." She added with a wry smile, "I think my nickname is funny." The pace of her speech accelerated, like when you're pumping the gas pedal on an old car, praying the engine will turn on and stay on. She talked through, over, and around the shame that sharing her nickname had stirred up. It was like watching someone play dodgeball. Denise was highly skilled at the game of dodging her shame, but I knew it was deadly. I was familiar with its rules and practices because I had played it myself for so much of my life. Denise had no awareness of the self-cutting language that poured out of her mouth or the high price she paid for her self-damning words. She had become numb to the pain of the shame. She didn't know the truth about her hunger, but her soul did. She couldn't imagine what to do to make her life better. I could see and hear that she believed if she got her weight under control, all her other problems would magically resolve themselves. "Dr. Robin, I'm desperate," she said finally. "What's my problem? What the hell is wrong with me? I have everything going for me, but I'm a big fat loser."

"You're starving to death," I replied.

She stared at me confused, as if she hadn't heard right. "Look at me!" she cried, gesturing to her body. "How can you say that?" Her face turned suspicious. At that moment, Denise was clearly wondering if the positive reviews she'd heard about me were accurate.

I understood why my words confused Denise. She thought her problem was the opposite of starvation. And yet, the secret cause of most weight struggles, depression, and loneliness is a deep, penetrating hunger that is not being acknowledged or satisfied.

Malnutrition is a terrible way to die. It's slow and it's brutally painful as it eats away at each organ, corroding the body until the stench of death prevails. I have known and been humbled to work with many women who came back from the brink of despair, suffering from anorexia, other eating disorders and weight concerns. I had just gotten off of a long plane ride from L.A., where I had been shooting a very demanding TV pilot. All I wanted to do was get home and plop into my comfy bed. It was late. I knew this because *Nightline* was on. I'm not a big TV watcher, and I seldom come into the house and go straight to the TV, but this night I did. As I was washing my face, my body begging me for bed and sleep,

I heard a voice coming from my TV. Her words awakened my slumber-seeking self. It was actress Portia de Rossi, talking about trying to starve away her sexuality. I had no idea who she was, or who she was married to, but I listened. I was especially moved by the accounts of her gut-wrenching struggle. She had written a book about how the denial of her true self had led her to starve herself. For Portia, extreme starvation of her core identity was manifested in physical starvation. She said, "When I was anorexic it just seemed like I literally wanted to disappear. And now I would like to reappear."

The problem that Portia had was not just that she was physically starving; rather she (and Denise) were suffering from what is referred to as *emotional anorexia*. Emotional anorexia is a real state of being. Psychologists recognize it and treat it right along with physical anorexia. Some of the symptoms and signs are suppressing emotions, including rage, lack of access to feelings, inability to cry, starving and neglecting needs, diminishing and/or minimizing one's desires, and the use of denial to repel pain.

Most people are trying to starve to death the parts of themselves that they or others dislike, dishonor, disapprove of, or disdain. Portia survived, filling herself with the nourishment of compassion, love, and truth. Trying to be someone other than yourself is like living on 300 calories a day and pretending it's enough. What I know for sure is that if you're starving and are actively in the process of dying, your life will show the evidence. You might be able to pull off being in denial for a time, and think you've covered up well enough that others don't notice. But even if you are a good actor and have learned to play dress-up and pretend, the Grim Reaper of your starvation will appear eventually. Starvation kills. There is no way out except to compassionately face and embrace the truth of your hunger directly—and with tenderness, begin to get the nourishment that your mind, body, and spirit desires, deserves, and needs.

You may think you can get away with stuffing your raw and real feelings in a back corner or locked drawer. You can't. No matter how big your pot of denial stew may be, you cannot starve without dying.

I was deeply moved by Carrie, a 46-year-old psychotherapy patient who was literally unable to speak about her pain. When she came into my office I would greet her, "How are you doing today?" And she would reply, "Fine. I'm fine."

When I'd ask her to tell me what was troubling her, she'd get very uncomfortable and start shifting around in her chair. "Oh, it's not that much, really," she'd say, before barely managing to choke out a few words. She seemed to be almost gasping for breath. If a tear slipped down her cheek she quickly wiped it away, ashamed that I would see it. Obviously, it's hard to get anything out of therapy if your primary goal is to make sure your therapist sees only your "together" self.

So many times I've met people who are hungry—ravenous to speak the truth—but who fear that if their loved ones, friends, bosses, fellow congregants, or even casual acquaintances knew the *real* them, they would be judged and rejected. Sometimes the hunger goes on for so long they don't recognize it. They've forgotten how to eat.

A friend's mother was widowed after her husband died of pancreatic cancer. They had been married for 55 years and she was devastated. Because she was frail, and her children didn't think she was able to care for herself, they convinced her to sell the house and move into a lovely assisted living center. On her first day there, the manager asked if she'd like to join a water aerobics class. "Oh, I couldn't do that," she said. "I haven't worn a swimming suit since I was thirty years old." Later, another resident asked if she would like to join the others for wine and cheese at the piano bar at 5:00 P.M. "Oh, I couldn't do that," she said. "We never drank wine." One Saturday night there was a dance and a nice gentleman asked her to dance. "Oh, I couldn't do that," she demurred. "I haven't danced since before I had children." Her view of herself was literally stuck in what "always was." Happily, however, the staff and residents of the center were patient and caring, and over a few months they gradually persuaded her to get involved in activities. Something very profound occurred: she rediscovered what she really liked and who she really was. "I feel as if I've lived two distinct lives," she told her daughter. "One was with your father, and it was a good life, but it was all about doing for others. Now, in my second life, which may be much shorter in length, it's about being who I want to be."

## THE DESPAIR OF SELF-DENIAL

Starving people are all around us. Rich or poor, in shelters or mansions that feel like solitary confinement. It doesn't matter. Self-denial and neglect is the road to starvation. Those who are starving don't fit any particular mold. There is no convenient stereotype. They're all around us, men, women, black, white, brown, yellow, rich, poor. Hungry.

Making yourself small is a sign of starvation. In one biblical story, Moses sent scouts to check out the Promised Land, which was said to flow with milk and honey. The scouts returned feeling demoralized. They told Moses, "We came to the land you sent us to, and it does flow with milk and honey. But the people who inhabit the land are large and powerful. We seemed like grasshoppers in our own eyes, and we looked the same to them."

This is a beautiful example of how feeling small and insignificant can warp our perception of reality. If we have a distorted view of ourselves or the world around us, we are naturally inhibited from making the right life choices. If we see ourselves as grasshoppers, and others as giants, we will allow others a power over our life that they do not deserve—and which continues to make us smaller until we disappear.

How do you make yourself bigger in your own life? Start by changing the recipe that defines you. Are you trying to bake a rich, decadent cake without using eggs and cream? Is that possible? What are the ingredients needed to build a self and life that is rich and filling?

## Are You Suffering from Emotional Anorexia?

I had all of the symptoms of emotional anorexia before I realized that I was *dying to be me*. These signs are not as cruelly apparent to others as traditional anorexia. You may look fine on the outside, while literally dying inside. Your life might look like the perfectly manicured gardens of the White House, but inside you are withering away.

The cure for emotional anorexia is to get our own voice in our story. It can't be our story if our voice is not in the room, in the conversation. Is your voice in your story dominant? Is it present, alive, awake? Quiet, still, dead, scared? When roll is called, is it your voice that is answering or someone else's? "The lion's story can never be told by the hunter," as they say, so we must tell our own story. The very act of giving voice to our true feelings and needs can be a tremendous release. It is the first step to joining the feast of life, where we are not an outsider but one who belongs. Finding a safe person to share our hunger and cravings with is important as we build a healthy and hearty self.

If you think you might be suffering from emotional anorexia, ask yourself:

- What do I *really* want, desire, hunger, crave, or need that I have been afraid, ashamed, fearful to admit and own?

- What thoughts, feelings, desires, longings, and needs have been in my mind for years, which I fight to push out?

Sometimes we ourselves don't know our own suppressed secrets, desires, needs, and longings. They hover over our lives, holding the blueprint for what lies beneath. But they are the key to what we really and truly are hungry for. So take a deep look. Ask yourself, "Where do I want more than I am getting?" Then use this information to build a healthy, rich, and satisfying life.

# CHAPTER 5

# HUNGRY FOR THE HIGH NOTE

*"Midway this way of life we're bound upon,*
*I woke to find myself in a dark wood,*
*Where the right road was wholly lost and gone . . .*
*It is so bitter, it goes nigh to death . . ."*

DANTE

I'm not a big believer in coincidence. One definition of coincidence I can get behind is that it is God's way of remaining anonymous; another definition calls coincidence, "A God-wink." One night I "stumbled onto" a television interview with Lionel Richie, an artist whose music I enjoy. I was busy writing this book and wasn't sure that I had the time to sit and listen to what he had to say, but I did—and I was ultimately grateful that I took the time. After hearing the interview, I felt I needed to call Lionel Richie and say, "Hey, Lionel, guess what I'm writing about? Something you seem to really understand . . . the cost of neglecting that we are hungry . . ." I never called him, but I appreciated the "God-wink" that came at a time when I was exhausted and needed a bold reminder that I was really onto something important that belonged in the world . . . that might soothe a soul, and maybe even save a life.

It was meant for me to see and hear this interview, not only for this book but also for my own self-care. As I listened to Lionel Richie's words, they felt like supporting evidence for my hypothesis about the dangers of being hungry too long—and the ultimate price of starvation and death that too often follow. With honesty, vulnerability, and articulation, he described the experience I call being "hungry to hit the high note." While most of us are not performers—having to do our "thing" in front of thousands, or even more terrifyingly, millions—of people, being hungry to hit the high note is something we have all experienced in some form. Lionel was so transparent about his experience (and what he knows is the experience of many performers like Michael Jackson and Whitney Houston) in this area. It is brutal and often crushing for a performer to have the torturous and unrelenting inner vocal coach pushing them to keep hitting the high note. Saying, "No, not that way, do it like you used to do it! You need to hit the high note that makes the audience scream and pay for more!" We see this with athletes who fly through the air making dunks that seem possible only for a superhero, or who land the impossible putt that travels around red robin's barn and smoothly slips into the hole. This action-hero status and hunger to hit the high note is seen in every profession, and shows up as much in the sacred world of ministry as it does in the secular world. It's everywhere. Parents are hungry and feel pressure to hit the high note and then demand that their children follow suit and chase it, too.

Like a drug addict, once we hit the high note, we seek and crave the intoxicating high of hitting it again and again. At its worst, we not only want to hit the high note of old, but our goal is to reach for one that's even better, even higher. This is the death of us all. We all know Michael Jackson was an absolute musical genius. He heard and saw things that the rest of the world had no access to. If managed well, Michael's gift was a heavy blessing to possess; if managed poorly, it was a deadly burden and a curse. Most of us could not begin to handle the gift of being so talented; so extraordinary, and yet still hungry and human. It was a quadruple threat for Michael, because he could sing, dance, write, and produce. He was the object of much attention and affection when he was the chosen flavor, but when his star began to fall it seemed to pull his essence—his body, life, and soul—down with it. It seems that Michael didn't know he was good enough, truly good enough, whether he got the thumbs up or down, whether his feet and energy could still float across the floor as he defied gravity. Who was he when he could no longer hit the high note that his audiences were so desperate for?

What happens to each of us, when we can no longer hit the high note? What happens to our identity? Who are we really without our latest success story? When we are dating someone average instead of a spectacular bombshell that will soon detonate and blow our lives to smithereens, who are we? What we are able to do in our teens, 20s, and 30s changes significantly in our 40s, 50s, 60s, and beyond. I watch my mother at the ripe age of 90—wise, witty, and a true piece of work and beauty—struggling because she is still hungry to hit the high note in her life. Her mind is active and her body, too, so she still wants to taste the high of the many high notes that she and my father hit in their lives. I watch her in amazement, and at times exhaustion, saying, "Mommy, I hope if I live to be anywhere close to your age that I will have discovered other ways of caring for my hunger and the grief of a changing and aging life and body." It is painful and at times scary to watch her so hungry, even after having lived an amazingly rich and full life. She reminds me that hunger is with us until the end. How we handle it is the question and challenge.

Refusing to face the fact that you can no longer hit the high note is about avoiding the grief that comes when something wonderful and special ends. I enjoy vacationing with my dear friend Kenya. But without fail, before we arrive at paradise, she is already grieving the end. She knows that we are going to have a blast, as we always do, but her hungry voice of loss shows up long before departure day is at hand. Embracing the reality of the aging process—and even bigger, our resistance to the fact that life is ever-changing, and that we cannot freeze the high notes and make them last forever—is a hard pill to swallow. But if we don't face up to it, life becomes painful and full of added loss and suffering. Life is ever-changing and so are we, in all areas of our lives. Whether we like it or not.

The ancient battle with aging has been on the scene at least since the Garden of Eden, and I suspect even longer. Our fear of mortality and our hunger to be immortal seems only to be increasing with advances in medicine and technology. Extending our ability to hit the high note is one way we dance with immortality—thinking we might actually take the lead. There are people who want to freeze themselves before they die, hoping someday they can be thawed out and never have to look death square in the eye. That is an extreme case of being hungry for the high note, of wanting life to always stay the same, but it shows just where our hunger and starvation can take us if it is not attended to and nurtured. Billions of dollars are spent every year as people try to keep themselves young. The hunger is to be young not only in spirit, but in appearance, too. (Actually, being young in spirit isn't worth much on the market these days. Most of the world is fixated on the outer persona, not caring much about the inner self.) Most cosmetic surgery is an attempt to fix and then freeze time; to defeat our mortality so we can keep hitting the high note. To shatter the crystal with a note that goes so high.

A former supermodel shared a personal and powerful story about what happened to her when she could no longer hit the high note, at least not in the way she was accustomed to. A delivery was made to her home. She opened her door, and the man leaving the package said, "I hear there is a hot model who lives in this building, who is she?" Ouch. The hot model was the woman answering the door, receiving the delivery, except she was no longer recognizable as her young, hot, and sexy self. This painful encounter brought her face-to-face with her reality, her mortality, and her hunger. She wanted to be the young and beautiful person she was many years before. She, like many of us, adopted and adapted to the world's standards for what makes us good enough and worthy; what makes us beautiful and sexy; what makes us smart and sharp. But like the rest of us, she struggled with internal standards of her own that could guide her to a place of inner peace, self-love, and acceptance.

If we're hungry for the high note it's either because we used to hit it and were bitten by the bug, or because we have watched others hit it and felt our own hunger stir. This hunger shows up in many ways . . . in our love relationships, family, and work life. It's everywhere. Our hunger to be spectacular, exceptional, extraordinary—or to be partnered with someone who is those things—keeps us running crazy, like mice in a maze. In romantic relationships the high note often comes with the intoxicating love cocktail at the beginning. To most of us that cocktail feels good, but it can't, won't, and doesn't last. Many people spend their lives trying to hit that high note in relationship after relationship, trading in partners like they'd turn in their car or cell phone—even when the old one functions perfectly well. This all taps into our existing hunger, and only makes us hungrier.

Hitting the high note is temporary. It doesn't last. What we are chasing is mostly an unobtainable illusion; in reality, it either doesn't exist or its existence is fleeting. This chase makes us believe that we can never be satisfied or full with anything less than the high note. In love relationships it makes us think that we need a filet—even when we ourselves are more like a French fry. The ego refuses any discussion of our being a fry, but most of us are just that. We all have moments where we are exceptional, and some of us have more than others, but at our core, we are not high-end airbrushed art. We are the priceless beauty of dust and clay, and we are enough. We can't imagine that we can ever be satisfied to be—or be with—a French fry. We think that a fry can't touch the experience we long for. But in our search to be something we're not, we are missing the boat of fullness and fulfillment that is right in front of and within us.

My journey to admitting that, on most days, I am a French fry, hasn't been easy. I've learned that whoever my partner is, he will morph from filet to fry just like me. But I have learned that a fry will nourish and feed me more than I ever imagined possible, and that the filet was, for the most part, a fantasy. A fantasy of hitting that high note.

Being hungry for the high note makes us chase the phantom of whatever it is that possesses our identity. This exhausting marathon only makes us more and more hungry. Hitting the high note once, twice, many times, can become addictive; it can make us think we can't live joyfully, full, and satisfied, with anything short of that, short of the filet. This deadly pursuit killed Whitney and Michael, and almost killed me.

When I hear people talking about drugs killing Michael, Elvis, Whitney, and so many others—those whose names we know and those we don't—I think, *No, it wasn't drugs that killed them, it was their hunger for the high note. It was the fact that there was no safe place to get help for that dis-ease.* There should be a Betty Ford Clinic for Hungry for the High Note. Drugs, alcohol, gambling, sex, pornography, eating, shopping, working, and working out are ways we medicate ourselves when running from the pain and terror of not being able to hit the high note. They are symptoms pointing to the core, root, and real problem. When nothing but artificial and frozen perfection can satisfy us, we are in big trouble.

When a woman who thinks her man is a filet discovers that she has a fry, she often feels disappointed and wants to get rid of him. She wants to hit the high note of being in a relationship with a filet. Men are in this same death trap. When a man chases the queens of plastic surgery, convinced that he can't be full and satisfied with anyone other than the perfect-looking woman, all bets are off for anything real and true. Women are having all kinds of procedures and surgeries done, simply trying to be someone's filet of the day. Being hungry for the high note makes us try and keep up with the Joneses of our youth; try to stretch, nip, tuck, and reach, hoping to hit the high note. I heard Robert Redford interviewed recently and he was talking about his appreciation for women who are embracing their wrinkles and creases. It's a much more organic way to live and love, to embrace what is naturally evolving as opposed to artificially manufactured.

Real love, emotional maturity, and security teach us that our filet order was more fantasy than reality; that we can be truly satisfied and happy being a fry with a fry. On most days, beneath the exterior, we are all simple. We are fragile, we are beautiful, and we are basic. We were not born to be perfect; we were born to be present, whole, and free.

## THE POWER OF EXPOSING THE LIE

One of the other things that struck me about the Lionel Richie interview was how he copes with not being able to hit the high note like he used to. It remains a tender place for him, but the way he faces it I believe could be medicine for us all: he names his limitations. He exposes the reality, and therefore doesn't live in the terror of a lie. Someone who is like a brother to me always said, "If I tell it first, then people won't have anything to tell. I will take away their power to hurt me by telling my stuff first." When we know the truth ourselves, and put it out for others to see, we can't be hurt in the same way. We don't have to hide or cover up our limitations as a hungry human being.

We render the hunger for the high note powerless if we admit it. When we reveal that we do have a note we can offer, but it's not that old high note. Exposing the lie that the high note is the best—or the only—note invites truth to be our trusted life partner. When we admit that hitting the high note is killing us, that it is no longer possible, or maybe even desired—when we allow the truth to shine—we lessen our own craving for the illusive and seductive fantasy. Lionel Richie says he knows he can't hit the high note anymore. All he can do is make friends with the person he is now, and the many wonderful notes he still can hit. When he performs onstage now and his voice won't go where it used to, he has the audience sing along. He lets them hit the high note for him! He's no longer under the pressure to be more than who or what he is. Instead, he's accepting that who and what he is right now is enough. I don't know how he feels when he hears his old songs from the Commodores or his extremely successful solo career, but he seems to have made friends with himself for who and what he is in this moment. To me, his voice is still magical.

As we heal and mature from chasing the high note and become more comfortable in our own skin, we see life, love, and loss differently. I received a so-called business opportunity that some might have said was insulting. In the past it would have stirred me up and I would have felt bad, but not this time. Over the years, I have been offered numerous television pilots—some were great opportunities and others weren't so hot—but never had I been asked to shoot a pilot where not even my travel would be compensated. It was to be entirely at my expense. For real? It didn't hurt my feelings or offend me, but I didn't have to think about or consider the offer, either. I am not starving anymore; I don't feel desperate. I'm no longer chasing or trying to hit the high note. I can think and feel more clearly because each day I befriend myself anew. At last, I am hungrier for the real note than the high note.

The taunting voices say, "Do it again and we'll love you . . . we'll like you, follow you, chase you . . . if you can't, don't, or won't do it again, we will throw you away. . . ." It would make even the bravest person tremble and break. The fear of not being special or chosen, of being erased and replaced, stirs up our hunger and sends us on a wild goose chase in search of the next high note. It makes us insatiable and inconsolable—until we make friends with ourselves. Which we can do, at every stage and age. The goal as I see it is not to freeze the experience of hitting the high note, but to allow a new note to be created within the realities of each moment, each day, each year, and each decade of our lives. So we can enjoy hitting the real note, not the high note.

## That I Would Be Good

I have always been moved by Alanis Morissette's song "That I Would Be Good." The first time I heard it I was at a continuing education training for psychologists, and it blew me away because that was what I hungered for in my own life, that I would be good no matter whether I could hit the high note or no note at all.

Feeling not good enough doesn't just happen to "regular" people. It may surprise you to know that the wound is sometimes even deeper for those who appear to have it all, those who have reached the pinnacles of fame and fortune. Morissette wrote this song at a time of great insecurity and self-doubt. After winning award after award, being feted as the new best thing, she emotionally collapsed. The pressure was too much, and she feared she would be unable to re-create her previous success. I identified with Alanis's fear; when you're in the public eye, praised for your gift, it can be the beginning of a lifelong battle to stay on top. It ultimately feels like the most torturous climb.

This is my prayer. It is my aching and arching hope. It is what I am deeply hungry for:

That no matter what comes my way . . .
Whether I get the thumbs up or down . . .
Whether I am embraced or rejected . . .
Whether I am number one or not on the list at all . . .
Whether I am healthy as a horse or sick as a dog . . .
Whether I am wealthy or close to penniless . . .
That I would be *good*.

CHAPTER 6

# THE SOURCE OF HUNGER PAINS

*"Since one's inner self is flawed by shame,
the experience of self is painful. To compensate,
one develops a false self in order to survive."*

JOHN BRADSHAW

We come into the world whole. You've heard about original sin, right? I'm talking about original *wholeness*. That's actually how the story begins. The "fall" happened only after humans were created in God's image. So we begin as complete beings, and then life chips away at our wholeness. The reason there are hungry adults walking around is because we learned at a young age that it's shameful to ask for too much, that it's unacceptable to be seen as needy, that it's rewarded to look happy when you're sad, that it's better if you don't act too strong-willed or express too many preferences.

67

Who would you be if you were who you were *meant to* be? What would you do, what would you eat, what colors would you choose, what interests would you pursue? Where would you live? Who would you love and make a life with? Do you know?

## CHILDHOOD WOUNDS, ADULTS ACTING OUT

Many of the expressions of hunger we experience as adults have their roots in a childhood feeling, experience, fear, or hurt. They are the result of a wound that never healed, a piece of our humanity that we were taught had to be mastered instead of tenderly embraced. We all have these wounds to a certain extent. They are the natural outgrowth of our development from complete dependence and vulnerability to independence and expressed selfhood.

When I was a child I once asked my father, "Daddy, if I died, what would you do? How would you feel?" What an odd question for a child to ask! What a *hungry* question for a child to ask. Only now do I understand my very important question to my father. I wanted to hear that his love for me was so great, that his attachment to me was so complete, that he would leap into the grave with my lifeless body, unable to go on without me. I felt that I couldn't live without *him*—a natural feeling for a child—but I wanted *him* to not be able to live without *me*. Would his world end if I died?

My father and I had a very close relationship. We talked all the time, shared meals, laughed, played games, and spent a lot of time together. We genuinely enjoyed each other's company. We hung out alone or with my tribe of friends, all of whom speak of him adoringly to this day. He had a wonderful gift for making people feel special and important.

My fears were about more than losing our bond. They were also about my father's distance—the way he could emotionally withdraw in the guise of being strong and steady. My niece's husband taught me a term that describes my father's steady and reliable way of being in the world. "Daddy was nine-fifteen," he would say. At 9:15 the hands on a clock are straight across, so this saying meant that he was always in a sound and solid state. His—and my mother's—style of coping was to make sure they could manage whatever was put on their plates—including the death of their children. They were both people who, while expressive, wanted to feel that nothing would ever devastate them to the point where they couldn't go on. My father had suffered the brutal murder of his brother before I was born, the unexpected death of his father during his first week in medical school, his mother going blind from diabetes, and then her death when I was nine. My mother suffered the death of two siblings when she was a child, her brother dying at the age of 4 and her sister at 15. Also as a child, my mother was hit by a car and almost killed. So both of my parents carried and survived great pain and trauma. The fact that they were African American and faced the assault of racism (and, in my mother's case, sexism) certainly made their lives challenging as well. They were both amazing survivors. While my father was loving and kind to all, his heart was guarded. I knew it, even though his smile was warm and engaging. Kids can sniff out their parents' fears, shortcomings, and limitations, but that doesn't mean that we can make sense of them. And it doesn't mean that they don't become *our* wounds—wounds we take along with us into adulthood, expressed in our own relationships and parenting.

The thing I feared most as a child was being erased and replaced. That fear stalked me well into adulthood. In existential terms, I was afraid of ceasing to exist, to *be*. I had an overwhelming fear of physical death, especially of my loved ones, that haunted me for years. I believed that I could not live without my father and I was terrified when he was diagnosed with diabetes and was hospitalized. I was only four years old at the time. I was so upset with him for being in the hospital that I refused to speak to him on the phone. I felt abandoned. I didn't understand what was happening, and my feelings of helplessness and vulnerability were overpowering. That terror of separation and aloneness was never addressed, and it stayed with me even after my father came home.

I acknowledge that today, 44 years later, that same ghost can float into my life uninvited and "get" me again. If my emotional state is weak, or if I'm exhausted, I can see myself automatically responding with that same old dread.

As Dr. Harville Hendrix so clearly explains using Imago therapy, we re-create the nightmare of our childhoods again and again in relationships of all sorts. Not because we like pain and disappointment; because it is a loving attempt on the part of the Universe to get our attention as it invites us to face and embrace our hunger pains. When things don't hurt that badly, we can ignore or rationalize them. It's not until the toothache, ulcer, or lump gets too painful or becomes too big that we can no longer ignore it. The problem is, we don't usually see this pain as having come to rescue us. We run away from and numb the pain, trying to distract ourselves from the real core issues, the real problems, the real deal. We self-medicate (using drugs, alcohol, sex, food, shopping, affairs, texting, talking, etc.), not realizing that the pain is there to deliver a life-saving message.

My initial adult response to the childhood fear of being erased and replaced was to partner with men who kept me constantly on edge about the possibility of abandonment. It so happens that I was also often waiting for them to get help with something in their lives—like an addiction of some sort. My hope was that they'd get help because they loved me so much that they didn't want to lose me. And when they didn't get help, I found fault in myself, not them.

## No Shame in My Game

Looking back, I no longer feel shame in making these admissions. I now understand that my self-destructive choices were an outgrowth of a hunger that had never been satisfied in my childhood. But these memories of being so desperate—feeling so small and without a real self—are still quite painful. I wanted a man who would love me enough to feel like he'd die if I died; a man who would give up his addictions and be emotionally and sexually faithful because he cherished me. I tiptoed through relationships that denied my longings, fearing that I would be erased and replaced. Each time, I would receive a big wake-up call from the Universe when the very thing I feared most would occur.

I've been involved in relationships that emptied me; that took much more than they gave, leaving me hungry and craving. I wanted something real, that could and would satisfy. Part of the pain of starvation is that we begin to hallucinate. We lose touch with reality, with ourselves and our surroundings. Out of all of this angst came the question, "Am I enough for myself? Can I exist to myself even if I don't exist to someone else?"

I realized that my life and presence may not have value to someone else, but *I* now valued it. Someone may be able to live without me, but *I can't live without me.* Now I care about myself, my health, my feelings, my hunger, my starvation, and my joy and peace.

There is very good news. This was the beginning of getting my life back and finding my real power. Many of my nightmares became my saving graces. More recently, a nightmarish dream showed itself as a metaphor. It represented the reality that I had not been seen for me, but for what others could *create me to be* for their own purposes. It showed me this had been the theme of my personal and professional life. I woke up in the middle of the night terrified, startled, and out of breath. In the nightmare I was in the background of a lavish and joyful party I had facilitated, orchestrated, and made possible. While I was at the center of its production, I was not a part of the party itself. I went from being an insider to an onlooker. The host ignored me, while enjoying all I had created—using the gifts and skills I brought to making this event special but not seeing me at all. I was invisible. I can still feel the shock and pain of that nightmare. I remember the smiles of everyone eating, drinking, greeting, and being merry and the host having turned his back on me, symbolic of having shut me out. I will never forget seeing the back of his head as he concerned himself with everyone but me.

A real-life example of the nightmare of invisibility happened when someone I felt connected to, who had been in my life for many years, came to my home when Kalle was sick and dying. I opened my front door sobbing because Kalle had just slipped on the floor and I was helping her to get up. I knew her time with me was limited, that I was losing her . . . that she would soon be gone from our home and I would be left to navigate the world without her. The grief of knowing I would be losing the one being whom I had always counted on was unbearable in that moment. I was coming apart at the seams. I walked into the arms of my so-called, almost lifelong friend and further dissolved into tears. I explained what was happening with Kalle. I said, "Can you sit with us and stay awhile? Kalle's dying." Not only could he not stay, but he was too busy to even sit down. When leaving, my so-called friend said he would call me immediately from the car. It was six months before I heard from him again, and at that time he didn't ask about me or Kalle, who had died four days after my friend abandoned us in the hour of despair and crisis. The incident felt like a drive-by shooting; my invisibility was never so evident or painful. That was the last time this person would be permitted to walk through the doors of my sacred space. I knew instinctively that this person was not my friend. Clearly, neither Kalle nor I existed to him. This was a lesson that was painful and necessary to help me distinguish those who are friends from those who are not. A requisite for friendship is that one be seen. That experience was a revelation for me; a turning point, a defining moment.

For the first time I chose not to run. Not to hide, but instead to sink down into the terror and despair that had been there most of my life. My fear of not being truly important to someone, of being erased and replaced, my terror of "not being," of not existing, was beginning to fade away. Freedom came when I could tolerate being let go. When I could handle the pain of a contract not being renewed, even though from all appearances my contribution to the team was meaningful and significant. When I could walk away from an intimate relationship where I felt more like a gas-and-go station than a human being worthy of love and respect. Freedom came when I could protect myself; step away without feeling destroyed. I wasn't going to die. I had value and worth, simply because I was *me*; because I was here, and I was a child of the Creator, and kissed by the Universe. For the first time, that was more than good enough for me.

## SAFETY IN TRUTH

When we lie, or cover up our true feelings, it is because we feel it is unsafe to tell the truth. If this is how we learned to keep the peace, we have no real peace. Our "peace" is built on having to hide to survive or have our needs met. There are times that people hide their true feelings in relationships to protect themselves from harm, and in that moment hiding can be wise self-care. But don't minimize how much danger can occur physically and emotionally when you keep yourself small. I'm speaking of the danger of losing your voice, losing yourself, and becoming what you're not. Even if in this moment it feels unsafe to change our circumstances, we can begin to be conscious and awake. And that's a good start.

One of my patients, Rebecca, was the child of divorce, and that experience stalled her personal growth and created a comfort zone around silence. Rebecca's task was to understand what in her history had prepared her to be so comfortable being viewed and treated like an object. Comfort connotes familiarity. Rebecca realized that her early home life was focused on making the wrapping of the package look perfect, no matter what the substance or quality of the content. Before entering therapy, Rebecca was unaware of the profound impact her parents' marriage—their mistreatment of each other in front of her and her five siblings and their volatile separation and divorce—had had on her. She was just beginning to understand how the wounds of childhood repeat themselves in adulthood. How they rise up over and over in order to get our attention, so that they may be laid to rest and we may find peace.

She asked me, fearfully, tentatively, but with a hint of excitement, "Who can I be?" Rebecca was both intrigued and scared that maybe her life could be different; maybe she would no longer be an object on the auction block for sale. She looked forward to the day when she could put up a sign AUCTION PERMANENTLY CLOSED.

## WHO TOOK YOUR POWER?

A colleague of mine once described a case involving Matthew, a very well-educated man who was being verbally abused by his wife. Matthew didn't recognize her tirades as abuse. His adult children did not call it abuse either, although they acknowledged that their mother's mouth was out of control and she felt overly entitled to "speak her mind," even when it was hurtful. Her behavior had chased her children away: They'd fled, first to college and then to jobs that were long plane rides away. Matthew was left to endure the abuse alone, and everyone wondered why he passively accepted it. He was quite accomplished, so as my colleague and I talked, I wondered out loud what was going on for him that he would allow this situation to continue. Who took Matthew's power and when did it happen? What trauma had he suffered that allowed him to be abused, but not to see it as abuse?

Thanks to his wise and compassionate therapist, Matthew was beginning to ask these questions himself. He was making tentative steps to discover how he had lost his power and how he could reclaim it. My colleague filled me in on the backstory.

As a child, Matthew had frequently seen his father physically and verbally abusing his mother. He also knew that his father had been unfaithful multiple times, and Matthew had witnessed his disloyalty when he saw his father with other women. Matthew never spoke to his father or mother about any of this. He thought that he was successfully keeping it all tucked away, shelved in a small corner of his mind. But it wasn't shelved, it was being acted out in his marriage and parenting daily. He hated conflict, and wanted to protect his children from experiencing the pain that he had endured as a child. So he decided not to argue, not to fight, not to make a big deal out of things that he felt were easier to let go. At all costs, he wanted to break the cycle of marital discord. What he didn't realize was that he wasn't breaking the bigger cycle of loneliness, silence, and pain. He had decided to give up his voice, his feelings, and his dignity, in the name of being a good husband and father. It is not surprising that he partnered with someone who victimized him. This was all he knew from childhood, and he felt just as helpless as he had when he was a child.

In order to heal, it would be important for Matthew to understand that not only was he being victimized, but by allowing the abuse, he was closing off the chance for him and his wife to build a healthy, loving, and respectful relationship. He was actively participating in his own downfall, as well as the downfall of his marriage. His desire to protect his children was not working. His children were caught in the crossfire between their parents' unresolved childhood issues.

There is no shelving of our childhood wounds. They show up as uninvited guests at every gathering, every occasion, every day. And they won't leave us alone until we properly address the source of the aches and pains.

## SYMBIOTIC ECSTASY

For many years I co-taught a class with a dear friend to doctoral-level students at a local seminary. The topic was diversity in marriage and family therapy. One of the goals of this class was to explore all the ways that differences create fear in relationships, and how that fear can bring out primitive and aggressive behavior. I coined the term *symbiotic ecstasy*, which is what I believe gets in the way of most of us creating mature, healthy, intimate partnerships. Symbiotic ecstasy is the need to stay merged with our primary attachment figure. At birth, this figure is our biological mother, simply because all human beings are attached in the womb by the umbilical cord to their mothers. At birth, this cord is cut quickly. Not only that, but babies are subjected to all sorts of medical procedures: the secretions are sucked out of their nostrils, they're turned upside down and spanked. What a trauma to go from being in the safe cocoon of the womb to being yanked into the world and greeted with a snip and a slap, surrounded by alien-looking people, some bearing video cameras. No wonder the first thing a new baby does is howl!

On some level, until we reach emotional maturity, most of us want to return to the very primitive form of connection we found in the womb. And sometimes that craving for the intimacy experienced in the womb follows us into adulthood. Many of us, as adults, seem to want to climb back in and make our worlds full of sameness to feel safe. We often confuse sameness with closeness. This confusion is born in childhood, but trying to build a healthy intimate relationship based on symbiosis is debilitating and destructive. In the beginning, symbiotic ecstasy is what makes couples feel close, but ultimately it is what chokes the life out of the relationships.

The job of every human being is to find our own divinity—our wholeness. When we put others on a pedestal, and believe ourselves to be incomplete without them, we are failing at our life's purpose. In relationships, we cannot make a covenant if we are worshipping a false idol. It is equally dangerous to put ourselves on a pedestal expecting others to worship at the shrine of our inflated self-regard.

Dependency, attachment, and fear are not love. They can get in the way of true love and connection. They are defenses learned by people who don't believe they can shine their own light. There is a huge difference between love and attachment. Love desires an individual to exist for who they are, and it invites that self into the relationship. Staying with someone because you cannot imagine your identity apart from them may mean you squander your precious gift of life.

## ARRESTED FOR HUNGER

Hunger pains are actually a gift—a big and necessary gift. We need hunger pains to survive and, even more importantly, we need them to *thrive*. Hunger pains get our attention. They are the alarm system that alerts us when our bodies are not being nourished. They warn us that it is urgent that we stop what we are doing and eat. The same is true for our emotional, relational, sexual, sensual, and spiritual hungers. When our needs are ignored or when we have not taken them seriously, our life and relationships grumble in quiet and loud ways. Life tries to get our attention, demanding that we not continue walking past ourselves, ignoring our truest and deepest needs.

Often we try to quiet authentic hunger pains with denial, shame, and blame, instead of filling our plates and relishing the fullness of the meal. We treat ourselves as lawbreakers, handing our fates over to society's enforcers: Police Officer Shame, Police Officer Denial, and Police Officer Blame. We beg these "officers" to reinforce society's norms, to frisk us, and see if they can find our enemy—our hunger. If found, the enemy requires an immediate and brutal arrest. We must silence this criminal. We want this bandit, hunger, thrown in a smelly police wagon, taken in for questioning, put in an even smellier cell, and interrogated until we make a commitment that we will go back into our lives and give it our best shot again. Until we agree to pretend to be full even when we are starving to death.

The pledge we have all taken to get out of the "Hunger Jail" might sound something like this:

> I promise that when I feel my needs and longings stir within me, when I want a real life, a real marriage, real joy, real connection, real sexuality, real passion, real faith, real forgiveness, real friendships, or real connection with family—when I want real *anything* that goes against what others want for me, or what society says is acceptable—I will first beat myself up for daring to want something real, and then I will deny that I need anything more than what I have. I will berate myself for being greedy and ungrateful and I will blame myself that I still haven't outgrown having needs.
>
> If that doesn't work, I will reach out to family, friends, clergy, neighbors, and even enemies, if necessary, who will reinforce the message that my hunger pains are wrong and that I am bad and weak because I haven't conquered them. And I pledge if that level of intervention and brutality

toward myself and my hunger pains doesn't do the trick, I will call 911 and turn myself in to Officer Denial, Officer Shame, and Officer Blame. I know that each time I call 911 for this intervention, the punishment will get worse, and my body, soul, spirit, personality, sexuality, and entire being will be attacked for the sole purpose of beating my hunger pains down until they are never heard from again.

It may seem melodramatic, but, in truth, many people live in this prison, pledging away all their rights as human beings. They make silent promises every day to "do better." But better at *what*? Not being themselves. I know this pledge all too well. It almost killed me and destroyed any chance I had to be my true and unmasked self.

## CAN YOU OFFER YOURSELF CLEMENCY?

Years ago someone in my life who had refused to speak with me for weeks dared to try to kiss me. I was enraged by his audacity and entitlement after having shut me out for so long. The same weapon he used to hurt me—his mouth, by staying silent—he was now using to objectify me. I was startled but thought, *You've got to be kidding me,* and I had the automatic reflex to close my mouth and pull away.

That was a healthy response. It was honest and it was appropriate, but almost instantly Officers Shame, Blame, and Denial showed up. They indicted me for having dared to stand up for myself; for expecting to be treated with respect and dignity. I took their deadly pledge, swallowed my truth, and apologized to the man. But even though I shrunk and evaporated in that moment, the cat was out of the bag, so to speak. My journey of running from my hunger was slowly but surely coming to an end.

We must retrain ourselves away from self-abuse, self-neglect, and self-rejection. We must learn to embrace the gift of our hunger. The life-saving growl of our hunger pangs, that prods us to be kind, gentle, welcoming, and inquisitive about our longings, needs, and desires. It is only when we can welcome *all* of who we are—the parts we're proud of as well as the feeble and limping parts—that we can truly be free.

# CHAPTER 7

# "I Want More!"

*"Wouldn't it be powerful if you fell in love with yourself so deeply that you would do just about anything if you knew it would make you happy?"*

Alan Cohen

I come from a family of do-gooders and pleasers, and from an early age I was taught to put others first. That was the motto of my household, and my parents went out of their way to make sure that we were thoughtful, considerate, and mindful of others' feelings more than our own. I can remember times when a school-mate would be mean to me and I'd tell my mother. She'd reply, "Robin, be kind. She looks like she needs a friend. Maybe she's having problems at home." I would silently scream and sometimes cry out loud, "Mommy, what about *me?*" But taking care of *me* at the expense of hurting someone's feelings was a big no-no. It would have been labeled as selfish, and in my family being selfish was the biggest sin of all.

I learned to see devastation and not call it that. I learned to re-language the disrespect that was shown toward me and others so that I didn't have to take action on my own behalf or theirs. I learned to be helpless as a part of my family legacy against abuse, meanness, and harm. We were the "good guys," who fought injustice with love—or so we thought. What did we do with all the knives in our backs, the betrayals of our loyalty, the gut punches to our dignity? I tried to make the best of bad situations, all the while wearing a smile. I have often used the analogy of trying to install central air conditioning in hell; it is an illusion to think a blast of cool air would change the hellness of it, but that was the way it was in our home.

I carried joy in one pocket and denial in the other. I was loading both pockets with more and more stuff. I had a privileged upbringing, went to great schools, took wonderful family vacations, and had no blatant traumas as a child. My parents supported and attended all my events. My father was a local and national hero. My mother was a professional who was afforded the luxury to stay at home with her children until we were older, which at times drove me crazy. She was around and available to participate in my life—to support my dreams, endeavors, and activities. But like any good mother, at times she got on my last nerve. I suspect that I got on hers as well. Later in life she returned to work out of her own personal, professional, and spiritual hunger to be fully and freely herself.

In my home, we were taught that it's more important to look good than to feel good. This means we were indirectly taught to cover up the truth, which in turn taught us that the truth was too big and too painful to face. We were taught to have compassion for others even at our own expense—but that meant we could easily be harmed and end up feeling bad for those who hurt us. This made relationships risky, because if something went wrong, we were conditioned to try and fix it. We didn't learn to extricate ourselves from bad situations, but only how to *manage* them; how to adjust the temperature in hell. But we were not taught how to get the hell out!

There were few messages in my childhood about self-protection. They were all about giving and loving. On the face of it that sounds wonderful, but the downside was that relationship reciprocity and boundaries were not taught, practiced, or enforced. No one seemed to know how to approach these tough but learnable skills. My parents were good people, smart and resourceful, and they loved their children. But in addition to their generosity toward others, they passed on to us their confusion about self-love and self-care. As a result, part of my master skill set was getting the short end of the stick and pretending it was long enough. Taking lemons and making lemonade was what I knew how to do best. It would not have occurred to me to say, "This is too sour, and, no thank you, I'll pass."

We all lived in the shadow of my larger-than-life father. He was a true legend and a magnificent man. He had the rare and unique qualities of being enormously kind, generous to all people, accepting, tolerant and embracing of differences, unassuming and approachable given his status of success by the world's standards. My mother has often said, "He marched with kings, but never lost the common touch." He loved God, humanity, and creation. He was sweet, tender, and available to my mother, my brother, sister, and myself . . . and to our dogs, guinea pigs, turtles, fish, and whatever other creatures found their way into our home. He was an advocate for human rights long before it was the politically correct or the expedient thing to do. He stood for justice for all people, even when taking such a stand got you put on hit lists.

But at some point, the shade from my father's giant shadow became too much for all of us. His godlike stature in our family and in the world had many consequences for our family, and for me personally. (I was always—and remain—the only one who ever dared to say so.) If Daddy was like God (albeit a very nice god), then who were we, his wife and his children? Were we to be little gods, or were we to not be gods at all? It wasn't clear, but what *was* clear was that there wasn't much room for any of us to become whoever it was we were created to be. We all got stuck, including my mother, as extensions of this god—my father.

The women in my home were all experts at starving ourselves and hiding it. My father's gentle power was simultaneously intoxicating and debilitating. He was not only a godlike figure in our own home, he was a leader in the civil rights movement who marched with Dr. Martin Luther King, Jr., and lived and preached about the power of working on behalf of others. I was and remain proud of my parents with their dedication to the movement and their messages of compassion and caring. I am who I am because of the positive messages they passed onto me. But those messages weren't the only ones I heard—or even the main ones. Both of my parents were quite skilled at managing the hunger game, at appearing to be full when in my opinion they were not. My mother had her own unique brand of denying and hiding her hunger. Her spiritual life, which was and continues to be genuinely rich, seemed to become a mixture of seeking God and a place of covering up profound sorrow, grief, loss, insecurity, and yearning. I learned many meaningful lessons from my mother that have enriched my life, but the lesson about hiding my hunger I learned all too well from both of my parents. I learned to suffer in silence and seem satisfied and full when I was dying to be fed. I was taught from an early age to hide my hunger (or displeasure or needs) at all costs—even if it meant living a life that was not mine.

My father died in 1990, and almost without my knowing it, his death gave me permission to acknowledge and face myself. And, in particular, my unconscious desire to remain Daddy's good girl even if it killed me. Even now, over 20 years later, I have been known to say, "When Daddy took his last breath, I felt like I took my first breath."

When I began writing this book, my maternal grandmother was 106 years old. She died at 107 just 6 months shy of her 108th birthday. My mother is a healthy 90 and her sister is 92, and their mother's death was a bittersweet time. I noticed how old issues revived themselves, as Grandmommy's death was near. The dance between resilience and fragility, strength and weakness, overcoming racism and yet still being oppressed, abounding joy and unrelenting sorrow, forgiveness and grudge holding—it was a sumptuous feast of emotion. There was love, laughter, grief, and tears. There were issues that seemed resolved, or at least resolvable, and reminders that there was a river under the river that held the real story. There was celebration, too, of the life of this remarkable woman, the daughter of a freed slave, who created and built an amazing life, both beautiful and flawed—the ground on which I stand, and sometimes fall. (I guess you could say that slavery and the hunger for emancipation run in my family's DNA.)

As I prepared to preach Grandmommy's eulogy, I wondered if my mother and my aunt were experiencing something of what I experienced at my father's death—the gift of being truly free. My grandmother was a strong and dominating presence, and maybe as Grandmommy took her last breath and made a peaceful transition into eternity, her daughters were taking their first breaths of independence, even in the twilight of their own lives. That's my hope and prayer for them.

---

## The Clock Is Ticking

As the saying goes, you can change the hands on the clock, but you can't change time. Time is the one commodity we can't get back. We all waste it. But just as we are learning to recycle plastics and glass to help save the planet, we can embrace this same change regarding the priceless gift of time.

I decided not to beat myself up anymore for what I used to call *wasted time*. Beating myself up defeats my very purpose and aim . . . it's pointless, it lacks compassion, and it further injures my heart. Being unkind to ourselves only wastes more of the precious time that we have left to live our lives more fully and freely. Dr. Maya Angelou says that when we know better, we will do better. So, I will do better, because I now know better. As Dr. Benjamin Elijah Mays so eloquently wrote:

> *"I have only just a minute,*
> *Only sixty seconds in it,*
> *Forced upon me—can't refuse it,*
> *Didn't seek it, didn't choose it.*
> *But it's up to me to use it.*
> *I must suffer if I lose it.*
> *Give account if I abuse it.*
> *Just a tiny little minute—*
> *But eternity is in it."*

---

## SMACK, CRACKLE, AND POP

Because I didn't know how to protect myself and discriminate between who was safe and who wasn't, I found myself in a physically and emotionally abusive relationship in my teenage years. As I briefly mentioned earlier, I graduated from high school and entered out-of-state college at age 16. I lived on campus, and like many freshmen thought I was able to care for myself. Enter Henderson, my first so-called real love.

I have examined—through therapy and years of living, growing, and grappling—what made me tolerate Henderson hitting me. I know I was young, and I know our love felt like "the real thing." He was the first person I had sex with, and we waited a very long time, for many reasons. Still I wasn't ready, emotionally, psychologically, or spiritually. I had been taught that the beauty of a sexual relationship was to be saved for marriage. While my parents weren't ones to harp on family values and principles, they lived them—which had a greater and more profound impact on me.

Not only did my parents support nonviolence in the civil rights movement, but they were also nonviolent at home. Fighting was not our style. This made the awful violence in my young relationship even more intolerable and perplexing.

I don't know how many times Henderson hit me, but once was too much. And even after his handprint disappeared from my face, my heart and soul were left scarred. And one of his hits injured my mouth so I literally was never able to whistle a tune again.

Because the life I had with Henderson was not the kind of life I was used to, I eventually got on a plane without his knowledge. I left and I went home to Philadelphia. My parents picked me up from the airport and we went out to dinner. They were really glad to see me and I was really glad to see them. We talked as we always did as a family, but I didn't know how to reveal my trauma. I now understand that being hungry can set the stage for destructive relationships. In my case, I hungered to be cherished and special. Henderson had made me feel that way, but that same hunger left me blind to his violent nature, his lack of appreciation for my innocence, and his ability to be cruel and humiliating. I am grateful that while I lost my whistle, I didn't lose my song.

As I came to understand myself more, I began to notice that many of my encounters with people left me hungry and feeling confused, as if something were wrong with me for wanting my needs met—for wanting to be taken seriously, for wanting to be loved and respected, for wanting reciprocity in my relationships. When I was around these people, I felt that I wanted too much and was too needy. I swallowed every bite I was offered whole— feeling insatiable—and when I walked away, I was bewildered, depressed, and secretly enraged.

My family didn't do anger well out in the open; as I've said, we were the peace seekers. What that means in real time and real language is that we hid our anger—often even from ourselves. We gulped it down like a dog who has stolen a piece of meat from the table, hoping to consume it before we were caught in the act. We felt ashamed of our anger and therefore we denied the powerful and healing gift that anger can offer. I had no idea how to pay close attention to my anger, how to listen for its lessons, because I didn't know that being angry was part of being human. This was a pattern that was taking me from bad to worse as my hunger intensified. Was I insatiable? Was I so needy that my hole felt as deep as the Grand Canyon? Or was it that I was legitimately hungry in relationships where I was being starved to death, trying to pretend I was full when I was empty? What was the truth? My life and sanity depended on exploring this raw and rocky question, and seeing what information came back to me. Could I ask for more?

We are afraid to say, "I want more." We fear the response—or the lack of response. So we tell ourselves that "less is more," which is sometimes true. But not when it comes to taking hunger and its messages seriously.

Putting men on a pedestal was my style. It's what I had learned to do. I made them wiser than me when they weren't, so that I could look up to them and respect them. So I could feel that being with them made sense, even though clearly it didn't. That hero-worship was a projection and an illusion. I believed that they had more going for them than I did, including more business savvy—despite the fact that I had built a very successful career. There are plenty of people roaming the world looking to feel big, and what better combination than to find someone willing to be small? It was the perfect storm, and boy, did it cause damage! From the north to the south poles of my soul, and from the east to the west coasts of my being, I was in bad shape. It was like I'd been struck by a natural disaster and had gotten no help from FEMA.

I performed the one-down act flawlessly. I made my shrinking away look comfortable, even though it was slowly killing me.

And what of the *real* me? What of the woman with the strong mind and kind heart? What of the woman whose wisdom runs deep and whose instincts are as sharp as a new butcher's knife? Well, here's what happened. When my instincts and wisdom gave me advice that I didn't like—advice that would mean ending a relationship—I turned my back. I drank the cyanide and called it Kool-Aid. I deliberately dulled my senses and knocked out the voice of wisdom. I didn't drink enough to kill me, but enough to numb the voice of truth. I made myself the wrong one—too demanding, too sensitive, too vulnerable. I did whatever it took to run from reality, not understanding that I could never outrun the truth. When I arrived at my new destination of excuses and exceptions, the truth always opened the door and greeted me.

A wise person said to me during this period, "If you would stop rubbing up against someone else's power, you'd find your own and no one could take it away from you."

When I began asking different questions, having to do with my real hunger and needs, a transformation began. The light went on and the truth about my hunger and longings set me on the path to freedom and peace. No longer did I spend time with people who required me to sit at the table hungry, watching them eat, allowing them to feast off me and my misguided love as the exorbitant price I paid for their company and false companionship.

I wanted to live, and that meant I had to learn to protect myself from parasitic relationships. I had to begin to own that "I want more."

I had to find my own divinity—which is the job of every human life. I had to reclaim my birthright and my true identity. Putting people on a pedestal makes life dangerous and feeds the lie—that someone in the world is better than you. There's a difference between admiring others, which is healthy and necessary to grow ourselves into better people, and making idols out of humans.

We all need to de-idolize and de-demonize our families. This is part of breaking the cycle of hiding and covering up the truth.

I no longer rub up against success, security, joy, and power to gain secondhand worth. I no longer play small so that insecure people will keep me around. I embrace more fully each day who I am. And I know that I can take care of and nurture myself.

---

### The lies that keep you down

These are three lies that keep a soul hungry:

1. I can't take care of myself.

2. I won't be okay alone.

3. I need someone else (a man, a woman, a friend, a parent) to be validated.

These lies played themselves out again and again in my adult relationships. Sometimes my "idols" were nice, sometimes they were mean, but the lies were equally debilitating. Most importantly, this story was mine to change. Only I could rewrite the script.

---

### DIRTY LAUNDRY

My openness and willingness to share is not a family trait. It is what I have chosen for myself, in order to claim my spiritual, physical, emotional, financial, and relational health. My way is very much not "the family way" of living in the world, as I share my warts and blemishes as well as my beauty and brilliance. I was definitely raised not to "air my dirty laundry" in public. I was the kid in my family who rejected that limiting message and rule. I learned that the dirty laundry is not really dirty. It is unacknowledged pain and shame, and denying it was never going to lead to my personal freedom and liberation.

In the process of learning, I also began to understand what it meant to care for myself and to set boundaries. What I owe and what I don't owe. What I want to share with people and what I don't. And, when I have done enough and am satisfied with my own efforts, attitudes, and actions, then I have peace. I finally have my own "good enough" barometer and it is working.

I have broken the rule to keep quiet about my pain or to deny its existence many times. I am done with the backdrop of my life being a "silent scream."

## "I Want More"

A close friend has this ongoing (and what feels to her like a never-ending) conversation with herself about wanting a hamburger that she won't permit herself to have. She also does this with her desire for a glazed doughnut. She knows what she longs for, what her mouth is at times calling for, and then she spends her time talking herself out of what she really wants. She looks for substitutes, surrogates, things she thinks are healthier and less fattening. The problem is, her true craving is never satisfied. She thinks she has chased it away, but it's not gone. It's waiting for her right around the corner with her truest needs. She pushes away her real desire by masking it with other unhealthy and ultimately unsatisfying alternatives, and then she is back where she started—this time feeling even worse for eating things that ultimately didn't touch her real need. She will eat almost anything but that hamburger, and she overeats trying to compensate; trying to satisfy her longing for that good juicy burger. She says that she buys a candy bar or some other sweet that does not satisfy her craving, trying to hush her desire, hoping it will go away. But it always comes back, and often with a vengeance.

So, not only does she add calories—and the pounds that go with them—but she does it with food that is nothing close to what she truly desires. Why does she torture herself this way? The denial of the hamburger makes the craving larger than life; it has taken on even greater power. She may think she is fighting herself about calories, but the issue has nothing to do with food. It has to do with ignoring herself, diminishing her needs, being mean to herself, and placing herself in a no-win situation. Sadly, that is never what she focuses on. Her focus is the hamburger, the doughnut, and her lack of discipline. She is big on calling for backup, hoping that each time Officers Denial, Shame, and Blame show up on the scene their arrest will deter her from doing it again in the future. Of course, this will never work. As long as she continues in this way, she is going to end up with unmet needs and a broken, hungry, and deserving heart.

What my friend did with substituting foods to chase away her true craving, we often do in other areas of our lives—especially relationships. But you can't fill a sacred hunger with a cheap surrogate. You only end up with a deeper unmet need that you can't shake.

Knowing that we have a right to get our needs met in a relationship is important. It's important to know that we can ask for what we want, and that someone who cares about us will listen and respect our desire. It seems so apparent, and yet many people think that they'll be fine if they can just convince themselves they don't want what they want. They even think they'll be happier! They believe they can fill themselves up on a mirage. Ultimately, if we're hungry and we don't eat, we'll die. No amount of positive thinking, praying, or pretending can change that fact.

In the past much time and energy were spent obsessing over how to address my wound—settling for crumbs when I wanted a meal, settling for an hour of time when I wanted a relationship—without *really* addressing it. I wanted to focus on my adult relationships, but that's not where the pain started and that's not where it was going to end. During the time of a major soul assault, I had one more empty encounter with a man. I remember looking at him across the dinner table, listening to his laundry list of excuses not to commit. This time, my inner voice was bigger than his. We quietly parted ways. I got in my car, drove down the highway, and all I could hear from within was, "I want more. This is not enough for me . . . it's killing me."

I began to truly understand that there had been a death theme in my life. I myself had been dead, and I had been engaged in dead relationships. I was exhausted by so many relationships that had been kept alive on a respirator. This particular relationship—its abuses and pain—had been co-created by me. I was still a bandit on the run from the real scene of the crime: my childhood loss, abandonment, and sense of being erasable and replaceable. I was never going to be free if I kept focusing on current dramas. I had to go back to the old landmark; to deal with the root of the issue. When someone gets cancer, the doctors don't play around with trying to get *some* of it, they treat with the sole purpose to get it *all* out; to get as much as they can, to remove it at the root.

I knew I had to have this type of spiritual surgery, but I went to the operating room kicking and screaming. My childhood wounds had robbed me of too much, and this was my chance to run like a captured slave toward freedom. I reminded myself it was like cancer: "Robin, to survive you have to remove every bit of it."

I have two spiritual fathers in ministry; both are loving, kind, smart, supportive, and generous with their wisdom, counsel, and time. I don't get to see them much because of their busy schedules and mine. One lives in California and the other is in Ohio, but several years ago, I had the opportunity to see both of them at the same time—it was a double hitter for me. They were both being honored at the same event held at Vanderbilt University in Nashville, so my friend Sandra and I surprised them by showing up for the conference and the festivities. While there, I had some one-on-one time with each of them. During a very early morning breakfast with one of these gentle giants, Rev. Dr. J. Alfred Smith, Sr., I heard the words flow with compassion and ease from his mouth, "Robin, sometimes you just have to let it die, let the whole thing die, all at once . . . grieve it, grieve the disappointment, grieve that you put so much in and got almost nothing out except for this major life lesson. Have a funeral, sit shivah, do whatever you need to in order to grieve this loss so you can fully and freely move on. Like cancer, let God go in and remove the whole thing." My green-blue eyes were now bloodshot red from crying. Right there in a public place! But what the heck, I was in trouble and needed help right then and there.

I did several things during this time of spiritual surgery . . . the first thing was to tell the whole truth and nothing but the truth to myself so help me God. The second thing was to "tell the truth, tell the truth, tell the truth," which means telling and trying to live the truth internally and externally in safe ways with myself, others, and the Universe.

Those words were medicine for me as I read Elizabeth Gilbert's book, *Eat, Pray, Love.* When I interviewed Elizabeth on *The Dr. Robin Show,* the radio show I hosted five days each week, the healing power of telling the truth was one of the topics we bit into and discussed. I was known for telling the truth, for being a seeker and truth-teller. In many ways this was accurate, but there was a deep level of truth that I had been avoiding out of fear. I had long feared what knowing the truth might require of me. Now I feared what *not knowing* it had done to my life, my hopes, my dreams, and my soul. So of course, during this time the person who knows it all—my best friend Sandra—and I had even more conversations than usual about the emotional and spiritual surgery I needed. We hashed out the pros and cons of having it or not. My therapist, who has walked with me for many years, was also on the front lines with me. When the pain was most excruciating and the fear bordering on unbearable, I saw her as often as twice a week. I have a loving and supportive village both of family and friends who supported me as much as they could, given that most of them didn't know just how bad off things had gotten for me. My pastor and church family, who pray for me just because they love and care, were with me . . . although they had no idea that my soul was hanging in the balance between life and death . . . and at this point, death absolutely felt like the kinder and gentler solution;

although, I had decided that I wanted to live and that even though I could drown in my despair, I had had enough of drowning. And, oh, yes, I had *Nature!* I don't know what I would have done without the woods, streams, deer who seemed to look deep into me and allowed me to stand and talk with them, the foxes who crossed my path, not once but many times in my backyard, the frogs in my pond and sometimes at my front door waiting to greet me. There was a time when the frogs were present in my life and it was so scorching hot that my mother asked if I thought I should bring the one at the front door inside. Clearly, this was one reminder of when my mother's big heart could get in the way of life being what it is meant to be. Creation knows how to care for itself. Needless to say, the frog stayed outside and survived.

What I know for sure is that it took a village of people, a tribe of creation, and the precious gift of silence for my life-makeover and inner transformation to occur.

We can identify the old thoughts, beliefs, and experiences that have continued to cheat us out of life's and love's best. We can stop the roller-coaster ride of unsatisfying intimate relationships, and turn our boat in the direction where dreams become reality. But what we get in return is not childhood-based dreams coming true. We get the dreams of a healthy adult—inviting and creating safety, security, passion, and respect in our intimate relationships.

Knowing our childhood wounds and where they began is necessary to understand the messages and themes that keep playing themselves out in our adult relationships. This is how we go about discovering the information we need to change the tide of our relationships. Our childhood wounds have cheated us all too long. We can begin a new chapter in our lives and invite ourselves to the banquet.

Wanting more requires taking back our power and reclaiming our divine birthright to *receive*. Wanting more is a rite of passage into an honest relationship with ourselves and others. Giving ourselves permission to speak of our hunger, needs, longings, and desires is one of the keys to ending the hunger strike. To setting our course in the direction of satisfaction and fullness.

"I want more." Three simple words, with life-changing power.

CHAPTER 8

# AN EMPTY FRIDGE

---

*"He who does not cultivate his field will die of hunger."*
GUINEAN PROVERB

Many years ago, my significant other collapsed on a beautiful white, sandy Caribbean beach. It was cardiac arrest, an uninvited guest that brutally interrupted our vacation and forever changed his life—and mine. I had never seen death sweep down and kidnap someone's breath and life in less than an instant. I know this kind of tragedy happens to people each and every day, but this time it was me, not someone else. I lived in a fog for a long time, even though I looked anything but fogged out.

Tyrone died twice. The first death came as he lay on the sand. Two strangers taking a late afternoon stroll on the beach knew CPR, and they managed to get his heart started. They worked on him until a doctor from the local clinic could reach this remote stretch of paradise gone bad. Tyrone suffered an anoxic brain injury. I learned this term and many others, as I grappled with the nightmare that had become my reality.

I kept trying to wake up from this bad dream, and then I would realize that I *was* awake—and this was my life. It wasn't a neighbor whom I was horrified for, nor a friend or family member whom I sensitively helped feel all their fears and pains. This time I wasn't the one entering the room to offer comfort. I was the one trapped in the horror.

Tyrone lingered in a severely brain-damaged state for five months. He kept beating back death, and looking back I often wonder if those months were a gift to help us prepare for life without him. They didn't feel like a gift then. At the time, I fell apart. I failed to practice what I had so often preached to others. My self-care was compromised, to say the least. I suspended my private practice and lived at the rehab center, sleeping on a cot for four months. I was so checked out from my own emotional state that, in spite of the dire circumstances, I was fully comfortable entertaining my friends and family who came to visit—as if we were sitting in my living room. I learned to eat fish, which I had hated all of my life, because I wanted to stay healthy and "alive" to take care of Tyrone, to be there for him. I didn't exist as a person. I wasn't taking care of my needs, because I would have had to face my overwhelming and profound terror and grief. I had faded away like an old newspaper that has taken a beating from the sun. The real question here is how much of me ever really existed? Would I have been able to live with such deprivation if I were not already intimately acquainted with it? Probably not.

This wonderful man never recovered his vibrant life as a father, son to his then-aging parents, brother, successful executive, my partner, lover, loyal friend, and a really great human being. His second death came on Christmas Eve, and this time it was for real and it was for good.

After his death, I was the walking dead. I was technically alive, but only technically. I dressed for success, eventually returned to work and tried to live again. Most people saw only my façade of vitality. I was warm, bubbly, engaging, willing to share my heart and feelings. I was still able to cry at the drop of the hat (which had always been my nature) and loved to laugh and be playful.

It all sounded good and looked even better. But underneath that exterior was a scared woman who was fragile, insecure, and afraid. I was dying a slow death.

The lights were on but no one was really home. You can't be home in your soul if you are living in fear. What I now understand is that I wasn't fully alive even *before* his collapse—I was full of hidden fears that were buried nicely and neatly in my insecurities. I didn't even know that they were there. I was buried alive, and dying by the second. Something had to be done. I had to see what was really true.

Trauma can uncover what is buried just beneath the surface. This is true for all of us, which is why weddings and funerals, births and deaths, marriage and divorce, conceiving children, trying to conceive them, having children, not being able to have them, financial hardship and financial windfalls, sickness and health, success and failures, hirings and firings—all bring to the surface what truly lives within us. Blessings and burdens show us who and what we are, and who and what we are not. Like an ATM machine, whatever is in us is what comes out.

Are you the walking dead? Are you on automatic pilot? Are you living but not really alive? Are you breathing but not using your breaths to create a life that you want to live? I needed to ask these questions of myself so that I would no longer pretend to be full when my soul's pantry was empty.

## RELATIONSHIPS ON A RESPIRATOR

Imagine being hungry for a delicious, fragrant stew, filled with fresh meat and vegetables, heaped over steaming rice—but instead you are served a plate of dry crackers. As you sit and eat, you smile and thank your host and begin to create a story in your head that this is what you really wanted all along. We do this all the time. We don't know how to get what we really want, so we settle for less and call it "healthy"—all the while, our cravings grow and go wild. It's not the settling that is the real problem, it's the pretending, denying, and hiding from the full truth about our hunger.

Being impoverished isn't always about money. Both the struggling citizen and the wealthy banker or celebrity are hungry for the same thing: permission to be who they are. The financially struggling person is hungry to not have shame for their position in life. The wealthy person is hungry to not have shame that they have so much and yet feel that something is missing.

When Vice President Al Gore and his wife Tipper announced that they were divorcing after 40 years of marriage, many people were surprised and deeply disappointed. They had always seemed like the perfect couple, a model for others. I was interested in how many people had opinions about the Gore marriage and divorce, even though none of us could really know what went on inside. Someone said to me a bit grumpily, "Why couldn't they just stay married? They have multiple houses all over the country. It's not as if they have to be in the same house together. They could stay married and almost never have to see each other."

I replied, "Maybe they didn't want to live their lives pretending to be full on something that was empty. Maybe they wanted to be full on something that was satisfying."

I was doing my radio show at the time, and people called in full of suggestions about how the Gores could manage their marriage without having to dissolve it. What they were really talking about was managing the emptiness so that the world saw it as fullness. I invited them to consider whether it was important to have a relationship that is not on a respirator—one that can breathe deeply of its own accord.

Some people saw it as a matter of morality, saying that keeping their marriage intact was the moral choice for the Gores to make. I wonder, though, if morality isn't a more complicated matter. Would God say that the moral path is to live your life as a lie?

## SKIPPING MEALS

Have you ever skipped a meal, thinking you would "save" those calories for later, even as you got hungrier and hungrier? Deprivation of any kind only increases the craving and makes one feel the starvation more intensely. That applies to life as well. Waiting for the "right" or "perfect" moment to live your chosen life is a miserable way to be. There's no magic in waiting. Waiting is overrated. Don't believe the old adage, "Good things come to those who wait." While waiting can have its benefits—emotionally, spiritually, financially, sexually, relationally, and physically—there are times when waiting is wasteful and comes from a place of fear. One day I was leaving a session with my therapist and I said, "Maybe I should wait a couple weeks to come in for my next session." My therapist looked at me with great compassion and replied, "Robin, you don't have to wait. What are you waiting for?" I burst into tears, suddenly realizing that there was no magic in waiting; that waiting, in this instance, was another form of punishment and further starvation. That it only made me hungrier. I was so accustomed to being told to wait for my needs to be met, needs that often got forgotten and left behind. I had started treating myself with that same dismissive behavior until I almost forgot that I was "there."

I was stopped short by the realization that day. I asked myself what I was waiting for in my relationships. I saw that I had been waiting for an otherworldly moment of true love and connection, when in truth there was nothing magical about it. What my soul was waiting for was to take myself seriously, to make myself a priority, to have my needs respected and, when possible, met. To be acknowledged, to receive compassion and nurturance so that I would not be hungry because of self-deprivation.

Patience is a virtue, as they say—unless you wait too long. Patience is only a virtue if you use it in the way it needs to be used. But if you are so patient that you can sit on the sidelines and watch the world go by without honestly engaging, waiting can be a form of self-abuse that's ultimately deadly. That's not patience! Self-neglect is sneaky, like a fire. One minute there's a whiff of smoke, and then you turn around and your house has burned to the ground—and taken you with it.

## SETTLING FOR CRUMBS

Imagine opening your refrigerator looking for something to eat and finding it empty, as if someone removed all the food as a punishment. For a time, I experienced that with my identity. I was hungry for an identity that was solid and secure. Not one that was given to me by another person—and thus could be taken away when the giver got angry with me for not stroking their ego. I was hungry for an identity I didn't have to beg, borrow, or steal. I was hungry to have a sense of myself that was solid; that could not be tampered with.

Many years after Tyrone's death, I became involved with someone I thought was alive but who was in the prison of their own exiled life. I had a big decision to make. I had to figure out whether or not I could or would choose life with my heart broken. Because I was one of the living dead, I entered the relationship in a zombielike state. I was so numb, I gave no thought to what this relationship would cost me. I got involved with someone who lived in a familiar prison, one that allowed me to remain locked up in despair. I think his plan was that we would be jailed together forever. If something hadn't changed within me, that deadly thought might have become a horrible reality.

As it turned out, he had no intention of popping the question. A future with me was never his aim, although it took me a long time to realize it. His life was full of activities that stroked his ego and his hunger for power and acceptance. A mutually loving relationship between equals was a commodity that held no value in his portfolio. From the beginning he had trouble making time for me. In fact, he once told me that one of the things he needed most was space—an almost comical admission since I rarely saw him. I can laugh about it today, but it hurt then. My options were either to wait on him and hope he would show up (he almost never did), or to accept from the beginning that he had no intention of honoring his word or commitment to me. I didn't understand that I had a third option, which was not to wait; to begin building my life without him. That is eventually what I did, but it was a long process. I walked around for a long time asking if I could taste and touch passion again. Could I live and love fully and freely, if I didn't exist to a man or to any other person?

One of my spiritual mentors said to me then, "Robin, not only is he a selfish lover, he is a terrible friend." I knew his words were true. In that moment I understood that I could no longer survive on this deadly, so-called relationship starvation diet. I was no longer willing to be the only one at the table not eating. I wanted never again to wither away as I watched someone gorge themselves. He left the table replenished and satisfied, and I left the table hungry and miserable. Something was so wrong with this picture. He certainly didn't care about my starving heart, body, or soul. But finally, I did.

When I left the relationship, it took him months, maybe years, to notice that I was gone. Who knows, maybe he still thinks I am sitting by the phone, saving my breath to live my life with him. It doesn't matter anymore what he thinks, or whether he cares. Whether he knows that I am alive, that I have a beating pulse and a pumping heart. *I* finally know that I am alive and that my life matters and counts.

There was only one thing left to do, I had to pop the question. It was time and I had to ask. I could no longer run from the question or the answer.

I took a deep breath in and out several times, building my nerve to ask what I was mortified to ask. I knew I couldn't put it off one second longer. I didn't want to ask a question about marriage, or the future. This one question was pressing on my hunger pains, making my stomach do somersaults and it had to be spoken.

So I popped the question. I asked myself, "Robin, can you exist to yourself, even if someone else sees you and treats you as if you are dead?" I was quiet, waiting for an answer.

After a pause, and very quietly, the voice of my soul whispered to me, "YES."

I had no idea what that meant, what it would look like, or how in the world I would ever pull it off. But the answer was "Yes." I could be dead to someone else and still be alive to myself. Wow!

I had a new option—to live because *I was worthy of life.* Not because someone else loved me, but because I loved myself, and I finally knew that I was worthy of love.

## SOMETHING FROM NOTHING IS NOTHING

The exact message from my father was, "Robin, if you work hard enough you can accomplish anything." How many of us were raised with this notion? The idea seemed to serve me well; I achieved goal after goal, placing checkmarks next to each success. But in the process I was being harmed, because I was unable to discriminate between what or who deserved my full attention and hard work—and what and who did not. There was no conservation of energy, no reflection. I was a busy bee.

My skills were awesome. You could give me almost nothing and by the time I was done with it, I had taken crumbs and made a full meal off of it. I even learned how to make myself full, when actually I was still starving. Fortunately, I stopped "making a meal out of crumbs." As I said earlier, I stopped drinking cyanide and calling it Kool-Aid.

When people tell me how much work it is to mirror, validate, and empathize with their partner, I say yes, you're right—it *is* a ton of work. It's hard to learn the new skill of not thinking that your way is the only way, that your decisions should be followed without being explored, questioned, and examined. It is work to share power. We have so few examples of sharing power. People either have power or they don't, they have a say or they don't. From government decision-making tables to family dinner tables, the issue of sharing power and privilege is all but absent, and real consideration that begins with respect seems to be like an endangered species.

If you never had any power, or if power was abused in your family—meaning someone had power and others did not, and those who didn't were subject to the one(s) who did—this power differential feels awful.

Unfortunately, marriage and parenting—and workplace jobs as well—are places where people act out their power needs. If you've ever wondered about ushers at the theater who tell you not very nicely what the rules are, or ushers in church who frown at you as you take your seat in the wrong pew, what you're seeing are examples of people who may have little or no power in other arenas of their lives, and are exerting it where they can.

I worked for many years in a juvenile detention center. It is a lock-down facility with many broken-spirited children. One of the saddest things about working there, other than seeing so many children of color locked up, was watching some adults use this setting to flex their muscles—to be powerful there because they had little power in other areas of their lives. This is often an unconscious attempt to meet our need for personal power, but in this instance on the backs of vulnerable children. A similar dynamic happens all the time in marriage, in parenting, and even in friendships. If power was abused in your home growing up, it's critical to know what your own issues are around power—how you use it, abuse it, and give it away. In order for any relationship to be successful, the issue of power is one that must be fully understood and addressed.

To be hungry for power isn't wrong or sinful, but to be hungry for power without being aware of it is dangerous to yourself and others. I have always believed that anyone who dares to run for the office of President of the United States, and is then elected, should immediately go into therapy—and stay in therapy for the entire time he or she is in office. This therapy would allow the most powerful man or woman in the nation to negotiate the tricky paths of power and vulnerability. A person who receives Secret Service protection should also be seeking protection for the unwieldy *inner* challenges that inevitably come with such a high-powered position. What a great example it would be for the whole country, to say, in effect, "I am powerful, but I am also human, and my hunger needs to be addressed for me to be the most effective leader I can be."

## Hungry for Love

We all crave love, but there are different ways of talking about it. One of the most profound aspects of authentic love is that the other person knows you—is a witness to your life. What do you want your life's witness to say about you? What's on your tombstone—no, what's on your *lifestone?*

Everywhere you look in the culture, people are pushing the idea that love means being swept off your feet. That's the prevalent definition of true love. From the "Real Housewives" to manufactured bachelor-bachelorette shows, to the perilous relationships of the latest stars, the love fantasy seeps into every pore of our society. I hear from men and women all the time who are looking for that grand and dizzying experience of love. I have some sympathy for the notion, having been its victim myself. I honestly think very few people escape it. The question is, why do these huge, grand-mal–seizurelike loves rarely last? Why do so many swept-away men and women hobble back years later as if they've been in a car accident? Well, think about it. If you're swept off your feet, that means—literally—you're not standing. You're falling. You're upside down. You're head-over-heels, you're dizzy and sick. Love is a loaded word.

How can you experience love when you don't know yourself? The object of your love is often a concoction—some combination between a real person and an idea of who you want them to be. Early love is a cocktail, which I wrote about in *Lies at the Altar.* People speak of "love at first sight," as if that were the greatest example of true love. But how can love happen at first sight, before you know a person? Attraction, maybe. Lust, for sure. But love? Rarely.

Another myth is that opposites attract because each person carries the missing part of the other, and together the two halves make a whole. The problem is, the equation doesn't work. The puzzle pieces don't fit. Only two wholes can make a partnership. That's not to say that the people we are drawn to don't possess a piece that is missing in us. But their job is not to complete us, nor is it our job to complete them.

This stubborn refusal to give up the fantasy, even in the face of irrefutable evidence, reminds me of my friend's son finding out there was no Santa Claus. He knew the truth, but didn't want to accept it. The fantasy was too wonderful. So he told his mother, "I know there's no Santa, but I want to believe it, and so I'll still put cookies and milk by the fireplace." It's a charming sentiment when voiced by a child, but not so charming for adults.

To ask if we are loving more like a child or a grown-up is an important question on the journey of reclaiming a healthy self. The sad truth—and what often causes pain in relationships—is that many adults are still looking at love through a wounded child's eyes. We're looking through innocence, trust, and great expectation(s); through all of the questions that were never addressed, let alone answered. In our intimate and romantic relationships—as well as in our parenting, friendships, and work relationships—many of us love and relate from the worldview of a hungry, neglected, helpless, and fretful child. We don't see from the bird's-eye view of a mature adult who knows his/her wounds and how those tender places show up. Emotional, psychological, and spiritual maturity has nothing to do with chronological age; it has to do with having the courage to open our hearts, minds, and spirits to truth even when it makes us uncomfortable, anxious, even scared. We don't have to be ashamed of our humanity, our hunger, or even our childlike ways. With tenderness and compassion, we can face the truth.

Sharon was ecstatic when she met Mark. They were both in their mid-50s and divorced, and Sharon had resigned herself to never meeting anyone special again. Mark, however, was very special, and Sharon felt full of gratitude that life had brought her a new man at her age.

"By the time you're in your mid-50s, you know yourself pretty well," she said. "That wasn't true for my first marriage. We were both so young, we didn't know who we were or what we wanted." The second time around, Sharon vowed, would be different: two strong, mature human beings joining together for mutual happiness. She thought Mark shared her dreams, but she began to see him as rigid and demanding. "I had my list of negotiable and non-negotiable items, but I just somehow got unplugged from them. I kept telling myself things were acceptable when they weren't."

Gradually, over a period of five years, Sharon reluctantly adapted to Mark's demands, even in areas that she'd thought were non-negotiable. When he complained about the noise and mess that accompanied a visit from her beloved grandchildren, she began meeting them in a park. When he said he didn't like a couple who were her oldest friends, she stopped inviting them for dinner. When he told her that taking vacations was a waste of money, she gave up her longtime tradition of heading to the beach for two weeks in the summer. When he chided her for splurging at the spa, she abandoned her monthly massage. Bit by bit, Sharon saw her true self shrinking into nothingness.

She didn't acknowledge it for the longest time. She kept making excuses for Mark, and telling herself that things weren't as bad as they seemed. But she was growing increasingly sad and removed from the confident person she had been. She felt as if she spent an inordinate amount of time tiptoeing around Mark, walking on eggshells and trying to keep the peace. The greatest pain was the distance that was growing between herself and her children and grandchildren. She saw less and less of them. One day she found herself sobbing in the shower, as she realized how much she was missing. She was barely around to see her gorgeous granddaughter grow up. She'd stayed with Mark because she didn't want to be alone again, but she realized with a shock that she was more alone than she'd ever been. Her concessions had grown and grown, while her happiness had shrunk.

Sharon dried her tears and approached Mark as he was watching TV in the living room. "If we're going to make it, I believe we really need marriage counseling."

He stared at her, not understanding. She went on. "I cannot live without my children being a major part of my life. I cannot live without seeing my granddaughter every week. It breaks my heart."

He grew angry. "You'd give me up for *them?*" he demanded.

"I don't want to give you up," she answered quietly. "But if I have to, I'll give you up for *me*. You have to understand that this is much bigger than my relationship with my children and grandchildren. It's about how much of me is lost and dying daily."

He agreed to go for counseling, and they're still working through their issues and doing well. Sharon is hopeful the marriage will survive and she feels new energy and peace knowing that she can now stand up for herself while still being a loving partner to Mark.

I often find that people enter relationships without knowing what their needs are, or how to ask for what they want. But even when you know your needs, it's easy to get sidetracked if you are driven by fear of rejection, loneliness, or conflict. Women often blame their partners and spouses for silencing their voices, when more often we abandon ourselves. We do it because we don't have enough self-esteem to love, honor, and protect ourselves. Placing the responsibility at the doorstep of your man—without owning your part of this disabling dance—will surely backfire.

## PRACTICE ASKING FOR WHAT YOU WANT

Many years ago, when I separated from my then-husband and was struggling to pay for a temporary furnished apartment in downtown Philadelphia, I considered asking my grandmother for help. I was doing my doctoral internship at Swarthmore College, which is outside of Philadelphia, working on my dissertation, busy with my active private practice, and attempting to purchase the home that my husband and I bought together several years before. When I bought the house back, I would need almost everything; at the very least, I would need a bedroom set and mattress, boxspring, frame, and all the basic trimmings so I didn't have to sleep on the floor. I spoke to my mother about asking my grandmother for money, and she smiled. "You can ask her if you want," she said, "but you know how she is about money. A gift at Christmas and your birthday, and that's it." I was well aware of my grandmother's frugality when it came to money, but what did I have to lose? I needed to buy a mattress and bedroom furniture and she had the money to help me. All she could say was no, and if so, it wouldn't kill me. I would have gone to plan B. Never mind that I didn't have a plan B; I would get one, if and when I needed it.

So I approached my grandmother and asked her if she would *give* me the money. I said, "Grandmommy, I'm not asking for a loan because I won't be able to pay you back anytime soon." She mumbled and grumbled, and finally said that she would have to see. Widowed at that time for over 30 years, she took care of her life, home, and money very well. She wasn't rich, but she was far from poor. Being the daughter of a freed slave, she had been an excellent steward of all that she and Granddaddy had worked very hard to accrue.

She did send me the money, a check in the amount that I had requested. But in the envelope she included an additional check, just for me. I was shocked. She said she sent me "a little piece of change" because I had the nerve to ask her to give me the money as opposed to borrowing it. I don't look at that card much but when I do it always makes me smile and reminds me that sometimes having the nerve to ask directly for what I want or need does pay off!

My grandmother gave me money because I dared to ask for it. It was that simple. She appreciated my courage and my honesty. That was all she had to hear. Given how many times many of us have been told "No"—and have had our requests shot down—it's understandable that we skip the necessary step of asking for what we want and need.

I have a close friend who is in a solid marriage, but she often complains about her husband's faults. He won't do this, he won't do that. One day I asked her, "Have you said anything to him about this? Have you asked him for something different?"

She got quiet. Suddenly she realized that she had never made the request.

Can you ask for what you want? Do you even know how to phrase the question? We can try to practice in small ways—managing our fears, shyness, shame, pride, and whatever else stands in the way of our asking for what we want. In doing this, it is possible that asking for what you want may become more natural and liberating over time.

The more generalized the request, the less likely it will be honored. The more specific, concrete, and measurable the request, the more likely it is to be met and taken seriously.

When we've had a big blow-up or a misunderstanding with someone important to us and we need to have a discussion about what happened, there are several ways to handle it. We can call on the toxic twins of blame and shame, which only makes matters worse. We can drop out of the real conversation and go MIA (emotionally or physically missing in action) to punish the other in the name of self-protection. We can placate the other and become a "yes" person to shut them up or close them down. Or we can take a new route. We can enter into a genuine conversation that makes room for both sides; for both perspectives to be heard and honored.

A request that would less likely be taken seriously might sound like, *"I'm upset with you and hope we can talk about what happened."*

A request that would increase the chances of getting a healthy and mature response might sound like:

> *"I am really stirred up about what happened between us. It would mean a lot to me if we could make time within the next two days to sit and listen and talk this through. What looks good for you and your schedule? This is what works for me. You mean a lot to me. Our relationship is important to me, and I want to figure this out with you."*

There are so many opportunities for us to practice making concrete requests to have our hunger acknowledged, our needs taken seriously, and our desires explored. But first we have to take ourselves seriously, and then learn how to wisely ask for what we want and need. Only then can we advocate for ourselves, as well as for what is best for the relationships we value and cherish.

## WORTHY OF LIFE

Can you exist—and have value and importance—if you don't exist to someone else? Can your life matter, your heart be considered, your feelings be taken seriously by you, even if they are ignored by others who matter to you?

If you were going to pop the question to yourself, what would you say? Here's my version:

> *Will you take me as I am*
> *And promise to love me for the rest of my life?*
> *Will you cherish me for my uniqueness,*
> *Care for me even when I'm not at my best,*
> *Support my dreams,*
> *Tell me the truth,*
> *Respect my hunger,*
> *Celebrate my being?*

There is only one acceptable answer, given fully and joyfully: I will!

Section II

# COMING OUT

# CHAPTER 9

# I Am Not My Hair

*"I am not my hair . . . I am the soul that lives within."*
India Arie

Hair is seen as a woman's crown and glory. The more beautiful it is, the more beautiful she is seen to be—and the more beautiful she feels. Our hair affects our psychological well-being; we have become dependent upon its appearance to impress others, feel better about ourselves, hide from feelings and fears, and meet the world's standards. At times our hair can feel like the only place we have control; it's also a way to get needed validation from others. It's as if we *are* our hair. This is not just the case with women; men can be as crushed about a botched haircut as women can.

Never before had I realized the power of hair as when I saw the movie *Elizabeth*, starring Cate Blanchett. At the end of the movie she shaved off her hair, symbolizing her full embrace of her power as the Queen of England.

Unlike Samson—one of Israel's chosen, whose hair was said to be the key to his strength—our strength is not in our hair.

But many of us believe it contributes to our worth. Hair can become a core part of our identity. This was me. Learning the lesson that I was more than my hair almost killed me. After many years of having truly enviable hair, I awakened one day to discover that my hair was breaking off. I panicked. *Not another thing going wrong,* I thought. It was a stressful time in my life; there had been too much loss already. There was a car accident that disrupted my physical well-being, waning professional dreams, the death of Kalle, and my burglarized home. My hair seemed to be all that was left of what I thought was the "acceptable" me. When I looked in the mirror, it was as if my broken hair mirrored my broken life and dreams. My hair was a bigger part of my identity than I knew. When it changed, so did my world.

When my hair debacle was unfolding—or should I say, unbraiding itself—a hair stylist I hadn't seen for years said, "Dr. Smith, just wear a wig. It will look exactly like your real hair. Your hair grows like an uncontrollable weed, you can wear the wig and no one will ever know that your hair broke off. You have beautiful hair and you can hide the damage until your own hair grows back." How was that for an invitation to live a lie out of shame? That stylist meant no harm, but his advice was exactly what my hunger demons wanted me to bow to. It was the opposite of what the Universe was calling me to face and embrace. Clearly, this hair stylist was alarmed that my "Barbie hair" had turned on me. He wanted me to cover it up (in shame). But doing so would have been the death of me. To cover up my hunger, fear, and shame one more time was the exact opposite of what my soul and life required. If I was going to walk in freedom and peace, I needed to expose the tender parts of me to the warm and loving light. This included my hair, which, at that point, I couldn't even recognize. It was like having an alien living on my head who taunted me with each touch or glance in the mirror. It didn't look, feel, or resemble anything that I, or anyone who knew me, could connect with.

Forget the straw, my hair breaking off felt like a whole *house* broke the camel's back.

Christopher, my hair stylist and beloved and trusted friend, has done my hair for years. He has done it for television, magazine articles, photo shoots, my ordination, speeches, and for everything in between. When I travel for big events he is always there not only to do my hair, but to watch over me. He's too humble to say that, but it's true. I can't count the times I have been preparing for an event when a decision needed to be made, and without anyone knowing, I have glanced over at Christopher. Without a word between us, I will read his expression and it will inform my decision. We have spent time together all over the country, growing from each other's stories, wisdom, love, sorrows, and laughter. He knows me, he understands me, he gets my gift, and believes that it belongs in the world . . . and he has gifted me to know and understand him. Our sharing goes into a bank vault that only the two of us hold the combination to. There it remains sacred and protected by a privacy act called friendship and trust. Actually, my closet friendships, all very different, share that common theme: *Mum's the word*. We live the motto, "What happens on the cruise, stays on the cruise." My relationship with Christopher goes far beyond my hair. It is loving, safe, and trustworthy.

Christopher has been with me during the best and worst of times. Over all of our years together, he cared for my hair and kept it strong, healthy, and looking great. His job never required him to be my *hair doctor* because my hair had never been sick. I know he has been the doctor for others who faced hair despair and dis-ease due to illness, stress, aging, hormones, and overprocessing, but that had never been my story. That is, until my hair went haywire. Then I needed him to put on his white coat. The only problem was, I was in Philadelphia and Christopher was in Chicago.

In this moment of deep despair, my friend Sandra knew what I needed. She encouraged me to go immediately to the only person I could trust—regardless of his location. She told me, "Go and do what you need to do. If it were cancer you would go to the best of the best. When Kalle was sick (or well for that matter) nothing was too good for her. When I've needed something, you've reached as far as you could. Do for yourself what you do for everyone else. Go to the rock, the only person you trust with your broken hair and heart."

Sandra was right. I would move the earth if I could for those I love when they are in need. So why was it so hard for me to honor and love myself in the same way? I was sharing Sandra's words with a very close friend, Ernie, who said, "Sandra is special. We all need a Sandra in our lives. It's rare to have someone bless our path especially when it's not the straight and narrow, easy-to-map-out way." There were no words from Sandra trying to convince me that there had to be someone closer than Christopher. There was no shaming or minimizing, just her loving support, guidance, and blessing—to go and do what I needed to do to take care of myself.

So I turned to Christopher to be my hair doctor. I was *scared to death* and Christopher knew it. Not only was my hair broken in unimaginable ways, but my heart was worse off than my hair. What I love about Christopher is that he cares for more than just my hair. Not only is he wise and amazingly gifted, he's also quiet and doesn't waste his words. So when he speaks, my heart and ears listen deeply to each word that rolls off his deliberate tongue. Christopher is soft-spoken and a straight shooter, a rare combination. Strength and honesty are his backbone. He's tender with me as he tells me what he really believes, thinks, perceives, discerns, and feels. Our relationship is a feast for me when my hunger pains are raging wild. I've trusted him with my hair and my hunger.

I had been sending Christopher text messages and e-mails bleeding with worry between each visit. Was I sick with cancer—or something even worse? By the time I arrived in Chicago at the salon, I had been to the doctor to make sure I wasn't physically sick. She ran lots of blood tests to check for everything and confirmed that all on the medical front was clean and clear. My doctor is superb and she knew that a lot in my life was stressing me over and out, but she didn't know my deep hunger pains. Or if she did, she didn't let on that my emaciated soul was airing my laundry without my knowing it.

Still, my hair felt terrible. I would say that to my closest friends and family, "Feel my hair, something is wrong with it. It feels like the hair of a corpse, a dead person!" How would I know what a dead person's hair feels like? I don't know. But nobody told me I was wrong. No one could imagine what happened to my hair, although everyone had a theory as did I. My hair had the reputation of living up to the commercial ad, "You can depend on me." Once I knew that I wasn't sick with a physical disease—that my 40-something body was still clicking and ticking quite well—I really started to wonder what in the world this was all about. I was sick and tired of this "now you see me, now you don't" theme in my life. I felt like saying, "God, you've gotta be kidding me that my hair had to go, too. Come on, enough already. Haven't I cried *uncle* loud enough yet?" I guess not.

I flew from Philadelphia to Chicago in tears, on a wing and a prayer. More like a single wing and a half a prayer. When I walked—really, limped—into the salon that cold December day, Christopher was shocked at what he saw. I was so scared and miserable that even though I hate cold weather, the frostbite from my fear, horror, and helplessness was far more formidable than the cold Chicago day in December. Like any competent doctor, especially one who knows their patient well, Christopher asked me all the pertinent questions. He was trying to get his own expert mind around the mystery of "what in the world happened to Dr. Robin's fabulous hair." He wondered, had I let someone else do something different to it? Had I let someone put chemicals in my hair? Through my fog, I remember looking up at him saying, "Christopher, you know that I wouldn't cheat on you." Neither of us could get much of a smile out at that point, but he was doing his due diligence—trying to piece together this jagged puzzle. He had done my hair only three months earlier, and all was great and appeared normal at that time.

The wing and a prayer that got me to the salon seemed gone. Sitting in his chair, I was a miserable mess. It was New Year's Eve morning and the salon was buzzing with the air of anticipation—everyone getting their hairdos to be glam as the New Year was ushered in. The salon had food and drinks flowing to go along with the festive atmosphere. I seemed to be the only one there for

117

*medical and spiritual triage.* The last thing on my mind was partying. I felt like I was preparing for a funeral—my own. I felt like the walking dead.

By the time I left the salon, Christopher and I had a plan. Truthfully I didn't like it. Secretly (okay, not so secretly) the only plan I wanted was regular access to Christopher whenever my hair demons threatened to overtake me. That wasn't possible. In the same way that the term *broken* described my hair situation, it was also befitting of my financial situation. I was broke everywhere in my life—or so it seemed.

The almost 700 miles between us felt insurmountable. Way too far for my broken heart and hair. I wanted to see him every week so he could sit shivah with me over my dying, straw-feeling, brittle hair.

My hair had been something I'd taken for granted all my life. At the time, way back when I was a teenager, Sandra reminded me, "You were never into your hair. It just was a part of you that other people loved, were jealous of, were attached to. But for you, it was just your hair." That was true—until it was gone. My friend Lynn, a breast cancer survivor, said, "Robin, it sounds so much like someone who had chemo and is starting from scratch."

"Your hair is like the rest of your life—virgin," Sandra said to me during another conversation. "Your whole life is being reborn. Your hair is an outward symbol of what is taking place on the inside. Something on the *inside* is working on the *outside*. You're not washed up; you're just waking up to live your new life."

"Sandra," I replied, "you know not everything can return to its virginlike state. For some things, it's too late to become a virgin again!"

"True," she said, laughing. "But your hair, like your *hungry soul*, is being reborn. For your new life, and the new you. Or maybe the *real* you. And the old—all that was in the way of your journey and healing—had to be taken away because it was no longer necessary. It was getting in the way of you being truly free. I'm sorry the process has been so painful. It's been brutal to watch you lose everything. But I know that your life is going to be sweet again. God is going to restore to you the years that the locusts destroyed."

My therapist and I had spoken many times about what I considered my dead life; my hungry self and soul. Now I was hungry for something else. I was hungry for my hair! I knew it, even when I didn't want to know it: my dead hair was the last straw. It was meant to break the Robin's wing, so that I could no longer fly away—away from myself, my soul's work, or the path that was mine to take.

I never considered wearing a wig, but I *did* consider having Christopher cut off all of my hair. Thankfully, he refused.

"Absolutely not!" he said. "Leave your hair alone; allow it to heal as you are healing. You and your hair will be *fine*. Dr. Robin, real healing takes time. You have taught and reminded the world of that many times. Now you must remind yourself what you have taught us."

Boy, oh boy, did God get my full attention with this hair breakage issue.

*Did it take all of this to get me to take notice?* I asked myself.

I heard a still, small voice reply, "Yes, it *did* take all of this to get your full and undivided attention."

I learned a lot about myself during this time of upheaval. I didn't know this before "all hair broke loose," but when all else failed in my life, I had always counted on my hair to be its robust, reliable self. When suddenly that changed, so did everything else. This was one of the subtler ways that identity theft made its presence known in my life.

Recently, as I sat with Christopher in his salon in Chicago, I said, "Only as a Monday morning quarterback with twenty-twenty vision can I say that my hair *had* to break off for the Universe to complete its job—stripping me of all that falsely kept me safe. I know in my soul that this had to happen. There was no other way that I could be sure of who I was. My hair had to betray me—and my money and life had to fall away with it—so that I could become *me*." We looked at each other through the mirror as he was doing my hair, and he said, "Dr. Robin, I think you're right, and when you tell this story it will only further touch people's lives and inspire them. Because you are willing to share your painful journey, not just about your hair but your life, people will know that they too can overcome whatever life has thrown in their faces or dropped off at their doorstep."

# CHAPTER 10

# I SEE DEAD PEOPLE

---

*"We wear the mask that grins and lies."*

PAUL LAURENCE DUNBAR

I was sitting in the parking lot at the grocery store talking with my assistant Kim on the telephone. It was a beautiful, clear, and warm afternoon, and we were discussing the exhaustive to-do list still in front of me. There was so much that remained on my schedule before my day could officially be called "over." I felt overwhelmed and I knew I would be working late into the evening. All I really wanted to do was to be out and about enjoying the beauty of nature and the day with Kalle.

I said to Kim, "I just realized something. I am a mortician."

She said, "Excuse me, what did you say?"

I replied, "I am a mortician, the best anywhere. I see dead people."

Kim was silent. I knew she was waiting for me to say something clever that would put into context what I had just said. The words themselves seemed totally ridiculous. Actually, *touched* might be a more accurate description.

"I realized something today," I explained. "I have spent a lot of my life trying to make dead people and dead things alive." I went on to explain that I had spent years with dead people, in dead relationships, in dead places playing the role of the most skillful mortician. By the time I finished with them, my handiwork had been so convincing that I believed—as did everyone else—that the dead person or thing had come back to life. But in reality they were merely embalmed in a mixture of make-believe, pretend, and false hope. Fear of reality was my partner in this booming mortuary business. How frightening and how dangerous to be dealing with dead things and acting like they were alive!

Kim got it, as did others with whom I shared the metaphor later. Many people are in the business of trying to make dead things alive again.

You, too, may know what it's like to be the walking dead. You might have been with a dead person in a dead relationship, or in a "dead-end" job, ministry, or household. A person who is sleepwalking through life is lifeless, detached from themselves and everyone else, uninvolved. They're living on the conveyer belt and calling it life; existing in their own world of tombs and graves and calling it peace and quiet. To be with a dead person when you are dead is no big deal—death begets death. But to be with someone who is dead when we are alive is deadly and painful. It can feel like you're in a coffin trying to catch your breath and find the light of day. It's no pretty picture. It's torture to be with someone dead unless you are dead, too. But it's a reality that every human being faces at some point. The problem comes when you have a dead-end reality in your life, but you pretend not to see it.

## DRESSING IN DRAG

I was good at dressing in this kind of drag—in my discreet, soft mortician garb. I went about my work, taking dead people, things, situations, and circumstances and making them look alive. Everyone was fooled, including me. I had been doing it for so long that I was losing my ability to know the truth from a lie— and to know the difference between aliveness and death. I had "relationships" (at least that is what I called them) with a number of dead people.

Being a mortician, I was a master makeup artist. I learned from an early age never to leave home without painting on a warm smile, touching up the sparkle in my eyes, and clothing myself in wit, intelligence, and approachability. I had my act together.

What a joke, a sham, a sad tragedy.

Even my closest loved ones never saw me without my mask. I hid my true face from the world, and eventually the pretense felt so natural that I began to believe it myself. What was so wrong with that? I was very successful, full of energy, and relatively content. I was the envy of my friends, colleagues, and acquaintances. The façade I created was like an impenetrable shelter that protected me from the truth—until the day it burned to the ground and left me raw and exposed. It felt like the end of my life, but actually it was the beginning of a chance at a *real* life.

You have to understand that this façade I created was not just about crafting a phony exterior for myself. My deceit went much, much deeper. That was the revelation I shared with Kim that day. I was effectively a mortician—the best anywhere.

Here's the real kicker, though. It takes so much hard work trying to make the dead look alive. Maybe you think that the opposite is true—that it's easier to embalm than to reveal the truth. But no matter how much you make the dead look alive, they're still dead. All the makeup and airbrushing in the world won't change that.

I had learned how to dress and re-dress my pain and brokenness in the most beautiful garb. I became so good at creating the window dressing that at some point I began to believe it was real. I learned how to look happy and joyful when sad, how to apply my smile along with my makeup, to laugh and play when my heart was aching and broken, to spiritualize my suffering and to top it off with some form of enlightened psychobabble. What's worse,

I got so good at shutting down and cutting off from my feelings that I actually believed I was okay even when I was miserable.

I remember being on vacation in my favorite Caribbean destination—a place where I go to relax, restore, replenish, and rejuvenate myself when I'm spent and empty. I was there with Sandra, and one day we were in the villa listening to music. The playlist included Luther Vandross, Stevie Wonder, Shirley Horn, Donny Hathaway, Nina Simone, Diana Krall, Lionel Richie, and the Temptations—and I always threw some gospel music in the mix, which invited a familiar smile from Sandra, as she shook her head and said, "Robin, you really do believe in true diversity." I was singing along at the top of my lungs, seemingly blissful, when Sandra asked, "Are you feeling what you're singing? Don't you feel sad from the longing in these songs?" I was surprised.

"I feel great, life is good, we're here in paradise, what more could I want?" I asked.

"A man!" Sandra replied. "Someone to love and who loves you back." Sandra had a loving man back home whom she was missing. And here I was, just fine . . . except for the fact that I was absolutely heartbroken and was running for my life from the truth. Officer Denial had me totally under his spell believing that I was *fine*. But the lie was making me desperate and hungry. I longed to be free from the suffocating grip of fear and the torment that came from playing small in my life so that others could feel big. I was sick of it. I had had it! And I was scared to death.

I hoped for rescue in the form of a therapist who would make it all better—a fairy godmother who would wave her wand and swish away my pain. Or better yet, a knight in shining armor who would save me. Much to my chagrin neither appeared. I finally realized that no one was coming along to fix me or my situation. The person that I had been waiting for had been there from the beginning, and it was *me*. This was great news. It was also a hard pill to swallow. I had to accept the idea that the help I needed had arrived, but it required that I get off of the stoop of "woe is me."

Yes, I had suffered, and the work I'd done did little to resolve my pain and grief. I decided that if I wanted a different outcome I had to change how I saw myself, and how I allowed people to treat me. Before, I felt battered by the way I had given my love so freely and it hadn't been respected or truly returned. I resented that the people in my life would take and take and give back so little. Now I had to understand why I colluded with disrespectful and non-reciprocal relationships. I had to learn how to fill my own cup with abundance, forgiveness, friendship, joy, love, passion, truth, and wisdom. If I wanted peaceful encounters—a meaningful love connection, solid and respectful relationships—then I had to do much more than wish or even pray for them. I had to plant the seeds in order to harvest the crop that I desired. The Bible reminds us that "faith without works is dead," and the Talmud says, "We see the world not as it is, but as we are." If I was serious about transforming my life and no longer living in a state of living dead-ness—i.e., self-righteous resentment, defeat, and regret—I had to take action. My breakthrough happened when I finally came to understand and accept the reality that my life, with all its joys and sorrows, successes and failures, was solely my responsibility to manage. And, of course, it takes a village to heal, so having the tribal support of my family and friendship village was essential.

---

### Ask yourself:

Where have you been a mortician—or known a mortician?
Were you raised by one?
Did it always seem to you that everything would be okay as long as you made it look okay—that even the dead would come alive if you applied the right makeup?

---

## WHO WILL WANT THE REAL ME?

Should we settle for the crumbs instead of insisting on being invited to the feast?

Rachel was practiced at settling because she had never believed she was lovable. Although this beautiful woman glowed with personality and good health, she thought she was ugly. "I was fat as a kid and although I slimmed down quite a bit, I still have a lot of cellulite," she told me in a soft voice. "I don't have good muscle tone, so everything is flabby." She thought her body might have been the reason why her fiancé, Francis, broke up with her. "Maybe he wanted someone with a better body. He never said that, it's just what I suspect. He never seemed to want me. Actually, my gut tells me he was ashamed of my body and of me."

I wondered, was Rachel projecting her own low self-worth on Francis? Further probing revealed that she was carrying around a heavy burden of self-loathing, which she thought was confirmed by her history of failed romances. "The men I've loved have always dumped me," she said bluntly, "and when Francis asked me to marry him I said yes because I was 28 years old and I wondered if I'd ever have another chance to get married." She admitted that she didn't love Francis, but was willing to settle. "Who will ever want me?" she said in despair.

Fear of rejection was so deeply embedded in Rachel's psyche that she couldn't even imagine getting what she wanted without pretending and settling. She had learned not to expect approval, and she felt so desperate that she would probably have accepted a proposal from anyone, just to get to the altar.

"What do you really want?" I asked Rachel.

"I want to be married and to have a family," she replied without hesitation.

"Even if it's marriage to a man you don't love?" I asked. "You told me you didn't really love Francis, and yet you were ready to marry him. That wasn't being fair to you, and it wasn't being fair to Francis, either."

Rachel cried because she had never thought of it before—never believed that she had a right to be secure, to live in dignity, to be loved for herself. She also had minimized the pain and trauma of the wound of not being good enough. If she had married Francis, the wound would have grown deeper. She would never have felt good enough, and the erosion would have continued. It also never occurred to her that her acting out of her "not good enough" wound could cause harm, heartache, and frustration to Francis and that his wound of feeling overly responsible and blamed when people aren't happy could be activated.

My friend Sophia's deep insecurity makes her hypervigilant. Recently we were driving to a party and she was a nervous wreck. The location of the party was the spectacular home of a mutual friend—a wonderful man, not the kind of person who would make you feel ill at ease. But Sophia was on edge.

"What if I spill something?" she worried.

"What if you do? That could happen to any of us," I replied. She shot me an anxious look, and was somewhat angry that I didn't seem to fully appreciate her concerns. Had I not known Sophia, I might have minimized just how big this all felt to her. If Sophia and I hadn't had the conversation about how anxious she was about attending the party, I would never have known the burden she carried. But I understood. It had been difficult to get Sophia to come to this party. She preferred to stay at home, reasoning that if she spilled something, broke something, or ruined something, it would be hers and she wouldn't get into trouble. Ruining something of someone else's would have given her unbearable angst, embarrassment, and self-blame even if she was reassured it wasn't a problem to them.

You have to know that Sophia is a remarkable, accomplished woman in her 60s, but even so she carried around some heavy baggage from her past. She grew up in a household where she was always made to feel inadequate and invisible. She was constantly reminded of her imperfections and never praised for her achievements. She was often told, "Sophia, *think, think, think!*" So she spent her whole life trying to think—and not trusting that she could. If something went wrong, she judged herself. "I must not be thinking enough. I need to think more." Instead, she needed to breathe, and trust that she was competent and capable.

Sophia went on to marry and modeled her early insecurities in her choice of a partner. While she has made great strides, she is still living with the fear of being a disappointment, concerned that if people knew who she really was they might reject her.

And no, Sophia didn't spill anything at the party that night. But I don't think she was able to relax and enjoy herself, either. The host loved having her, and his friends adored her and hung on her words. Even so, Sophia held her breath the whole time, and only let it out when we were safely in the car on the way home. I asked her how she was feeling.

"Exhausted," she said. "I love Daniel, but it's too much work for me to worry about getting into trouble. Staying home is lonely, but it's much easier."

My heart went out to my beloved friend. I wanted to protest, to say all the usual things one says—"Oh, no, you're wrong! Everyone loves you. Don't be silly." But I respected the depth of Sophia's wound and was careful not to fill her ears with platitudes she wouldn't believe. All I could do was continue to reach out to her, hoping she would in time begin to see her enormous worth reflected in the love of her friends.

## BORN TO PLEASE

Women are socialized to please—yes, even in these modern times. What that means is we are raised to be separated from our true needs and to mask our authentic hunger. We go along to get along. Sound familiar? Dorothy was a stay-at-home mom to two active children under age five. She loved her children and she was a great mother, but her days were full and exhausting. When her husband Jack ("the breadwinner," as he often reminded her) walked in at the end of the day, he dropped his briefcase on a chair and barely uttered a word of hello before collapsing in the living room in front of the television. Dorothy corralled the eager children away from him, whispering, "Daddy's tired." But she resented his indifference. It was as if they were two separate families.

When she spoke to me about it, Dorothy asked with great hesitation, "I know he works hard to support us, but does my husband have a right to come home at night and have little to say to me and to our children? Does being the breadwinner make it okay for him to be a jerk?" She really wanted to know. She wasn't sure.

I asked her, "What do you think?"

She was quiet for a while, and then admitted, "He doesn't think my feelings or the children's feelings matter."

"I'm sure that's a painful realization," I said, "but the real question I want you to consider is whether or not your feelings matter to *you*." She was focused on getting her husband to care about her feelings—and that was important—but the first step was to care for herself. She had never even considered that before, and the question was a big breakthrough for her.

## WEARING THE ROBE THAT FITS

Everyone is familiar with the story of David versus Goliath. But one aspect of the story is especially meaningful to me. It's the point before David went into battle. King Saul brought him an elaborate suit of armor and urged him to put it on. David tried on the armor and found that it felt awkward and uncomfortable. It didn't fit right. He couldn't breathe or move freely. So he took the risk instead to go into battle wearing his own clothes—wearing what suited and fit him. It wasn't fancy like the king's armor, but it was authentic for David and it worked.

Why do people pretend to be what they're not? Do you notice this in your circle of friends and acquaintances, people pretending to be wealthier than they are (and going deeper into debt), people pretending their kids are flawless, people saying they never ever fight with their spouses? Where in your life do you pretend?

The biggest lie is pretending to be full when we're starving. We must be careful and protect ourselves in relationships with people where we are hungry for their validation—and they look through us like a freshly cleaned glass. The more we engage in these relationships—work, family, lovers, friends, faith community—the more likely their rejection and coldness will lead to obsessive, destructive, wasteful, and addictive behaviors. The bottom line is that pretending gives others way too much power and makes us way too small. It's the fact of being way too small in our own eyes and in our own hearts that is the place of first injury—and the place of needed repair. This is what turned life around for me: Becoming important to myself, caring about my own feelings and needs, taking my desires and passion seriously, and not pretending to feel respected and loved when I was being mistreated.

I am reminded of a time I had to protect myself from mistreatment. During a very tough time in my life a "friend" called to say he was coming to Philadelphia for an art exhibit and wondered if I would be free for breakfast. While at one time we had been involved, by this time our relationship had been purely platonic for years with very little contact. In planning for his visit, we talked several times about how hard life was for me and what had been going on in his life. I was feeling anxious and afraid because my future, both personal and professional, was in flux. I was waking up each day and going to bed asking the same questions: "Am I going to be okay?" "Am I going to make it?" "Will I end up losing everything I've worked so hard for?" Also, I was beginning to realize that even with all of my brave and desperate attempts, a secure love connection had always eluded me. My major meltdowns most often happened in my kitchen. I'm not sure why, but it always happened that way. Not the bathroom, bedroom, or car. The kitchen just seemed to invite the floodgates to open. I remember one time crying hysterically as I literally collapsed there and was caught by the coolness of my limestone floors. While their texture is far from soft, in my darkest hours of despair, its nooks and crannies held me. I love the old hymn "Rock of Ages," and the chorus that proclaims, "Rock of Ages, cleft for me, let me hide myself in Thee." My kitchen has a feeling of being a cleft for me—a refuge where it is safe to have major meltdowns and live to tell the story.

I was cooking breakfast in my kitchen for my friend, because it felt easier to eat at home where we could really get caught up. I had some of everything, that's my style. When I cook, I love to have a large spread where there is enough for seconds and a doggie bag for later. As I was making the pancakes, some with fresh fruit and nuts, he came over to me at the stove and said, "This is trash, and so is this one." I looked up, startled by his disapproving look. He had two of my spatulas in his hand. He was shaming me for what he felt were sub-par utensils! He went on and on and on. I remember thinking—and eventually saying—"You are out of your mind." I let him know that I was barely surviving, and my focus was not on my utensils or any other external thing in my life. It was a miracle I hadn't gone crazy; that I had a portion of my mind and life still intact. How dare he try and shame me—and then think we were going to sit down and eat breakfast like all was well! He also insulted Kalle, which insulted me. I realized in that moment that he was a miserable man. His life had been far from what he wanted, and he decided to pick on broken-down me to ease his injured self. Sandra has a saying that the rest of our tribe has adopted: "Not with me!" That is exactly what I felt. "Not with me . . . never again, not with me."

Breakfast was very quiet, and I knew something had changed in me. I knew he would never be in my home again. I knew why our relationship was flatter than my pancakes. When he left, I remember saying to Kalle, "Don't worry, he'll never be in this house again." To this day, that remains true. I never saw him again, nor did I have the need to discuss his horrible behavior. What I needed to know was that I was no longer available for him or anyone else to take their misery out on me.

I kept the spatulas for many years as symbols of self-honor. Eventually they both fell apart, but not before I had become more whole.

Our lives fall into shambles when we're pretending to be full. If you don't nourish yourself, you can't escape starvation. Eventually, it will catch up. It will kill your relationships. It will kill your parenting ability. It will kill you.

In a very real sense, it is like having a distorted body image. You're looking in the mirror and thinking you look fine, while others are whispering, "What's wrong with her? She's emaciated." You can ignore the signs for a while, but in the end they will show up.

Often these days I find myself in conversations with middle-aged people—usually women—who are faced with the issue of caring for aging parents. In many cases they've just finished rais-ing their children and/or are close to retirement from their jobs. They never planned ahead for the time when they might have this new responsibility. Now they're struggling with how to handle an overwhelming burden. Don't get me wrong. This isn't about love. They love their parents very much. But it can be too much to once again find yourself in the role of a caretaker when you long for freedom.

The biggest issue I see around caretaking is the silence—the in-ability to voice one's needs and struggles. You'll hear people saying with admiration, "She never complains," as if that is a badge of honor! They say, "She's always pleasant. She's never short on pa-tience. She does it with such grace." When I hear that, I think, "Uh-oh. That's dangerous." Because deep down I know this woman is starving. No one is thinking about her needs, least of all herself.

## THE STUMBLING BLOCKS TO AUTHENTICITY

Sometimes I think it's in the water—*if something is wrong just hide it.* I remember a deodorant commercial that said, "Never let them see you sweat." But in our hearts we know there is more to life. This fantasy is based on pride, arrogance, immaturity, and fear.

By pride, I mean that you are full of yourself; you think that your "stuff don't stink." That so-called pride, which really isn't pride at all, masks a ferocious insecurity. The most insecure people in the world walk around thinking they're better than others be-cause of how many expensive toys they have, or what they use as props to hold up their fragile egos—youth, beauty, bucks, bling. If they lose their toys or their fleshly armor, they panic. Who are they then?

Arrogance can be manifested in righteousness. Sometimes in faith communities, people are very self-satisfied. They think they have a higher moral code and are worthier than others. They use their superiority as a way of shaming those who do not follow the same path. In my opinion, this form of arrogance is every bit as damaging as the reliance on material and physical facades.

Immaturity leads you to embrace the fantasy of being rescued by the "right" man or the "right" woman. There is one exception that makes finding the "right" person not fantasy, but a reality. That is when you begin to look for yourself with all of your heart and energy. When *you* become the treasure that you are seeking, instead of making someone else the answer or solution to your problems, the quality of your life will begin to improve.

Fear is at the base of pride, arrogance, and the immaturity of choosing fantasy over reality. Most people are so afraid of being judged as not good enough that they spend the majority of their lives trying to prove themselves—and then die, having never lived the life that was theirs to live. What a tragic waste.

If we want our life to change, then we have to report for active duty now, show up like a grown-up and do the necessary work to build, yes, *build* the life that we desire. If we are waiting for something to happen to our life—the right partner walking in the door, the right job becoming available, the right diet that will finally help us lose weight—we need to rethink the dynamic. Rather than letting life happen to us, we'll need to vow to happen to life.

# CHAPTER 11

# Living with the Hole

———————•———————

*"The naked truth is always better than the best-dressed lie."*
Ann Landers

We all live with holes. Holes are the cracks and crevices in our minds, souls, and relationships caused by painful life situations and circumstances. Sometimes these holes remain a painful cavity, but most often they get filled with the sludge of misinformation and unfounded judgments. One TV show I contributed to was about horrible racial and sexist insults made by a public person toward a group of African American female champion athletes. I talked about the hole in the soul of America. Thousands of people connected with my term "hole in the soul." I think that's because deep down many of us know that there is also a hole in our own souls. We make up our country as its citizens, so if there is a hole in the soul of the country then we must check out the individuals who comprise this body we call America. The same is true of parents and their children. Parents want their children "fixed" and whole. But those same parents are often unwilling to look at their own brokenness and the holes that their children inherited from them.

Having a hole in your soul is nothing to feel ashamed about. It is something to attend to. The holes in our souls highlight the key elements that are missing in us, and become a trusted guide to find the root of what is broken and injured in ourselves. Holes don't just go away of their own accord. Some remain empty, while others get filled in with imitation fillers or inferior substances—which always cause bigger problems later. But they may just as easily be filled with life-giving materials. These life-giving materials are the nourishment we need and crave.

We nourish ourselves by establishing and maintaining healthy, substantive relationships with self and others; by having boundaries that foster respect and allow authentic "yeses" and "nos" when necessary; and by practicing good self-care as we nourish and nurture ourselves. Yet too often we go hungry.

When families choose to mask their pain and suffer in silence, they are filling the hole with a temporary, inadequate substance. They're busy applying spackle to a crater, hoping people on the outside won't notice their suffering. They're terrified that others—even perfect strangers—will see the truth of their sleepless nights, loveless marriages, addicted family members, angry parents, despised siblings, and internal conflict. They'd rather fill these holes in, cover them up, than let anyone know they are human, hungry, and imperfect.

## CREATING A DEATH TRAP

Grace came from a very traditional Christian family, and she grew up believing that it was an important value to only have sex with one man in her lifetime. It was a value she also wanted to pass on to her children. This was a worthy goal, of course, but the problem was that Grace let it overwhelm all the other values in her life—especially the value of being a whole and respected human being.

Although faithfulness meant a lot to Grace, it unfortunately meant little to her husband, who had affairs throughout their marriage. He was a distant and withholding partner, but she stayed with him, believing she had no choice. She had made her bed, so to speak, and now she had to lie in it. Or even worse, die in it.

Grace and her husband had three children in quick succession, and she was consumed by their needs. Grace was unhappy, but the idea of leaving wasn't even part of her thinking. Speaking the truth wasn't an option, either. She struggled to maintain the marriage, even though she didn't feel as if she existed in it. Over 20 years she became smaller and smaller and smaller—existing less and less.

Sometimes she felt as if she was spending her life digging a hole that would eventually be her grave. The grave felt more comfortable and easier than finding her voice and beginning to speak up for herself. She was resolved to being voiceless, and she blamed her husband for her helplessness and silence, not seeing that no one can take from you what you refuse to relinquish.

What shook Grace out of her big dig was when one of her children was diagnosed with a life-threatening disease. Suddenly, seeing her precious son fighting so hard to live, Grace thought, *My baby is fighting to live, and I walk around like I've given up.* She promised herself that if her son survived she would never allow herself to accept a death trap again. As time moved on, Grace expanded her promise, vowing that whether her son lived or died, she would from now on choose life.

Grace's son recovered, and after much therapy and couples' counseling, Grace summoned her courage and did the one thing she had vowed she would never do: She left her husband. She escaped the death trap. Later, reflecting on her choice, she said, "When I vowed to be with my husband until death, I didn't realize that it might be *my* death." And she might have said that, by extension, she would have passed on that death to her children.

## THE HOLE OF GRIEF

The dog of very dear friends died almost a year after my beloved Kalle's death. They were devastated and knew that I would understand, given how much I missed Kalle. One day we were talking and they shared the advice given to them by people who said, "You really should get another dog. It will help you feel better and relieve your pain." I had received this same advice many times from well-meaning people. My friends made it very clear to me: "We don't want another dog, we want our dog back. We're not looking to replace him, we're looking *for* him, we're longing for him, we're wanting *him*, not a fill-in." Their pain was so evident it broke my heart. I heard them loud and clear.

There is no right or wrong here, but I was aware of how uncomfortable we are with grief. We have a hard time living with the hole—or seeing others who are. So we look for something worthy to fill it.

About a year later, my friends did get another dog. But not to escape the pain and loneliness of losing their beloved pet—the new dog was not a surrogate or a replacement. She was a symbol that they were ready to open their hearts again for love.

Years ago, I was talking to one of my closest friends about someone in my family who was in a relationship that we all judged to be painful and unhealthy. My friend asked, "Why do you think she is with him?" I replied, "I think she got tired on the journey and just set up house with the person at the point where she ran out of gas. She filled the hole of her life with a particular person, not because he was the desire of her heart, but because her heart was tired and worn out and he happened to be there at the right (wrong) time."

Sometimes we do feel so weary it's hard to fight for ourselves. Do you give in because you have reached your limit of struggle? Inevitably, when we lay down what feels like the burden of living an authentic life, our hunger increases and we become saddled with a greater burden.

## DIMMING THE LIGHT

A friend told me that every time they argue, his wife punishes him by remaining silent for a week. She literally will not speak a single word. My friend hates the silence, which feels like oppression. How did he address his wife's need to punish him in such a cruel manner? He told me he was trying to "work on" himself, so he didn't say or do things that triggered an argument. He said, "I need to work on my tendency to overreact to little things instead of just letting them go. I need to grow up and pick my battles."

"What are you working on?" I asked. "To learn to suffer with a smile? Don't confuse suffering with maturity. Don't say, 'I'm building my relationship muscles.' You can't pretend to be happy and think you're going to get 'better' by covering up your true feelings."

This was an interesting case, because the person suffering was a man. More often, I hear about the insecurities and fears of women who desire to "do the right thing"; who are trying to have it all and be it all.

It's a human trait to want to fix things. Women especially are wired to run interference in order to keep the peace and calm things down. Whether it's in the household or in the office, we're supposed to be good at soothing people's feelings—always with a smile, of course. The woman who wears a smile as a mask becomes fractured in her sense of self. Having access to her smile can cause her to become plastic, less authentic and real. Accessing her hunger, anger, and other real feelings may be much more difficult because she has too long masked her true feelings. And if she does have access to her hunger and true feelings, then she feels like something's wrong with her.

As I write this we are in the midst of a very long and brutal political season before the presidential election. I watch the various candidates try on new masks to appeal to different populations. It's no secret that there is lying in politics—the actual term is *pandering*. Voters often get frustrated because they're not sure they're looking at the real person. What do the candidates really believe in? They're not sure. Many politicians are chameleons who are terrified of saying how they really feel for fear it will cost them votes—and therefore, their jobs. But if you win an election by being only partially yourself, or by totally creating a new public persona, how can you claim a victory?

It isn't just in politics where people adapt their beings to the prevailing winds. How many times in the course of a week do we adapt our story to fit our audience, whoever they may be? If someone asks us how our kids are doing, maybe we say, "Great!" Or maybe, if we feel safer we admit that Billy is struggling. That adaptation is fair enough. Nobody spills their soul to everyone who asks, and I'm not saying we should. We need to be selective about who we are vulnerable with, but we also need to know that vulnerability is an essential part of humanity and wholeness.

However, what is the barometer for being real? What do we need to feel safe with the truth? And do we find that most of our relationships are safe, or do most of them require the adapted self?

If the adapted self shows up too often that's a problem. It makes us hungrier because it pulls us away from the true self. And the hungrier we get, the more dangerous it is to our survival.

Alice Walker once wrote, "In search of my mother's garden I found my own." But what if we stop at our mother's garden and call it our own?

The fundamental question is: Do we dim our light so that our world and ourselves disappear from view? And what would it take for there to be an awakening?

I once purchased lights to install around the exterior of my house, but I was busy and I didn't get around to having an electrician put them in. Every day I passed the boxes, and I thought I was waiting for the right time to call the electrician. There were a number of reasons I was waiting. I was too busy; I wanted to redo my office and there were some structural issues with my roof, so I thought I'd do it all at once, etc. Meanwhile, it was getting dark around here. One night, coming home late, I saw that all the remaining lights had gone out around my house. As I stumbled around in the black night, I was finally determined to make the call to the electrician.

Later, when I had light again, I found myself reflecting on how long I'd had what was needed—the boxes of lights that I had passed each and every day to the point of forgetting they were there. The lights were there; they were waiting. But I chose to ignore the darkness as each light extinguished until I couldn't ignore it anymore because there was only darkness. I was moving so fast that I just passed myself and didn't realize it.

What is true for all of us is that we hunger, ache, and suffer. Our lives get filled to the brim with despair, and then we go within and pretend to be okay—which is the furthest thing from the truth.

Speaking for myself, my pain will no longer be the secret that my family knows but has almost never spoken of. It will no longer be a secret at all. I had enough sense to long ago share my raw pain with my small carefully chosen village. To this day, this was one of the best decisions of my life. My well-being depended on it. Because my closest friends really knew me, they could see past my upbeat words to how much I ached. At times I pulled off the scam of being okay when I wasn't. I now look back at that time in my life and think how sad it was. What a waste of time. But that's what fear will make you do. It will make you run and hide while pretending to be big, secure, and important on the outside.

Our pain and voice will no longer be sent to its room as punishment without supper. Our pain demands to be heard. Our feelings and wounds want to be put on the witness stand in the court of authenticity, where we can tell our true stories to someone who is safe.

The first person your life wants to call to the witness stand is *you*. It's giving you the invitation to come out of hiding, into the marvelous light—with the right people, in the right place. The time is now. It's uncommon for people to share their raw despair. Most of us are taught to dress up our despair with fancy toys like cars, clothes, people, degrees, credentials, ideologies, trophies, and finery. And for those of us who don't have the funds to play in the big leagues of the hiding game, using money and external props, we use whatever is available—drugs, alcohol, sex, anger, depression, domestic violence, street violence, and phoniness. Most of us have learned to do anything but face the facts of how to build a real life from the basement of ground zero and its sacred and holy ashes.

---

### You could ask yourself . . .

What would I do if I were brave?
How would I live if I weren't afraid of judgment?
What would I do if I had a choice to live any way I wanted?
What would I see if I turned on all the lights?

---

W.E.B. Du Bois, a great, early civil rights leader and scholar, once declared: "The most important thing to remember is this: To be ready at any moment to give up what you are for what you might become." People are so invested in what they *are*, that they often fear what they may *become*.

They are so mired in their present lives that they can't open their eyes and envision the possibility of a different—better—future.

How often do we find ourselves stuck in our past—staying loyal to old rituals, behaviors, and obligations that no longer have meaning or feed our souls? Are we tied to behaviors, relationships, or people that don't pave a path to the future we wish to have? This is an opportunity to reclaim and reinvent our lives.

## HOLY SUFFERING

I heard a sermon once where the preacher talked about Jesus being scarred and having the wounds to prove it. I have always connected with not only the divinity of Christ, but His humanity, too. Jesus cried and wept, He got ticked off with those closest to Him as well as the erudite sophisticates of His day (in today's terminology, the "beautiful people"—the ones with the "bling"), and He lived with terrible disappointment about those He felt he could count on who let Him down. He was heartbroken and grappled with feelings of abandonment and aloneness with regularity, yet somehow He still did His work with joy, power, passion, and purpose. Ultimately, He got the job done. It was a last-minute dialogue in the Garden of Gethsemane that most of us, regardless of our faith, can identify with. Jesus wondered at the 11th hour of His mission if He could get out of His commitment and find some other way to accomplish His lifelong purpose and calling. I love this. Jesus even had the courage, while in His despair, to ask God if the plan that was best for the masses could be altered or amended because it was going to cost Him too much suffering. We have all hoped for such a stay of execution.

Oh, how I wanted to find a way to rise from the ashes of my rubble without any additional suffering. If we suffer day after day, and we don't learn what we need to in order to attend to our hunger, then much of the messiness of our lives—the losses we have suffered, the problems we have endured—may seem to be in vain. While I suffered a lot over the course of my life, and at times it seemed I wasn't learning the lessons, the truth is I *was* learning—over time. If we suffer and we learn—no matter how long it takes—then our suffering has not been totally in vain.

## THE QUESTION

Something funny happened on my way to living my life. A good friend called me and said, "Hey, do you want to go to a fun party with me at what I hear is a very cool house?" I said, "Sure." In those days, I was young and always game for something new and fun. Wherever something was going on, I wanted to be there if I could. I was at political events, fundraisers, concerts, birthday parties for close friends and people that I barely knew. I went to various churches, synagogues, street fairs, and community events. I would travel to Washington, D.C., for a fish fry and New York City to have dinner.

My friend and I were at this very happening eclectic party where I knew a few people, but not many. The house was amazing. It was a tucked-away treasure just on the outskirts of Philadelphia. The owners were warm and seemed happy to have good friends and strangers mingling in each corner of their rustic yet elegant home. People were perusing and wandering all around, and food was everywhere. There was no way to avoid caloric intake unless you hid in the bathroom—which was itself breathtakingly gorgeous. The energy in the house was hot—hot in a good way. It made me want to *be* at this party. Something about the environment made me want to be my whole and real self.

I had no idea that on this night, I would meet someone special. And through him, I would meet someone even *more* special: Me. I was going to meet a part of *myself* that I had not been awake to. How could I "meet" *me?* I knew myself so well. Or so I thought—until that night.

The man in question was an astronomer by profession, but he also dabbled in the less scientific world of astrology. He knew from his extensive academic training that his area of expertise, astronomy—the study of the universe—was deeply connected with his area of personal interest: the horoscope. As people nibbled and ate, I found myself in a corner with my girlfriend and this astronomer. We were chatting and he said, "I really respect your work." I thanked him for his kind words.

Now you have to know, I'm accustomed to having certain things happen at parties, and one of them, as predictable as air, is that people come up to me—sometimes apologetically, and sometimes with a look of desperation in their eyes and a tremor of fear in their voices—to ask me a relationship question. Or share with me a struggle they or someone they know is experiencing. (Sometimes the *someone* is themselves, standing before me "in drag"— their exquisite evening gown or perfectly fitted Armani suit serving as a disguise to hide their hunger. I know this look so well. I know the tremor, from personal experience. I know what it is to dress in drag, sometimes designer and sometimes the blue-light special. Whatever the costume, it is what lurks underneath that is most important.)

"Does everyone do this to you when you're out?" they often ask. "Do you get sick of hearing people's problems? Of having someone come up to you and ask a question or acknowledge that they watch you on television or listen to you on the radio?"

With the astronomer I flipped the script. Rather than waiting for him to ask me about my life I asked *him* about my life! I don't remember the exact question—the question was irrelevant—but his answer was a silent, in-my-face scream that I have not forgotten all these years later.

He regarded me with a steady expression before replying, "Robin, why do you ask questions that you already have the answers to?" He went on to read me like the front page of *The New York Times*, saying, "This is something that you do a lot. You ask about things that you know the answer to."

I was silent, stunned. This stranger knew a truth about me that I didn't know myself. His words were truth, clothed in compassion. The question was pregnant with meaning for me. "Robin, why *do* you do this? Why do you pretend to not know what you know? Why do you ask questions when you already have the answers that you are seeking?"

I had to breathe deeply. I realized that this was a divine set-up. Waiting for me at this party had been a stranger, bearing good tidings that could bring me great joy and freedom. I had an appointment with the Truth that night. I wasn't at this party to enjoy the house, eat delicious food, or to meet and greet people. I was at this party to meet and greet a part of myself that I really needed in my life.

I found myself back in my hosts' beautiful bathroom, working hard to catch my breath. I splashed my face with cold water. I didn't care about messing up my makeup. I cared that my makeup had failed to conceal the blotches of my humanity—which I had wanted so much to cover up.

There was something about his words that soothed me. I was relieved: Someone had seen through me, tenderly and with care. After

I recovered from my shock, I accepted his gift of self-knowledge with gratitude and wonder.

Every person has the potential for this kind of real, deep wake-up moment. Have you ever had one? If you have, what did you do with that moment or revelation? Did you utilize it, minimize it, tuck it away, dismiss it, deny it? Even if you missed the original opportunity, you can return at any moment and receive the revelation. It's okay to revisit these places, or to have them revisit us like unexpected "pop-ups." We never know when they will show up with a fresh message for our consideration. These moments can be the catalyst for change and the alleviation of hunger.

## Now, Face It—and Feel It

I had to face what I had learned. The old, debilitating message from my childhood was ringing in my ears: "If you can't fix it, don't feel it." I had to learn to feel, face, and embrace the many things I couldn't fix, the many hungers that made me ache. I had to get out of my head (where judgments were fixed) and into my heart. I had to feel what I had been afraid to face. I had to feel how hungry I was for a straight answer from those I loved or worked with. I had to move on, through the morass of things that didn't make sense. And so many times they didn't make sense! I thought about the time when I was supposedly loved and cherished by someone, but then was not the woman he chose. How subsequently I believed that I had misunderstood and misread the relationship, and that I had wanted too much. I thought about the time I was at the top of my game, with ratings reaching toward the sky, and then the phone stopped ringing. I thought about the times I tried to ask my mother, or my father from the grave, "What's up with this? Why is nobody talking about our real situation?" I thought about the times when everyone went silent and politely looked at me, hoping I would stop naming what was real.

Fortunately, this only made me hungrier for truth.

# CHAPTER 12

# The Road Out
# of Hunger

---

*"Always remember, everyone is hungry for praise*
*and starving for honest appreciation!"*

DAVID BRANDT BERG

The road out of hunger is not the same as the road in. That's self-evident. You can't get fuller by starving more. Someone once defined insanity as doing the same thing over and over and expecting a different result, and that's the case for those who try to heal by burrowing deeper into their nothingness. I've experienced this when I'm hiking in the woods and I decide to explore a new path. When it's time to go home it becomes clear to me that the way I entered the woods is not how I'm going to find my way out. It would be a waste of time and almost impossible to retrace my steps. I have to search and find a new route.

On many occasions I have heard people who are struggling in their relationships promise to "try harder." And I ask them,

"Try harder at what?" They don't understand that trying harder is often another form of sabotage. Usually, when someone says they're going to try harder at a relationship, it means their partner is exerting control and passing judgment. The one who is working so hard is living in fear of not being able to satisfy the demands of the other: that they will never be able to make things right, or be good enough.

Relationship isn't the military; we aren't soldiers in combat. It may sometimes *feel* like combat, but the enemy is within. We're fighting against our authentic hunger—for real love, real joy, real connection, real passion, genuine respect, and someone who listens to us and cares about our heart. Military troops I have spoken with say that soldiers get a bad rap. They are expected to be tough, without fear and feelings. It's not a question of whether soldiers cry, experience fear and hurt; it's that they try to contain, mask, and swallow their grief until they can find a safe place to let it out.

A wise person once said that "love without boundaries makes victims." That's right on the money. It should be a bumper sticker on all of our cars. Without boundaries, it is impossible for anyone to be a good partner, a good parent, a good friend, a good colleague, a good sibling, a good son or daughter, a good citizen of the world. If you show up as a victim, you are inviting others to victimize you. If you're a victim this way—where your basic needs for love, respect, being cherished, being included, or sharing money—are not being honored, then you are helping to create more hunger.

## A BAND-AID ON A GUNSHOT WOUND

You can't heal something that's wounded, unless you know how the injury was created and which organs, muscles, and bones are affected. Same goes in relationships. For example, your injury may be that you feel disrespected. But in examining the wound, it's crucial to determine the source of the disrespect—and that includes the lies that went into making you feel disrespected in the first place. If you don't understand what lie went into creating the disrespect, rage, or victimization, you really can't fix it. That's what I call putting a Band-Aid on a gunshot wound.

Living in the lie of hunger means constantly fighting off the truth and not seeing it. Many times people are comfortable in their illusions, and they no longer see that they are striving for the most ludicrous impossibility. To give a vivid example, if your partner didn't have a leg, you wouldn't say, "I hope she grows a leg." Yet when your partner is emotionally lifeless, spiritless, mean, and selfish, you might say, "I hope she becomes loving"—refusing to see the situation as it is. If a relationship is solely based on hope, and not reality, there is no true relationship there.

## TELL THE TRUTH

Arlene was nearing age 62, and she was looking forward to retirement with great anticipation. She had been in an unhappy marriage for many years, conscious of continually putting her needs on hold. But now, with retirement approaching, she had made an important decision: She was going to make the coming years about *her* needs, for the first time in her life. As she drove home on one of her last days at work, she was thinking happily about a long trip abroad she was planning with friends. "Now I'll live," she thought. Then her cell phone rang. It was an emergency room nurse calling to tell Arlene that her husband Jack had just suffered a massive stroke and had been brought to the hospital. Stunned by the news, Arlene quickly drove to the hospital, where she remained by her husband's side through long harrowing hours and days.

Arlene's husband survived his stroke, but it soon became clear that he was severely damaged and would need full-time care. At first she just felt shock, but as the reality sank in, she could feel a wrenching despair. One day a nurse said cheerfully, "It's so lucky you are retiring. You'll be there to help Jack. He'll need you now more than ever."

Arlene nodded mutely, but her sense of grief and terror was growing. She had been starving for many years in a lonely and empty marriage, and then she had been invited to a banquet where she would experience fullness. She was excited that she was going to finally enjoy what was left of her life, and she didn't feel the need to divorce her husband. Arlene's plan was to focus on herself and her desires, and let Jack take care of himself for a change. But when Arlene arrived at the door of the banquet hall, she received the shock of her life: The price of admission would be to abandon her sick husband. What was she to do?

As Arlene would later whisper to a friend she trusted, "I can't believe that I've been in a marriage that sucks for 30 years. Now I'm 62 and retiring, and I was finally going to have something of my own, and he had a stroke."

Arlene was fortunate that she had a safe person with whom to share her true feelings. "I want to stick my head in the oven," she exclaimed one day, and her friend embraced her—assuring her that those feelings were understandable and acceptable. Arlene felt mildly guilty for expressing such feelings, but little did she know that breaking the silence and speaking the truth to her friend was a first step in resolving her crisis.

For all the years of her marriage Arlene had lived as if everything was okay when it wasn't. Her retirement dream was the big secret that she guarded jealously and that gave her hope. Now everything had changed and her secret was out.

Arlene's situation might seem dire, but there's a secret she didn't know. In speaking the truth, something almost magical happens. When we speak our truth to a safe person, a new possibility opens up. Stating the truth out loud creates an internal reaction that grows and spreads. Arlene's crisis allowed her to break the silence and speak of her hunger after 30 years.

So, how does telling the truth then progress to *living* the truth? It's a process that begins with a tiny kernel—maybe having a thought about truth, then moving to knowing what is true, then speaking the truth (often with fear and trembling), and then beginning to live the truth. The more we spend time with the truth and allow it into our lives, the more our lives change. Alternatives begin to appear, ideas begin to blossom. In Arlene's case, she found services that could support her independence. The last time I spoke with her she had hired a nurse so she could take a five-day cruise with friends. And she had a blast. The issue wasn't about Arlene abandoning her sick husband; it was about Arlene breaking a 30-year cycle of abandoning *herself.*

Another blessing that came with speaking out was that Arlene's friends formed a nurturing shield around her. They had been waiting for the opportunity. As one of them said to her, "I have been concerned about you for a long time, but I was afraid to say anything because you were so closed—always acting like you were fine and things were good. I didn't know if it was my place to speak up."

One of my dearest friends, Louise, who died in 2009, had a phrase that drove our friends crazy: "I'm good to go." She said this when life was at its worst and it was obviously untrue. But a few years before her death, E. Lou, as we affectionately called her, gave up the false line and began to speak honestly about her true feelings and hunger. This changed her final years for the better. When she died, it was in truth—and set an example for us all.

## TAKE BACK YOUR DIGNITY

No one has the right to control you. A man I know, Kevin, took charge of his life when he confronted his 26-year-old stepson, John, who was disrespectful and often verbally abusive—not showing up when promised, and criticizing Kevin loudly in public and private. Kevin had been nurturing him since he was ten years old, and had given him everything he needed. His wife, Janet—John's mother—never corrected her son. So finally Kevin took matters into his own hands.

"The relationship we have is unacceptable to me," he told John. "You're abusive, and I'm not having a relationship with you anymore." John was stunned.

"You can't do that!" John retorted. "You're my stepfather. You're married to my mother."

"You can't tell John you're not having a relationship with him," Janet later concurred.

"I can, and I just did," Kevin responded calmly.

When John complained that he still had to visit his mother, Kevin agreed. He told John he was welcome in the house, and that they would inevitably see one another. But Kevin was not going to have an emotional relationship with him any longer.

He put his foot down, deciding that until John showed the respect he needed and deserved, Kevin would no longer support his stepson. It took a year and a half, but John finally came to Kevin and apologized for his behavior.

Kevin had not only taken a stand for his own dignity, he taught his stepson a valuable lesson about true connection, respect, and love. He didn't put Janet in the middle, and he stopped blaming her for not fixing the situation. Instead, he took responsibility for his own hunger to have his dignity honored.

## THE CRUEL POWER OF HUNGER

Polly had been seeing a married man for several months. He was something of a player and a scoundrel, and he didn't treat her very well. She was very easily manipulated by him.

She told a friend, "I know he's married, but I just need to hear somebody tell me they love me. It's been so long, and I just really need that."

Her friend felt empathy for Polly, and appreciated her honesty. But she asked for clarification.

"You don't really believe that this man loves you, do you?"

Polly hesitated for a moment before answering.

"Well, I believe it when I'm with him, and that's good enough for me right now." Her voice dropped to a near-whisper. "I don't need a lot, just that. I was depressed before I met him, and this has been helping me get over my depression."

Polly clung to her inauthentic relationship as if grasping for her last "lifeline" on a game show. She didn't see the danger she faced: That this faithless, untrustworthy man could cut the cord at any moment and leave her spinning back to the bottom of her depression. In hearing this story, it got me thinking: Is a lie enough, if you are desperate? Is a taste enough, if you are starving? When faced with that situation, it can *feel* like enough—at least to survive.

There's a biological phenomenon that occurs when a person is starving. Doctors often see it with people who are on extreme weight-loss diets. If you eat less than you need for health and sustenance, your body's survival instinct will kick in to try and keep you alive. Sensing imminent danger, it will slow down your systems to conserve precious energy. This starvation response is the reason why some people can't lose weight even when they eat very little. Emotional starvation is no different. It tricks us into believing that we can survive our unattended hunger. People like Polly will say, "I don't need much. A little something is better than nothing." Others might say, "I don't need a relationship at all."

Jennifer married a man 30 years her senior. In the aftermath of their bitter divorce, she acknowledged that she had never loved him. Her husband had treated her badly, and he ultimately left her for another woman. Why was she with him in the first place?

"I only wanted to be able to say I'd been married—that someone once had wanted me," she said.

In her view there was a stigma associated with being single.

"At least with a divorce, I can say that once someone found me desirable and worthy enough to marry me."

Jennifer was overweight when she met her husband, and overweight when they got divorced. He said that he was repulsed by her body. As horrible as the breakup was, she could at least say, "I'm divorced. Somebody chose to walk down an aisle with me."

"That's huge, isn't it?" she asked me.

Is it? How "huge" is it to be a partner in a soul-crushing relationship? It was huge to abdicate her dignity and honor to try and satisfy her hunger. As some point, we've all tried to satisfy our hunger with junk—or drunk the poison, calling it Kool-Aid.

## OUT OF THE BUNKER

A longtime family friend lost her husband after 55 years of marriage. When I visited her a few weeks later, I expected to see a fragile, grieving widow of 80. But the woman who answered the door seemed to be glowing with a light from within. When I hugged her and told her how sorry I was, she smiled and thanked me, saying, "I'm doing fine. Don't worry about me."

We sat in the living room, and as she poured tea she told me about what she was up to. The list seemed awfully long—volunteering at an animal shelter, joining a book group, getting involved in local politics. She seemed happy, and I found myself staring at her in wonder. Finally she let me in on a secret. "For 55 years, I served and catered to him," she said. "I gave him my whole life. And now, whatever years I have left are going to be about me. I am relieved and grateful to have a little time on the planet to focus on myself." Her daughter stood mortified as her mother told her truth, that she was hoping to finally satisfy some of her own hunger.

I had never known that so many of her needs had gone unmet in her marriage. I doubt many people did. It was her secret, as she put on the mask of dignified contentment. How sad that her liberation had to come so late. But how wonderful that she could experience it and speak about it unapologetically. Some people don't live to be free.

## Lot's Wife

As I've mentioned, in 2010 I was in a serious car accident. An SUV totaled my car—and almost totaled me. Parts of my life *were* totaled; others changed forever. I now live with permanent, chronic pain which will likely be with me for the rest of my life.

Activities of daily living are now real chores. Things that I did for fun are either forbidden to me, or I have to walk on eggshells when doing them. Swimming and diving, running, tennis, hiking, yoga, and even a leisurely stroll all exacerbate my pain.

One of the most obvious signs of the accident is that my neck locks in place, making it difficult to turn in either direction. While this is a painful daily reminder of the accident, it's also a powerful reminder about the danger of looking back. In this way, the pain carries a spiritual and psychological lesson: It reminds me to learn from the past, but not to live in it. It helps me take the *would have, could have, should have* CD out of the player in my mind.

One night my neck totally locked. I could not turn to the left or to the right and I was scared to death. I cried my heart out hoping some of the pain would leave with the tears, but that didn't happen. "I can't live with this kind of piercing pain, I just can't bear it" were my words in the middle of the night. I longed for Kalle, and at the same time was glad she was gone. How would I have ever cared for her when I could no longer take care of myself? I was terrified about what had become of my fiercely independent and healthy self. "Is she gone?" I asked myself. Had I lost Kalle *and* myself?

As the days turned into weeks and weeks into months, I realized that even if my life and body as I had once known myself was kaput, over and done with, I could learn the lesson of keeping my gaze forward. Too much backward glancing can give any person a stiff neck. For me, it was much worse.

Rev. Dr. J. Alfred Smith, Sr., my other father in the ministry, told me in a very raw time in my life, "Robin, keep your eyes on the Conductor." He was telling me not to lose myself in the pain, hunger, and distractions, but instead to keep my gaze looking forward toward God. I came to realize that looking back is a waste of this moment's gift. I wish I could have learned this some other way. Being hit by an SUV seems drastic; but being stuck in a past I can't change might be even worse.

## WORTHINESS

Brené Brown, a researcher and lecturer on the themes of vulnerability, courage, authenticity, and shame, conducted a research project to find out what distinguished people with a high sense of self-worth from those who were paralyzed by shame and low self-esteem. She began to evaluate what those with high self-worth had in common and found only one variable: they *believed* they were worthy. That's it. They didn't have more status or money or love. They weren't better looking or more extroverted. They simply believed they were worthy. Brown goes on to say that these "wholehearted" individuals also had the courage to be imperfect. They fully embraced their vulnerability. They let go of who they thought they "should" be and acknowledged who they *are*.

At a conference I attended, one of the speakers said, "Truth precedes love." I thought, if only that could be written in every heart that seeks love. How often do we use the expression *true love* only to mean false love—love built on lies and fantasy, love built on desperation and deceit? Imagine a different scenario: true love being grounded in truth.

# CHAPTER 13

# GOOD TOUCH, BAD TOUCH

*"The wound is the place where light enters you."*

RUMI

It was a beautiful spring day. My life felt like it had gone through the shredder at the highest speed. Not only had my most recent love interest betrayed me, but he lacked remorse for any of the pain he had hand-delivered to my heart. I had spent a lot of time trying to get him to "see" how much he hurt me, to no avail.

I was supposed to be writing this book, but I couldn't because my wrists were full of fluid and very swollen. My hands, fingers, arms, neck, shoulders, and back were in terrible pain. I could barely move, let alone write or type! As my nieces said to me, "Aunt Robin, you're a hot and hurting mess." They were right, but I was in too much pain to even enjoy their warm and well-meaning humor.

My massage therapist has anointed hands. All of the people I have sent to him agree, singing his praises for both his seasoned expertise and his gentle and tender spirit. I knew that I needed to see him; this was an emergency situation. I made an appointment and he was able to see me immediately. I was so beaten down in my body and spirit and hurting everywhere that our greeting was more quiet than usual. I did the usual—slipped out of my clothes and laid, covered, on the table in the dimly lit room. Soothing music played in the background and various aromas floated though the air, offering comfort simply by their smell.

He knocked and asked, "Are you ready?" His voice is as smooth and steady as his hands are.

"Yes," I whispered.

As his hands did their job, moving over each tissue and muscle, my cells seemed to thank me. I felt the tears rolling down my face. The room felt like a safe, warm womb that I wanted to never leave. I realized that I needed good touch—safe touch, touch that asked nothing of me other than to receive its gift and to breathe. I was hungry for just this kind of touch. I've had enough demanding and selfish touch to last me two lifetimes, I have lived through too much bad touch. That day, my body and soul were starving for good, nurturing touch, and it was at this point that I realized the power of this kind of personal interaction.

And my understanding of this power was deepened by a story told by a judge—a tall and distinguished-looking man—who had a memorable encounter with a little girl on a mission trip to Zambia. On first sight, the girl ran toward him, flinging herself into his arms. She trusted that she would find safety there, which she did.

As he told the story to our congregation, I thought how we are all hungry to find the right arms to run into. We all need someplace to fling all of our troubles, cares, worries, joys, and sorrows, trusting that we will be met with wide-open arms. When church was over, I went to the judge and thanked him for reminding us of how much we all need good touch and the safe arms of someone to run, climb, or fall into. He seemed a bit surprised at my take on how big his message was. Not just for me, but for all humans.

As our conversation ended, we shared a smile and an embrace—a moment of good touch between us.

I know in the past that I have settled for bad touch because I was so hungry for good touch. But I didn't know that I was starving, and therefore couldn't acknowledge what I wanted and needed.

The research has long shown that babies who are not held or touched don't thrive. Ultimately they can die, even if all their other needs are met. We are hardwired to need good touch to grow, develop, and thrive. If a baby's growth can be stunted due to touch deprivation, what in the world happens to us as children and adults when we go without good touch?

Both my massage therapist and my physical therapist—who also blesses my body and soul with gifts and healing—have become key players in addressing my body and soul's hunger for good touch. You, too, need this kind of touch. Just be sure to stay tuned into yourself and to respect what you feel, what you know. Tune in to what makes you comfortable and uncomfortable, the energy around you, and the vibes people give off—whether positive or negative. I have a photograph in my home of a wolf with a caption that reads, "Trust your instincts." When it comes to touch, do the same. Once you trust yourself, you can have access to all the safe, nourishing touch you need.

CHAPTER 14

# CHANGING LANES

*"But one thing I do: forgetting what is behind
and straining toward what is ahead . . ."*

PHILIPPIANS 3:13

When the church leader—the man in charge—and I first met,
it was all good. I needed a church home, a place where I felt safe
and where my talents and gifts would be utilized, appreciated, and
respected. That worked for a while, but as time went on, I realized
that being a woman seemed to get in the way of my having full
access like men did. Before I joined this organization, I asked the
leader about his position regarding women in roles of leadership.
I believe to this day he answered honestly, but I find my question
more telling than his answer. Why did I ask this question? What
had I picked up in the climate of this very welcoming and kind
environment that made me wonder if there was *room at the inn* for
women at the top? I asked this very smart, highly accomplished,
and statuesque man—the very one who had warmly pursued me
to join him and his extremely successful and competent all-male

staff—because that was what I did at that time in my life: I asked questions that I already knew the answers to. I didn't want to face the truth. This was one of those times. I liked the man in charge. I still have a sweet affection for him. I respected him and he respected me—as much as he could given whatever his gender biases were at that time. I was willing to "wait" until he felt more comfortable, until we knew each other better, until, until, until. I waited until one holiday morning when I sat crying, an outsider once again, and watched what felt like "all the king's men" carrying out their assignments without including me or any women. This scenario had become unbearable. I simply could no longer carry the pain of my invisibility. I was hoping it would get better; that my soul would not keep reminding me, in the words of David Whyte, "The soul would rather fail at its own life than succeed at someone else's." I waited week after week, month after month, and year after year. Until one day I realized my violet was no longer shrinking, it had officially *shrunk*. And so had I.

I arranged a time to meet with the president of the organization. He was always super-busy, and yet was always willing to make time for us to connect. He had no idea what was on my heart and mind, nor could he have imagined that enough emotion to fill Grand Central Station was about to walk into his office for our 8:00 A.M. meeting. I remember showering that morning and getting dressed. I felt like I was going to a funeral. I guess I was, but who had died? It didn't seem to be me that was dead, nor him, so who or what was dead? My fantasy and dream was that he would value my work, my calling, my way of being in the world enough to change his usual way of doing business and how he captained his ship. But it became clear to me that he wasn't going to change how he did things. That even if he did, by that time I was going to be all dried up—even more injured from many years of waiting, longing, and hungering. Given my resentment at not being seen, the pain of my starvation as others ignored my needs, and the further injury and damage that were bound to result if I kept it to myself, I had no choice but to walk in there and share my heart with him that day. So I did.

My mouth was dry like the desert. Fear had gripped each cell in my body. I walked into a church office wondering what or who would encourage me—or at least prop me up—so that I could, in the spirit of John Mayer's lyrics, "say what I needed to say." In spite of my parched mouth and my terror of saying "I hurt because of what is happening here," we were both honest and open.

It was huge for me to do this. Some of my friends said, "Okay, if you have to, if you feel it will help . . . you know he's not going to change . . . what's the point? What do you hope to gain? Do you think it's really worth it? Aren't you scared to face him especially since you already know his discomfort with women in the very top positions of leadership?" I was petrified. My mouth mirrored the dryness of the Arabian Desert. This was one of the few times in my life when fear showed up boldly in my body as I have heard many people describe it. I didn't have the sweaty palms, but the dry mouth said it all. I was conscious of my fear in a way I don't remember before.

I could no longer live with the fear and pain of not being who I was, or being halfway affirmed for my gifts, talents, and abilities. I needed to be fully acknowledged. If that couldn't happen in this environment, then I needed to say how badly that felt, how much I loved it there, and that I would begin looking for a new position where all of me would be welcomed without exception. As Flannery O'Connor said, "The truth does not change according to our ability to stomach it."

I stayed with this church for a few more seasons while I looked for a different position. My passion to be me full-time was too great to stay. I wanted to find a home where I could live out—fully and freely—what I was in the world to do. I wanted all of my credentials to be used to help create and build peace on earth and goodwill toward all creation.

That experience happened many years ago. I have often reflected on how huge and scary it was to go to the president and share my need and desire to be treated fairly and have my gifts, skills, and education fully utilized. The whole experience was connected to my hunger to be fully me. I told him, "You brought me in, you've nurtured and loved me, and you gave the illusion of inclusion. But in truth, there's a sign you hold that says *women not allowed any further.*" I told him that this hurt me deeply. I think he understood, and even felt bad to some extent, but he had to be who *he* was. Unlike my old self, I didn't feel the need or desire to convince him otherwise. The days of "old Robin" weren't over yet, but they were beginning to wind down. I no longer felt that being the first woman to reach my level of leadership was enough. I wanted to be in an environment where justice for all people was upheld, and clearly this was not that place. As a black woman, issues of human rights and justice mean everything to me. As I've said, my father and mother marched, sat, picketed, prayed, funded, and were almost sprayed and arrested for the cause of justice for all people. I was known as the civil rights baby, because I was in a stroller as my parents marched for equality for black people everywhere. When I got older, I sat on my father's shoulders, holding the picket signs around Philadelphia's Girard College and other marches. I have a photograph in my library of me as a little girl, helping the NAACP raise money.

The words of Rev. Dr. Martin Luther King, Jr., are etched and ingrained in my soul and mind: "Injustice anywhere is a threat to justice everywhere."

Many years later, I became friends with one of the most powerful and influential men in the country, who many say wields power and brokers deals all over the world. He had been very gracious and supportive of me, my life, my ministry, and my very big dreams. After not being in touch with him for almost two years I *awakened* one day and realized that I needed to reach out to him and ask for his help. I was having a very hard time with my career and—with knowing what I really wanted to do, as well as what I really *didn't* want to do. I experienced the awful crash of all things valuable in 2010—I was shattered financially, relationally, spiritually, physically, emotionally, and professionally. Life as I knew it came crashing in on me. In a conversation with my friend Sandra and beloved cousin Kim, I said, "I need to contact him." They both replied, "Him *who?*" I spoke his big, bold, and brilliant name aloud. "I need his help. I need to tell him that I've been living life out of my lane, that I've been cheating on myself. That I've been treating myself like a part-time lover or worse yet, like an unpaid prostitute." Sandra asked, "What will you tell him?" And I replied, "I will tell him the whole truth."

I sent him an e-mail saying that I wanted to meet with him and of course would come wherever it was most convenient. I didn't expect him to respond immediately because he's so busy. But I received an e-mail from him just a week later, apologizing for his delay in responding. He told me to contact his office and I would be put on his calendar ASAP. I traveled to his fancy sky-scraper corner office. When I walked in, we embraced and both smiled warmly. He looked terrific and I suppose for the shape I was in, I looked much better than I felt. We got caught up on family, and then I just cut to the chase.

"I'm in trouble, and I need your help," I said. He looked alarmed. I explained how the floor—and all of its contents—had fallen out from under me, and I was in jeopardy of losing the little bit I had left as well as the career that I had very successfully built over the last 25 years.

"I was living and working out of my lane and it didn't work. I know my lane and I want to be in my lane. It's the only thing that I desire to do, but I need help getting fully back into my lane, the lane I was born to breathe and live in."

"Robin," he said with great compassion, "why did you wait so long before calling me for help?"

"For two reasons," I replied. "First, I have been half out of my mind dealing with one loss after another. Each time I thought I was coming up for air; that maybe things were going to be *okay*. But each time the storm of some new loss would dunk me under again. The undertow from the grief and trauma was simply too much to bear. I didn't know how to call anyone for help.

"Secondly, I have come to understand something very impor-tant about myself. I don't know how to ask for help when I need it. Unless I can pay for it! And clearly the help I need from you can't be bought."

"Okay." He smiled. "So how can I help you?"

This meeting with my friend was ultimately helpful in several ways. But what was most meaningful was that—other than Sandra, Kim, my mother, and, in a smaller way, my beloved lawyer and friend—I had not told anyone that I had been living out of my lane. That my *life* depended on changing lanes.

That day my mouth wasn't dry, and I had no fear. I knew who I was. I had no idea what he would think of my situation, if he would help me, whether my words and desperate pleas made any sense to him. But I knew that I was finally back in my lane—and it felt good. I felt free and liberated to ask for his help; to say, "I'm in trouble." Humbly, and without any prior notification or outside authorization, I safely put on my turn signal. I waited until all the busy traffic had passed me by. And I changed lanes.

## THE END OF AN AFFAIR

I spent years having an empty affair with things and relationships that I thought were *something*, but turned out to be little more than "Nothing." "Nothing" is the name I've given to empty, vacuous expectations that left me hungry and always wanting more. What did I expect that "Nothing" could give me? Good question. "Nothing" can't give anything. "Nothing" has at times been a man, a job, friendship, my own homegrown fantasy. And whichever it was, it would not and could not deliver anything. It only emptied me out. "Nothing" was a force that took up residence in my life and refused to leave—claiming squatters rights, because I allowed it to abide with me for so long.

As you can imagine, my affair with "Nothing" was bloody, brutal, exhausting, empty, and left me deeply lonely.

When I've shared this, people have asked me for "Nothing's" real name—assuming I'm really referring to a man I want to keep anonymous. But "Nothing" is not a man; in fact, it does not exist. It is an illusion. It refers to the hopes, dreams, and expectations that are not realized. "Nothing" is a ghost, and not a friendly one. Its vanishing always left skid marks on my heart.

So often my encounters with "Nothing" have been connected to my need and hunger for love. The wise and challenging words of Vietnamese monk Thich Nhat Hanh often return to me when I think about what love is—and what it's not. For me, it has been as important to know what love is not, so that I could understand what love *is*. He says, "Do you have time to love?" and goes on to say, "The most precious gift you can give to the one you love is your true presence."

It has taken me what feels like forever to quietly, without pomp or circumstance, change lanes. To end this painful affair with "Nothing." But I am grateful and relieved to have finally ended my romance with my hunger. To live a full life free from my affair with "Nothing." Deep within, I heard the famous words of the Rev. Dr. Martin Luther King, Jr.:

> *Free at last*
> *Free at last*
> *Thank God Almighty*
> *I'm free at last.*

## Who Do You Say You Are?

There is an African tribe who at night whisper in their children's ears, "Be who you are." Too often we've had just the opposite whispered—or shouted—in our ears: "Be someone else! Be like your brother, your cousin, your neighbor, that other one who is not you. Please be anyone other than who you really are."

No wonder people are so desperate to escape themselves, and rush to create a better façade. No wonder so many people are wrapped in the daydream of *if only*. If only I were:

   . . . prettier
   . . . taller
   . . . richer
   . . . more talented
   . . . luckier
   . . . more extroverted
   . . . smarter
   . . . thinner
   . . . more successful
   . . . white
   . . . younger
   . . . better!

These longings are a sure pathway to hunger, and eventually to starvation. They create an enduring ache, as they put your real self in competition with some idealized version of you, and your real self is always found wanting.

Who do you say you are? Are you the embraced self of your birthright, or are you the longed for and never achieved self of your fantasy?

The activist and author Parker Palmer, who founded the Center for Courage and Renewal, is a favorite author of mine. Parker always speaks to the heart, challenging people to be themselves. He created the term "birthright gifts"—what we come into the world owning, yet often spend most of our lives abandoning. He wrote, "What a long time it can take to become the person one has always been. How often in the process we mask ourselves in faces that are not our own. How much dissolving and shaking of ego we must endure before we discover our deep identity—the true self within every human being that is the seed of authentic vocation."

People are hungry for someone to say, "Be yourself." Their divine birthright has been stolen from them, as if someone stole their birth certificate. As I've said, it's a form of spiritual identity theft.

It behooves each one of us to check in and see if we are who we were born and meant to be.

## SAY MY NAME!

A friend of mine tells the story of getting married and having her mother-in-law constantly call her by her husband's first wife's name. It was funny at first—just one of those slips of the tongue that happens to everyone. But she kept doing it, and finally my friend confronted her husband. His response? He thought it was cute.

Cute to be called by someone else's name? Cute to be denied an identity of one's own? Cute to be the victim of this underlying hostility? When I heard that story, I shuddered. It was perhaps a small thing. A tiny indignity. But I could look ahead with a clear vision and see that 10 or 15 or 20 years down the road the indignities will have piled up in my friend's life. That's because an isolated incident of disrespect often becomes the norm, not the exception. If we are disrespected, and we ignore, minimize, or dismiss the reality of how we are being treated, it often takes over and becomes a regular item on our life's menu.

When my friend told me that she didn't know what to say when her mother-in-law called her "Jane," I made this suggestion: "Say who you are. Say, 'I'm Ruth.' And keep saying it every time, until it becomes your own identity chorus. You can't make her stop or change, but you can be clear that you know your name and that you know who and what you are."

## HAS ANYONE SEEN YOU?

As I've said, I love David Whyte's question, "Has anyone seen David?" It seems to show that David understood that most of our identities were stolen early in life. It's as if we're forced to take membership in a country club that requires each of us to wear "the mask that grins and lies." Standing in front of his co-workers that day, David's mask was shattered. Although he had been working in an organization where he was considered to be an effective leader, and gave the appearance of being in charge of both his work and personal life, internally he felt like a chicken with its head cut off. It was as if he was running around, directionless. On

this day he was pulled over by the Universe and felt the humiliation we all feel when we realize we have lied to and cheated on
ourselves. That we have become part-time lovers, sometime lovers,
or no-time lovers to the one who deserves our all: us.

A question that all of us need to be asking of ourselves regularly
is, "Has anyone seen *me*?" At work, at home, at the playground, at
worship, at parties, funerals . . . everywhere. We need to check in
with ourselves to see whether we are being authentic, so that others
may truly see us. This question has been an important part of my
journey into living the only life I could genuinely live: my own.

I have grieved about all the years I was lost, searching for myself in relationships, in work, in fame, in play. For so long I was
nowhere to be found.

Has *anyone* seen YOU, *ever?*

Have you seen yourself?

When was the last time there was a sighting?

Have you ever felt invisible?

Are you there to be found?

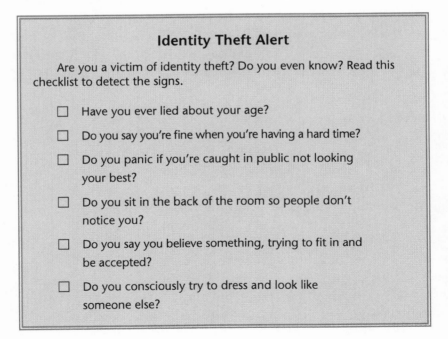

### Identity Theft Alert

Are you a victim of identity theft? Do you even know? Read this
checklist to detect the signs.

- ☐ Have you ever lied about your age?

- ☐ Do you say you're fine when you're having a hard time?

- ☐ Do you panic if you're caught in public not looking
  your best?

- ☐ Do you sit in the back of the room so people don't
  notice you?

- ☐ Do you say you believe something, trying to fit in and
  be accepted?

- ☐ Do you consciously try to dress and look like
  someone else?

## LOOK WITHIN

There is a saying, "The lion's story will never be known as long as the hunter is the one to tell it." In order to fire the killing shot, the hunter must close his eyes to the worth of the lion, the nature of the lion, the living value of the lion. Only the lion can express his true nature and tell his own story.

Can you live in your own truth? Can you lay down the denial and fear and accept yourself? I know it might be hard, especially if your habit is to cover up. When I was growing up my mother was clear about not revealing her age. She was in her early 40s when I was born, and for as long as I could remember she believed that it was downright rude to ask a woman how old she was. Many women feel that way and carry shame about their age—no surprise in a youth-obsessed society. I'm sure my mother worried that people would judge her negatively if they knew her age. Sometimes it seems that we treat aging as if it were a disease—worse than cancer. How sad is that? Probably the most objective reality of who we are is that we were born into the world on a certain day and date. Studies have shown that people who have healthy attitudes about aging live longer, because they aren't burdened by the stress of denying that they will die. Truth is, if we don't grow older we're not living. At 90 my mother now rejoices in her age and even boasts about it, but it took her becoming an elderly, vibrant woman to begin to appreciate the beauty of her age. As I watched my mother's long dance with the aging process—from denial to acceptance to enjoyment—I have concluded that I only want to be me if I'm being the *real* me, at every age.

Looking inside can be painful and confusing, so sometimes people find it easier to evaluate their situation from the outside—maybe to blame others instead of really looking at themselves. A friend told the story of driving to a doctor's appointment and being stuck behind a huge truck that was spewing noxious fumes. The fumes were so overwhelming that she could hardly breathe, and she kept praying for the truck to make a turn. But it kept clattering along in front of her, and she felt sicker and sicker. Finally, shortly before she arrived at her destination the truck made a turn and disappeared down a side street. To her astonishment, the fumes were just as strong. She pulled into the parking lot and stopped, still feeling sick. And then she noticed that she'd been driving the entire way with the parking brake on, and the fumes were being created by her own car. What a powerful lesson!

How many times do we look outside ourselves for the source of our problems, thinking that there has got to be an external explanation? How would things change if we always started our investigation by looking within?

## GROWING YOURSELF

Suzanne is a wonderful homemaker in a loving 25-year marriage. She loves to bake, and her home has always been a busy, happy place, with delicious smells emanating from her kitchen. Now her kids are married with children of their own, and it is just her and her husband at home. "My house feels like a tomb and a place where there's no light," she told me.

This is a difficult time for Suzanne. But I also notice something else. She's waking up and thawing out—for the first time becoming attuned to herself. One area where she is becoming more attuned is her relationship with her father. He has always been critical of her and sometimes downright mean, but in the past she'd shrugged it off. "I had my nest," she explained. "I was protected from his jabs because I was involved with my kids. I didn't have time to be bothered." But now it's all coming to the surface. As Suzanne thaws out, she feels the sharp pain of her father's meanness. She knows she cannot tolerate it anymore. She admitted to me that in some ways she preferred the years when the conflict was on ice. She hates conflict! And yet, as she experiences the small awakenings of selfhood, she is amazed and proud of how strong she is. She'd never known that about herself before.

When we are asleep, we hide in shame—fearing that if others knew our truth, they would reject us. It's as if we've made a deal with the devil to remain silent, in exchange for the comfort of belonging and being free of conflict. (Although that rarely works out.) We cede our souls to the isolation of being unknown, and adopt the identities we are given. But it's not the real you or me. It's who we thought we had to be to receive love, care, and acceptance.

What is the greatest fear of all—the one that is so powerful that it compels people to give up their true identities? *Being alone.* The desire for an undivided love, companionship, and secure love is so powerful, so overwhelming, so dizzying, that we often fear or forget to be ourselves in the face of it.

## WHAT DO YOU NEED?

Over dinner one night, my aunt's husband told me a story from his childhood. He'd be sitting at the table eating and would want a second helping. His mother would respond, "No, you don't need all that." He was confused to be told that he didn't need seconds when he wanted more. He said to me, "Okay, maybe I didn't actually need all of the food, but I thought I did, and I also thought that there must be something wrong with me that I thought I needed it." His confusion was not about food, but need.

If people tell you that you don't need what you think you need, it's confusing. As a child you're self-centered, which is developmentally appropriate, and you don't have the brain wiring yet to figure out boundaries. So, learning the balance between self-involvement and caring for others is a lifelong process. Most people lean a little too far on one side or the other, tipping the scale toward selfishness or selflessness. The initial learning comes from parents, caretakers, and other teachers. When they tell us to do or not do something, we obey them because we have to. Often we believe them, even if it doesn't make sense to us.

We think, "I need this, I need that," while our parents and caretakers say to us as children, "You don't need this or that." Children pay close attention to verbal and nonverbal cues as to what is and is not acceptable. The situation can lead to confusion, as a child tries to resolve the conflicting voices of their desire and what others say. As children (and adults, actually) we try to read faces, minds, and many other signals as to how we are supposed to think, feel, and act. What often gets imprinted is that "my needs are not important." Or worse yet, that "I don't have needs." A conflict can develop between what someone else says we need and what we want—which can compromise our sense of entitlement. All of this leads to inner turmoil and confusion.

If our wants and desires are always dismissed as a child, we may dismiss or minimize our hunger and needs as an adult, finding it easier to acquiesce to someone else's agenda.

## It's Okay to Say, "No, Thank You"

In 2009, I decided to buy my mother a new TV. Hers was old, and it was threatening to go dark at any minute. I decided I'd get her a replacement before it went bad. I was already in the store buying a TV for myself, so I figured I might as well take care of it while I was there. Plus, I love to save money and there was a great sale at the Sony store! It was a win-win situation.

I wanted to surprise Mommy. So I loaded the TV in my car, and I also bought a table for it to sit on. I took the TV to my mother's house and set it up while she was out, thinking what a great surprise it would be for her when she got home.

A few hours later, my mother called. I was expecting an outpouring of gratitude and excitement—or at least acknowledgment for how incredibly thoughtful I'd been. Instead, she said, "Honey, I don't know how to tell you this. I don't like this TV. I like my old one better. Can you take it back?" She hurried to add, "I feel bad, and I appreciate your effort, but I don't want it."

I felt briefly deflated and a bit stunned, but I also realized that I was being handed a good lesson. I had jumped in without being asked, and without asking—assuming that she had a need she didn't have. Reflecting on the incident, I wondered, why had I done that? Why had I expended my energy and resources without even knowing if my gift was wanted?

The truth is that over-investing, over-doing, and over-giving all create unnecessary hunger and they cover up the real longing underneath those actions.

## THE COURAGE TO NEED

A couple years before she died, I interviewed Elizabeth Edwards for my radio show. This was before the scandal over her husband's affair erupted. At the time, John Edwards was running for president, and Elizabeth was struggling with a reoccurrence of her cancer, which had a poor prognosis. She was getting heavy criticism in the media for going out on the trail to campaign, instead of spending time at home with her children. People said, "These may be your final years. What kind of mother are you that you don't want to spend them with your kids?" I asked her about the criticism, and she was very honest. She told me, "Yes, my kids are my priority, but I have other desires, too." She didn't want her life, or her children's lives, to be reduced to a deathwatch. She chose to not have her illness paralyze her, and in this way she was modeling for her children the importance of having a purpose in life.

I admired Elizabeth's courage. When she did die, I felt that her children were better prepared to cope because she had passed on the model of strength, courage, and self-care to them—and also showed them by example the importance of following their own paths, regardless of what others were doing or saying. This was an example of someone who paid attention to her hunger and listened to her inner voice.

In what ways are you listening to yourself, your heart, and your needs? In what ways are you not? It can be a frightening challenge when we first find ourselves at the bottom—the "ground zero" of our identity—not knowing who we truly are. The awakening can be painful as we begin to wonder what our own voice would have said and done if it had not been chased away by external influence. If the world had not demanded we be someone other than who we are. And it is difficult to tease out our truth as we try to untangle the many messages from family, friends, neighbors, and the world that bombard us. While it is no easy task to discern our true identity, it is necessary in order to live fuller and freer lives.

Compassionately understanding our hunger pains so we can embrace our true identity is a lifelong journey. Ask yourself these questions: If I had no fear . . .

- . . . how would I respond to words, requests, or actions from a family member, lover, friend, boss, co-worker, or stranger that stir up hurt for me, bring discomfort, or invite or provoke me to be angry?

- . . . how would I get married, remain married, go for that trial separation, or get the divorce that I daydream about?

- . . . how would I move away from the familiar, my family and friends, to live in an emotional and physical climate that more suits my hunger, preferences, desires, and needs?

- . . . would I practice the faith of my family—or any faith at all?

- . . . what would I be doing that I'm now afraid to do?

When I was doing *The Dr. Robin Show*, I had a caller who had married a woman who deeply shared his Christian faith. Recently, however, he had embraced the title "agnostic"—which was causing serious problems in the marriage. They loved each other and thought that their marriage was for life . . . forever. They were sure they would not add to the rising divorce statistics. But life happened in an unplanned way, and they found themselves at that potential crossroad.

His wife felt as if she had been betrayed by him. She felt she was sleeping with a true stranger. That she had lost her husband, lover, and best friend. God had been their anchor; their faith was something they each felt was necessary for their marital union to succeed. So what did his changing lanes mean for their marriage? The question was no longer, "How do we keep our marriage thriving?" Instead, the question at hand was much more basic: "Can our marriage survive this major shift?"

As the caller answered the question of his authentic identity, he could not deny his evolving truth. Pushing away his questions and disappointments with God would require him to live a lie and betray himself. Yet after we discussed the situation, he realized that he had left little to no room for his *wife's* identity to be honored. His feelings and devotion hadn't changed toward his wife and their marriage, even though they had changed toward God. We talked about what it might mean to his wife for him to own that he changed a key part of their marital contract without any discussion. What would it mean to his wife to know that her position made sense to him—that he understood why she felt blindsided by his newfound path? What if he confessed that he had not known how to include her in his confusing and soulful evolution, fearing that it would cause a rupture in their marriage?

It was now time for him to grapple with claiming his true identity while still honoring hers. Our brief on-air discussion that day opened up exciting possibilities for him. He realized that he didn't have to throw the baby out with the bathwater. Seeing and honoring his wife's true identity became as important as seeing, embracing, and honoring his own.

One of the biggest questions in life is, "Who do you think you are?" Everything is up for grabs, including the kitchen sink, when we begin to explore who we are—versus who we thought we were. So:

- Who are you?
- Who are you *really*?
- What is your heart's desire?

CHAPTER 15

# BLESSING THE BROKEN ROAD

———•———

*"Two roads diverged in a wood, and I—*
*I took the one less traveled by,*
*And that has made all the difference."*

ROBERT FROST

*The Dr. Robin Show* lasted three years. It was an amazing experience, talking to callers from all around the country and a few
outside of the U.S., interviewing the rich and famous as well as
ordinary people, learning and being inspired from their stories. I
had the privilege of growing as a person from the courage, resilience, tears, and fears of each person who called or sat with me in
the studio. My radio show was a great example of what is possible
when safety and respect are the foundation of all interactions.
While the rest of the country was fighting about the issues on the
left and right sides of the political aisle, *The Dr. Robin Show* was
an example of what is possible when the hearts of the left and

right showed up together to learn, support, and challenge in a safe heart-to-heart dialogue. When hearts and minds are open—when we slow down to listen to a viewpoint other than our own, when our need to be right is not always in the driver's seat of our life—we can decide that being in relationship has more value than being right.

In *Lies at the Altar* I said we can either be right and alone or be connected in a relationship with someone we love who loves us back. When I'm in my right mind, meeting my need for connection is what is important to me. Being right and alone leads to starvation; I want to feast at the table of love and connection.

It's not a rare thing for me to say, "We're all in recovery from something." People hear that and want to say, "Not me." They wonder what scoop of gossip they missed about me if I'm talking about being in recovery! Recovery has been defined far too narrowly for my taste. Recovery is a broad avenue—actually, it's more like a freeway. If you've been to LA, then you know the 405 is a formidable highway known for gridlock, accidents, and other traffic-related delays. Well, life can sometimes feel like we've been traveling the 405. To find a different road, we need recovery. Even if we have never struggled with addiction, life itself leaves enough on our doorstep that we all need help clearing the way.

The most well-recognized addictions are drugs and alcohol, sex, pornography, shopping, and food. But there are others that have people strung out and imprisoned: addiction to rage and bitterness, unforgiveness and meanness, anger and resentment, and the "toxic twins" of shame and blame. We can be addicted to lying, to cheating ourselves and others, to betraying the truth and to staying in relationships that are being kept alive only by a respirator. The list of possible addictions is endless; each of us can find ourselves on the list in more than one location.

Music was a big part of *The Dr. Robin Show*. I love all kinds of music, my producers and engineers loved music, our whole team were music lovers. One day before I went on the air, my radio producer said, "Dr. Robin, I have a song I want to play for you. I think you'll love it." Through my headset came Rascal Flatt's song, "Bless the Broken Road"—a song that immediately pierced my heart and unleashed my tears. I have pretty easy access to my tears—I cry when I'm happy and when I'm sad—so crying isn't unusual for me. But what I heard this day was each word, each note, each chord that spoke volumes to my hungry heart. What this song invited out in me was a fresh impression about love—not only romantic love, but the love I hungered for most of my life: The gentle and uncompromising love I wanted to feel toward myself. This song invited me to experience forgiveness and receive a pardon for all the time I wasted in love and in life.

I often said on my radio show that the broken pieces of life are the floatation devices we need to make it back to the shore of our destiny safely. This song said it all: There was redemption for my waste, that my suffering could be recycled, that the plastics, papers, and shredded pieces of me were not for naught, that something useful and good could and would be birthed from what often felt like my life's wreckage.

In the New Testament there is a story I love to share. It comforts me in raw and rough times. A shipwreck occurred. While some people were able to swim, others were only able to get back to shore safely by floating on the broken pieces from the wreckage.

I've joked with my best friend Sandra that I must have an amazing, super-size float because my life has so many broken pieces. I have learned through lots of good therapy, loving support, prayer, play, and meditation to fully honor the broken pieces of my wreckage—and myself. It has been a hard road. Not only the suffering, but learning to be tender with myself as I offer myself the compassion that I generously offer others. When we can do better, we will.

My many broken pieces got me back to shore alive . . . limping, yes; shaken, yes; crying, yes; hungry, yes; but they returned me to my own loving arms.

*God bless the broken road!*

# CHAPTER 16

# Match Made in Heaven

————— • —————

*"Before I formed you in the womb, I knew you."*

JEREMIAH 1:5

*Bashert* is a Yiddish word that means "meant to be" or "predestined." I use it sparingly and with care. It is most often used when speaking of a romance, a love connection, or a union that feels like a match made in heaven.

My ordination into ministry and my intoxicating love relationship with Kalle set a new standard for my intimate love relationships. Actually, they set the bar high, where it belonged, for *all* of my relationships. Both changed my life forever.

In their own unique ways, my ordination and my relationship with Kalle showed me what deep and abiding love, clarity, respect, and joy look, taste, sound, and feel like. Each gifted me with the authentic experience of knowing when the "hookup" was "meant to be," versus a setup for a mess-up full of disappointment and misery. Like everyone, I have learned many lessons by trial and error and from getting a fleetload of things *wrong*. C. S. Lewis said, "God whispers to us in our pleasures, speaks to us in our conscience, but shouts in our pains: it is His megaphone to rouse a deaf world." These words sometimes float into my head as I grapple with and feel the remorse and regret over all the cartons of spilled milk in my past. God sure knew how to get my attention. I wish the megaphone didn't have to be so loud . . . it hurt more than my ears, it hurt my heart. And yes, like any child who hates to admit their parents are *right*, God's megaphone saved me and gave me my real life to live.

I've learned my most helpful and meaningful messages about who and what I deserve in my life through baptism by fire. I was dunked in and out of life's river more times than I wish to remember. All of the beauty and debris have scrubbed me and rubbed me until I was washed of my many illusions—illusions that only made me hungrier, and caused more harm and suffering.

After all the devastating losses and events of 2010, my life and I fell into a million little pieces. Like Humpty Dumpty, I was shattered. I couldn't imagine my life ever being put back together again.

This cleansing process happened until I cried "uncle" and would no longer settle for less than God's best. My life was far from perfect, and my hunger was still very real. But I no longer felt crazy; I didn't want to die from heartache or heartbreak. The fear of being *me* had subsided. I wasn't dying to be me anymore, I was *living* to be me. What a huge transformation. There was no fixed formula for this healing; I had just limped along the road of life and kept learning as best I could.

My lessons at times have been brutal. There have been family losses and tragedies, and as I've said the floor of my career and employment security fell out from under me—taking my hopes and dreams with them. But I kept breathing, even when I wished that my breath would stop. Over time, life got better and so did I.

When I give a keynote or sermon, and things seem to have gone *well*, I often finish by saying, "I am human. I suffer, I struggle.

Don't drink the Kool-Aid about me or anyone else being anything more than human and hungry. We are *all* trying to find our way. Some of us know that, others think that they have arrived." Most of the time, I'm not bothered when people pretend that they have it all together. I know that either they are scared to death to take their masks and costumes off like I used to be, or they are un-plugged from reality. The best thing is to have compassion for them, knowing that *that was me*—and it could be again, if I don't remain awake to myself, my life, and my world.

I was sick and tired of selling myself short. Learning the lesson, no matter how difficult, was in my best interest. I learned how to feed myself real food, and how satisfied I felt when I was with the right person in the right place. There is no replacement or surrogate for the real thing. Ashford and Simpson got it right when they wrote the blockbuster song, "Ain't Nothing Like the Real Thing."

It feels like I got married a gazillion years ago. It has been 26 years since I walked down the aisle to meet my handsome young groom. I remember a lot about that day. The details are still clear in my heart and mind—how I felt, how I looked, the sweltering heat of a spring day in May. The sun was expected to shine and there was supposed to be a breeze, but nothing about that day was cool. There were butterflies in my stomach (they felt more like hornets) and weakness in my body. Everyone said it was just my nerves. Of course some of what I felt *was* normal. The "what the heck am I doing" nerves show up even when a marriage is "all good." Both the bride and the groom are hoping this is the "right" person to be taking this step with—one small step for mankind, and one giant step for both people at the altar. That day both of us were hoping, praying, and wanting it to be and remain true that "you are the one." In time I discovered that what I called "nerves" that day were actually messages from my intuition, telling me that I wasn't ready. My close friends and I always say that asking yourself "am I sure?" is a sign of wisdom, not weakness. Whether you're moving toward the altar or even once you're there—no matter how sure you are. Better to have a close call than to make the wrong call.

Kalle was a Portuguese water dog that I rescued at a time in my life when I was the one who most needed rescuing. She was almost eight when I adopted her. People always said, "Kalle really lucked out," or "Kalle is truly blessed, Robin, no one would do for her what you do. . . ." People were right. No one would do for Kalle what I willingly and joyfully did. And no one could do for *me* what she willingly and joyfully did for me. No one knew that *I* needed to be rescued, that *I* was emotionally withering away. I told people, "Actually, Kalle rescued me." People smiled, thinking I was just being gracious and kind, but I wasn't. I was telling the whole truth and nothing but the truth so help me God.

Kalle showed up in my life at a time when my hunger was raging out of control. At the time, I didn't know that I was hungry—that I was starving to death. That I was close to passing out from emotional and relational starvation. Spiritually, my situation was a bit trickier to understand. In many ways, my pot was overflowing with good people and good energy and sweet connections. But the rest of my life had such holes in it that all the good that was pouring in was swiftly running out.

It took me a long time to realize that I couldn't neglect myself and continue to eat crumbs in relationships. My relationships were cheating me and draining me. Somehow I thought that if I could remain spiritually full, keeping my connection with God intact, I could stay checked out from reality. But the Universe doesn't work like a smorgasbord, where we can pick and choose our lessons or our teachers. I now know that I was using my spiritual practice and my relationship with God to cover up a lot that was going wrong. The Bible says that "Love covers a multitude of sins," but it does not suggest using love to cover a mound of mess.

Kalle rescued me and helped me build my courage muscles so that I could begin to clean up the sad and complicated mess I had made in my relationship life. My ordination and my relationship with Kalle were powerful examples of how clear and uncomplicated a worthy choice can be. That doesn't mean they were without effort and commitment, but these two choices didn't feel like I was doing hard time in prison. I felt alive, full, and free. I knew this is what a lifetime commitment should feel like—peaceful and real. As I shared with the congregation on the night of my ordination, "I believe this is what a meant-to-be union feels like."

Kalle had been physically abused, and I guess from one abuse victim to another, we understood the long road home to a healthy and whole self. My relationship with Kalle taught me to call abuse what it is—abuse. And that when meanness shows up, to call it by its rightful name. Like many girls and women who are abused, I was able to dilute the enormous suffering and toll that my teen-age "first love" relationship took on me. But when I had to witness Kalle's post-traumatic stress, I was able to begin to see my own.

I had come from a family where we weren't spanked. We weren't a family of screamers, either. Not that we didn't have arguments, but we knew how to carry sorrow and rage with suffocating elegance and gravelike grace. We knew how to hide our hunger and our pain. With Kalle, neither she nor I had to hide anything from each other. We were safe and sound . . . finally.

There is no debate that Kalle was on her last leg when I rescued her and there is no doubt that I was in the same condition. It takes one to know one.

I nurtured and restored Kalle back to the status of her divine birthright. Yes, I blissfully over-indulged her and spoiled her "sweet rotten"—and she did the same for me.

Thanks to my ordination and my life with Kalle, I now know what it means for something to be a *bashert*—a match made in heaven.

# CHAPTER 17

# KALLE'S LAST LECTURE

———◆———

*"Can a mother forget the baby at her breast . . .*
*Though she may forget, I will not forget you. See, I have*
*engraved you on the palms of my hands . . ."*

ISAIAH 49:15–16

I was in big trouble.

Our home—mine and Kalle's—had for eight years been a place of play, running wild, chillin', and eating great food. Food-wise, it was even better when I was on the road and my mother was baby-sitting Kalle. Kalle loved for Mommy to watch her. Instead of three meals a day, she basically had six: Her standard three, plus some portion of Mommy's breakfast, lunch, and dinner—plus snacks. "A treat for Grandmommy, and one for Kalle," I once caught my mother sweetly saying as Kalle danced around the kitchen. Kalle was adored and catered to in every way when she was healthy, and even more so when she became sick.

Kalle died at home in our bed on April 24, 2010. It was peaceful and dignified, and she was surrounded by love. She was failing and fading quickly, and when death showed up, he took her in a whisper. I wasn't sure that she was really gone. I asked her doctor and our beloved friend, Dr. John, "Is she gone? Are you sure?" With such compassion in his eyes, he quietly said, "Yes, I'm sure. She's gone." Tears flowed and flowed from my eyes as they had been for days prior. I kissed her still-warm body. She looked like all unharmed, freshly dead beings look: as if she were stretched out, taking a good snooze. I thanked her for our almost eight years of the best loving and living that I could have imagined. I thanked her for staying until I got the lesson. I didn't really know what that meant when I said it, but I said it anyway. Our life together was amazing, joyful, and so much fun. We did almost everything together.

The morning of Kalle's death was full of rites and rituals. I didn't know the hour that she would take her last breath, but I knew she was leaving me quickly. The house had become more of a hospice wing, with all that she needed—including her beloved groomer, Jennifer, who helped Mommy and me care for Kalle in the end. We would all have drowned without her love, patience, huge heart, and enormous skill.

Kalle's body was taken from our home shortly after her death to be cremated. I walked through the bone-chilling stillness of my house wondering if this was real. Was she really dead? I was asking, "How would I live without her? How would I bear the pain?" I was grateful that she was no longer suffering. I had known this feeling before, as those I love grew sick and put on the garments of immortality, but the pain of saying good-bye even when "it's best" is brutal.

I walked down the hall to the laundry room. Each room I passed felt more still than I had ever experienced in all my years living here. It was peaceful—and in an eerie way, so was I. As I was standing in front of the washing machine, in somewhat of a stupor, I heard a voice. Was it Kalle's voice, my voice, God's voice, the

Universe, the voice of my friends? I don't know and I don't really care. What I heard was truer than true.

*"Mommy, if you take care of yourself the way that you took care of me, you'll be fine. If you don't you're in big trouble."*

Those words were, and remain, true. I bent over backward for Kalle; the question was, would I now do the same for me? Did I have the courage to love myself unselfishly like I loved Kalle, or would I hold back, play games, and make excuses of why today isn't the day to love myself like crazy?

Kalle showed me what was in me, what was possible, what I was capable of giving and receiving. Now the question was, would I step up to the plate for myself the way I did for her?

I started calling this "Kalle's Last Lecture," and over time it has led me to know, own, and embrace without apology that I'm hungry—and that I want more!

## The Good Mother

When times were rough and rocky in my life, my beloved therapist taught me the concept of "the Good Mother." Regardless of who has raised us—whether or not we have received loving and healthy parenting, whether or not we were hurt, neglected, or harmed as a child—we all have a Good Mother living within. Most of us don't know she's there. Her job is to whisper; to offer words of wisdom, self-care, and encouragement; to correct and redirect without shame; to exhort, admonish, and discipline with dignity; and to restore us to our rightful relationship with God, nature, creation, humanity, and, most importantly, ourselves. This inner Good Mother is the guide for the child within who is always going to be with us, who never grows up or goes away. The Good Mother is always truthful, dependable, and consistent. We always have access to her wisdom and care. While she tells us the truth like any good parent, there are many times when our inner child chooses not to listen and heed what she says. We dismiss, ignore, and often can't or won't believe her. But still she remains.

She helps us to live and learn, versus live and *live without learning*. She never gives up on, abandons, or forsakes us. We only need to allow her to speak truth to us.

We don't necessarily know how to access the Good Mother, and it's hard to believe that there is a loving and wise presence that is always available to us. But the Good Mother's influence grows as we grow; as we listen to and allow her to guide us. Whether we are aware or not, the Good Mother is with us in our joys, mistakes, sorrows, successes, and failures: what has worked out for us, as well as the dreams that have exploded in our faces.

I am more grateful every day that the Good Mother is walking and talking with me all along my path. We all need to invest time, energy, and effort in getting to know or reacquaint ourselves with the Good Mother . . . She is ready, willing, able, and waiting for each one of us, and she always leaves the porch light on.

# CHAPTER 18

# MY WALK
# FOR A CURE

---

*"No matter where I run, I meet myself there"*
DOROTHY FIELDS

I hate cold weather, and the frigid chill of the East Coast winter days at their worst penetrates through me. Once I feel a shiver, it is hard for me to warm up and shake it off. So, what in the world was I doing walking for miles when there was a code blue in Philadelphia? "Code blue" is when the temperature goes well below freezing, and when homeless people as well as all others are advised—and at times mandated—to remain inside until it is safe to come out again and face Old Man Winter.

I was hiking in the woods a lot that year. There had been several snowstorms and ice storms, but nothing could deter me from walking, roaming, and hiking. My friends asked me, "Why are you walking so much? Is it helping you? I know you hate cold weather . . ." It was an interesting question, since at the time no one knew my "dying to be me" diagnosis—including me. Indeed, the winter weather was brutal, but not as brutal as the arctic cold of the pain I endured from invisibility, fear, and rejection.

Honestly, at the time I was doing all of this walking, I had no idea why I was doing it or what it meant. But I did know it was important that I do it. Sometimes I would go walking twice in one day—I couldn't help it. All I wanted was to be outside with nature, with the natural running water of the Wissahickon, with the icicles more beautiful than words could describe. At times, an icicle would appear on my cheek as the tears flowed and then froze.

Once I even walked from my home to my best friend's house, ten miles each way. I walked for months in what felt like an aimless wandering, like someone lost and numb—from the cold, from the pain, from my unmet hunger needs. Sometimes when I walked, I would hear words or phrases connected to thoughts for this book, and when I heard and felt anything inspirational, I would quickly pull off my gloves and try to type it into the draft section of my phone or call myself and leave a voice mail before I lost the thought. Feeling alive was rare during those days, and feeling inspired to do anything was even more rare. So when something special came to me, I figured I'd better record it. Because as quickly as it came, the coldness and what felt like death in my soul would soon return and capture me. I didn't want the fresh and alive thought to become stuck or frozen in the recesses of my pain. I didn't want to lose my musings. I wondered if there was any point to my walking or if anything I was writing in the frigid dead of the winter woods would ever be felt, heard, or embraced in the warmth and light of spring.

As I walked I reflected that the dial to my inner world had been locked on "winter" for what felt like forever. Although there were moments where the sun peeked out at me, teasing and flirting with me with its bright and brilliant rays, seducing me with its warmth, as soon as I would crave one more glance or touch, it vanished—and left me feeling the stark reality of the long and barren winter. I was sure that a few of these sun sightings were the promise of spring being birthed anew; that it would soon bloom in my life again. But winter said, "No, my work is not yet complete in you. I still have work to do before spring bubbles up from the frozen earth of your life. I am doing something in the underground of your body and spirit. I am pruning your deepest roots, resources, and wounds, and fertilizing your soil with manure that reeks of suffering. And yes, there is only one path out of the valley of the shadow of death and that is to walk, waddle, wade, wander, and limp through this season."

In the black church, there is a saying: "God may not come when you want Him, but He's always right on time." This may be up for debate, but I believe that winter was His presence, and right on time.

Walking was my meditation and my medication. I discovered over time that I was "walking for the cure"—the cure to my starving soul. In the process I was getting stronger and more alive. It was active meditation; what's called "walking meditation" in yoga.

Active meditation had always put me back in touch with my spiritual core and aspirations, but this was a journey unlike any I had ever traveled. I share the dark desperation of my journey with you here not because I still feel the sting, but because I want to normalize this dreadful place as one that everyone visits; that everyone roams around and runs from. It comes with being fully human. Many people have told me that when they acknowledge their hunger, they feel less shame. And that's a good thing.

## THE CENTER FOR REFLECTION

If I catch myself struggling with myself or with anyone about anything—and I mean *anything*—I check myself into "the center for reflection and time-out." My friends and family laugh, asking, "Where is that center located? I may need to go, or I know someone who needs a room immediately. Do you know who they can contact to get a slot? Who is in charge?"

I laugh really hard because that so-called center isn't a physical center. It is the place I go to within me when it is clear that I have left myself again, when it is clear that I have fallen off the wagon, stumbling headfirst into a lack of clarity, fear, and confusion. I go to the only place that can help me; to—in the words of Psalm 61—"the Rock that is higher than I." It is where I go when my heart is faint, and I check in for as long or as short a time as is necessary for me to breathe again without fear. And to know what is true. Sometimes I am only there for seconds or minutes, and other times more intensive work is required for me to know that I am free, safe, and joyful. This place is available to all who will go within, so they can hear all they need to know to move powerfully and passionately in their lives as they attend to their hunger.

What's even better about this "center for reflection and time-out" is that it is free; it travels with me wherever I go; and I can never be without it. I can forget that about it, but as soon as I become conscious that it is always with me, I have full and unobstructed access.

## ATTUNEMENT

We strive for attunement. We want to be able to say to ourselves, "I see you, I get you, I feel you." Once we have that, we can reach out and experience the blessing of having others be attuned to us as well. This is the real, felt experience that we are understood; that someone truly gets the *real* us; that we are not crazy for how we feel or what we want; that someone is "tuned in" to our unique frequency—the channel of our truest feelings and deepest longings. This person hangs on to our words and feelings because they are interested in who we really are, not who we pretend to be. This is true connection and intimacy—a place where we are truly known.

For years I dragged my masks around with me, stuffing them into my purse, packing them in my suitcase, loading them into the trunk of my car. I kept them crammed into my front door closet in case an unexpected visitor appeared. It is amazing how much freedom I have without them—how much room there is in my closets and my heart. The best part of it is the joy I experience at being truly known. The joy of feeling that we are not alone in the world—that someone is our witness, that our life matters, counts, is valued, and will not go unnoticed and unrecorded by at least the person attuned to us.

True connection and intimacy are essential to growth and health, and that's why one of the first steps on our journey is to find and surround ourselves with those who tune into our frequency. To nurture relationships with people who desire more than our airbrushed façade, who want a relationship with a living, breathing, unique, and flawed but glorious human being.

So how do we weed out the destructive voices in our lives? How do we evaluate our standards and requirements for friends, colleagues, and lovers? We have the power to assess the people in our lives and to decide which of them are true friends. We also have the power to decide which voices we are going to listen to—those living or dead, personal or societal. We can surround ourselves with voices of support, encouragement, honesty, and approval. We don't have to be stuck with the negative voices that have long made us feel we weren't good enough. Here's an additional benefit: Our true friends are the best support system we can have. If we are struggling with the weight of unwanted self-hatred, our friends are our backers, committed to our success.

A friend of mine who was trying to lose weight found a "diet buddy," and they vowed to hold each other accountable. They devised a no-shame, no-BS zone. They knew what they had to do, and they were quick to pick up on it when the other person faltered. The buddy system worked. I reflected that we all need those kinds of buddies in our lives.

## YOU ARE ALIVE

A troubled man wrote to me: "I hate my life! I have a dead-end stockbroker job. I'm in a dead-end marriage but am afraid to leave because I don't want to lose my child. We're financially struggling. I can't take much more. All is a mess."

I felt his pain, and I appreciated his honesty. It takes a lot of courage to speak your despair out loud. I understood perfectly the hole he was in. Life sucks sometimes. It's full of burdens that seem unresolvable. What could I tell him? Noticing his repeated use of the term "dead-end," the first thing I had to say loud and clear was, "YOU ARE NOT DEAD." I urged him to look for signs of life. "You want love, mutuality, respect at home and work, a partnership, personally and professionally, where you are appreciated, because you are ALIVE!" I said. "How do you begin? One step at a time. Decide which area of your life you want to work on first: Your marriage or employment. Find a qualified therapist who will walk with you, help you remember your worth and value, as well as help you create an overall redesign for your life."

The truth is, none of us can do this alone; we all need help when we're surrounded by dead things and we want to *live*. If you feel that you are being swallowed by the deadness, don't give up on yourself. You deserve to live with love, respect, fairness, and peace. Nothing is perfect, but all the dead-end people and situations around you are not the answer. Sometimes it takes us really owning that something has to change; at first reminding ourselves, and then admitting it to a few safe others. Moment by moment, over time, we breathe and build a new life into existence for ourselves.

In the words of the great Alice Walker, "No one is your friend who demands your silence or denies your right to grow." Step one is that we have to become our own true friend. The rest we will figure out on the journey.

---

### Water, Not Ice

It's easier to be water than ice, Mark Nepo writes. When trees fall on water, they don't crack and break. When a tree falls on ice, it breaks the tree and often cracks the ice. In my life, I have been hungry to let the icy parts of me melt into flowing water, so that what is meant to be in my life will remain—and what is meant to move on, will float away to its rightful destination.

Sometimes I go down to the flowing waters near my home just to remind myself. I remember that when I have been cold and hard like ice, life was much harder and kept me hungry. When I see the river moving, I am encouraged to go with the flow of life and trust where it takes me.

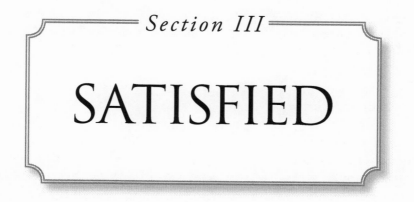

*Section III*

# SATISFIED

# CHAPTER 19

# RESET YOUR TABLE OF LIFE

*"This being human is a guest house. . . ."*

RUMI

My friend was determined to lose weight. She told me the first thing she did was clean out her cupboards and refrigerator. She was ruthless, tossing out bags of chips, cookies, breaded frozen foods, cans of cola, even a leftover slice of her birthday cake. She told me, "If it's not in the house, I won't eat it."

It felt a bit extreme—not the fact that she was cleaning out her cupboards and refrigerator, but her lack of compassion for herself. We see this all the time with weight-loss programs that are based on shame and blame—where self-compassion never makes an appearance. The idea is that people can be forced into compliance with a heavy dose of self-loathing. But lasting change requires self-compassion—feeding the hungry soul that is crying out for acknowledgment. Shame makes us withdraw and constrict. It leaves us sneaking around, cheating on our promises to do better. Shame leads to gorging in hiding.

We need to practice compassion with ourselves, be gentle with ourselves, and careful about how we approach change. My friend told me that she was disgusted about her weight, and had vowed to "beat myself up until I lose it." She related how a personal trainer at her gym had remarked, "You keep talking about losing weight, but you never do. Your credibility on this subject is zero." The trainer was no doubt practicing a form of *tough* love. I'll agree he was being tough, but where was the love? Listening to her, I wondered if it were possible to see change with a warm heart—to not base it in shame. Has shame ever truly motivated anyone to change, or does it just lead to a never-ending spiral of guilt and failure, which in turn leads to deeper shame and hunger?

"Whatever you do to lose the weight, self-compassion is number-one in making the pounds melt away," I told her. "As the shame melts, so will the weight. Be gentle and tender with yourself, and motivation will have more room to show up in your life and help you in many ways."

Having said that, my friend's kitchen cleanup project got me thinking. What would it look like to clean your life cupboard of all the junk "food," knowing that if it wasn't in front of you, you wouldn't consume it? What would it mean to undertake this project with humility and self-respect? Let's face it, the biggest and most widely ingested junk food is our own self-loathing. It not only crushes your spirit, but damages those around you. People who hate themselves can't help lashing out at others—strangers, friends, children, spouses.

Maybe getting rid of the junk means moving, changing jobs, or getting healthy. For many people it means getting rid of relationships that don't feed their souls. I recently saw a friend and noticed how fabulous she looked. She explained that she had dropped 180 pounds. I looked at her as if she was crazy, because she's always been slender. It took me a minute to realize what she was talking about—the weight of her ex-husband, and the years of drama, trauma, and abuse that were no longer weighing her down.

## TOSS THE BLAME

When we are hurt by the words or actions of another, there's a deep part of ourselves that wonders if we had it coming. We think, *Maybe if I had been a better friend, she wouldn't have spread that rumor about me. Maybe if I had been a more supportive wife, he wouldn't have put me down in front of his buddies. Maybe if I had been a better daughter, my mother would have loved me more.* A big part of the sting of an insult or betrayal is our fear that we aren't good enough. We feel diminished, ashamed, and unlovable. The process of healing involves learning to recover our sense of self-worth. As long as we see ourselves through the eyes of our offender, we can't heal.

## UNLOAD THE SHAME

When a person hurts us—especially if it is someone we trust and look up to—the deepest cuts are betrayal and shame. You may mask it with anger or thoughts of revenge, but the hurt itself is based on a feeling that you are not good enough to be treated well and with respect. One way to free ourselves from these painful feelings is to engage more fully in life and to not let our offender cripple us. A patient of mine, who was shattered when his fiancée abandoned him for another man, told me, "Dr. Robin, I will never have love in my life again." When we dug in a little deeper, we discovered he was overwhelmed with shame. As a result, he had given his fiancée the power to make him feel unlovable and unwanted. I suggested that one way to address his shame was to focus on the lesson of his experience, and to understand that his feelings of humiliation started long before her. She was just his most recent reminder that he didn't feel good enough or worthy of love.

One of the most debilitating wounds is the "not good enough" wound. Not feeling good enough is at epidemic proportions; it's something we all grapple with at different points in our lives. It's shocking how many people on the top rung of any ladder of success experience it.

Keep in mind that we are all vulnerable to shame. In fact, it's hardwired in our brains. Brené Brown described research that was conducted on nursing infants. It was found that when an infant missed its mother's nipple or had trouble attaching, he or she would hang their head in shame as if they'd done something wrong. It was an automatic response, showing that human beings are wired to experience shame. As we get older, the shame becomes conscious, but there is still an automatic quality to it. The good news is that we have the power of consciousness to manage shame and replace it with a different response.

## RESET AND RENEW

A friend called me, grieving over the breakup of a close friendship. "She was my best friend for 40 years," she said, "and now we're not speaking." The breakup happened because the two women's husbands couldn't get along. They were always at each other's throats, and after one big blowup at a barbecue, her friend just stopped speaking to her. "This argument didn't even have anything to do with us," my friend moaned. "Now she won't respond to my calls. Were the last 40 years worth nothing?"

"I wonder," I said, "if there was an issue between you that was kept under wraps for all this time—something that has gone unaddressed. Figure out if this relationship is something you want in your life, before you try to win her back."

Before I learned to make my own needs important, I was in relationships that were full of self-denial. Because I felt I deserved so little, I naturally attracted men who wanted too much. They were only interested in filling their own bellies, while I told myself, "less is more." Once I discovered the truth about my hunger, and learned to respect my longings, I was no longer willing to spend time with people who required me to sit at the table hungry, watching them eat, allowing them to feast off of me and my misguided love. It was too exorbitant a price to pay for their false companionship. In the words of Oscar Wilde, "No man is rich enough to buy back his past."

So, what did I do? I reset my table. The names on the place cards were new, especially the one at the head that bore my own name. The plates were full. It was a new experience—dizzying in its rich and luscious gratification.

When we choose to live a full, authentic life, we will need to reset our table, filling out the place cards with names we trust, and choosing heaping platters of the "soul food" we require and crave. Never underestimate the power of your village!

## REACHING OUT

A woman I know told me the story of going to visit a friend who lived a thousand miles away. She hadn't been to her home for a long time, and she was shocked to see that things were falling apart. Not only did her friend seem depressed and very shaky, but her husband was very quiet and hostile. She could see that something was terribly wrong, but she didn't say anything. She didn't know if it was her place to interfere, to speak up. She left without saying a word, and when she came back home she felt miserable. "This was my best friend," she told me. "How could I not speak the truth to her? How could I not reach out to her? How could I join her in the pretense that everything was okay?"

She was describing the code of silence that we take: If you're willing to pretend, I'll do it with you.

"You can't save her," I said. "But you *could* say to her, 'I care about you and we have been through a lot together, many ups and it feels like even more downs. I'm worried and these are the reasons why,' and then see what happens."

It's a real challenge to find people in our lives who are willing to speak the truth. Not to overstep their bounds, but also not to collude by going along with situations that are destructive without compassionately reflecting what they see. Are you willing to speak the truth in that way—to yourself and those you love? Speaking truth with tenderness and compassion is the only real way to create genuine and intimate connections with ourselves and others. Unfortunately, most of us are not taught to responsibly or respectfully speak the truth. In fact, we are taught the exact opposite. Most of us learn to nurse our lies the way you would an evening cocktail you've craved all day long. I have seen it again and again. While the truth may feel scary, foreign, and even painful at times, we are attracted to it and the relief it can ultimately bring. Often when I am preaching in a church or speaking at an event, I will reference the New Testament scriptural reminder, "You shall know the truth and it shall set you free." I remind people that the *promise* of those words isn't that the truth will make us happy (although sometimes it does). The promise is that truth will make us *free*. Truth is freedom. Truth is love. Truth allows us to grow and heal. Light and darkness are needed for growth. We need both day and night, waking and sleep, work and play, speaking and silence, giving and receiving. Truth abides in all.

When we know ourselves, trust ourselves, and surround ourselves with loving, healthy, and honest support, we are able to create the life we are worthy of living. There is something almost intoxicating about being in the presence of compassionate truth-seeking and -speaking people. It's an incubator for growth, healing, and wholeness. Truth draws our hungry souls. It calls to our tormented minds, bombarded with who and what we "should" be. It cries out to our exhausted bodies, longing for permission to rest and play. It woos our longing and weary spirits to return back home—to the only place of true rest. Truth is a place where communication and connection are shared in love, compassion, and safety—emotional, physical, and spiritual.


### FORGIVE TO LIVE

Linda lived for 20 years with a controlling, emotionally abusive man. He constantly put her down—mocked her comments, criticized her appearance, insisted that up was down and down was up, to the point where she didn't even know what she thought or who she was. Her entire focus was to avoid setting him off on one of his angry tirades, not realizing that it was impossible to achieve his standard of "perfection."

In time Linda's pain and loss of self showed up as an eating disorder. She stopped eating because she wanted to disappear. She stopped eating because, in her confused mind, she wanted to please her husband who had always been critical about her weight. Maybe she stopped eating to gain a tiny measure of control in a life that afforded her none.

Linda's sickness led her to the brink. She was hospitalized with heart problems at the age of 46, and it was a wake-up call. Her treatment included therapy, and for the first time in her memory Linda was being encouraged to talk about her own needs and desires. During this process her husband reacted badly, continuing to blame Linda for her illness and reminding her, "You're a mess." But Linda was growing stronger. As she gained control over her eating disorder, she also began to take charge of her life. She decided she could no longer be married to a man who didn't value her, and she left her husband.

In the end, this story had a happy ending—Linda escaped into a new life. But there is one sad problem. Linda couldn't get over the anger and resentment she felt over her wasted youth. A hard knot of fury lived inside her and it was stopping her from moving on. We discussed that resentment is a pernicious killer and eats away at the soul.

I told her what I wrote in my book *Inspirational Vitamins:* "Resentment is like taking poison and expecting the other person to die, unaware that you are dying too. A woman at peace with herself has stopped looking for someone to blame."

Linda's journey was to rock back and forth with all of her feelings as she worked toward learning how to forgive herself and her husband. The path to forgiveness is often unchartered, rough, and rocky. It's not for the faint of heart. I am not talking about phony forgiveness, but forgiveness that embraces with compassion and accountability the fact that we all have a story that has made us who we are.

Forgiveness is a hard pill to swallow. I have lived enough life that the invitation and necessity to forgive has rung my doorbell numerous times, and I've tried to answer it as best I could. Sometimes I acted as if my doorbell was broken, calling back silently, "I can't hear you." As I sit now, older, wiser, more scarred and more victorious, I know that without choosing to forgive when we have been wronged, we simply remain stuck in a corner of spiritual stagnation and emotional disrepair. It's also harmful for our physical health. We end up being owned by those who betrayed and hurt us. They control our energy, our time, our minds, and our health. As long as we are more focused on them and how they've "done us wrong" than we are on our right to be free, the power remains in their hands.

When we are wounded by another person, the instinct is very strong to curl into a ball and hold onto our hurt. This inflexible position becomes a distorted and destructive form of what we wrongly define as honor. We want the one who injured us to "get theirs"—to suffer as much as we are suffering. There is a warped, yet bitter comfort in fantasizing about their downfall. When cruelty and injustice tilt our world out of balance, our innate reaction is to want to even the score—to make things right by holding a grudge or seeking revenge. But these emotions only tilt the scale more steeply, and not in the favor of the wounded and injured one. Our wounds are not healed and it does not relieve our suffering. Only the tough road of genuine forgiveness can accomplish that, and many of us are still trying to get our hearts and heads around how to really do the act of forgiveness in our daily lives. It's a hard thing.

Forgiveness is one of the toughest—but most necessary—jobs in life. Please don't think I naively underestimate how huge the task of forgiveness can be. Forgiveness, if it is authentic, is hard work. At times, it can feel more difficult and unobtainable than holding on to the pain and bitterness. It is a journey that evolves over time. C. S. Lewis wrote, "Everyone says forgiveness is a lovely idea until they have something to forgive." I agree with him wholeheartedly; it's easier said than done. But the hard work of forgiveness, of self and others, is one of the essential tools needed to get our lives back.

Being unable or unwilling to forgive will stop us dead in our tracks and prevent us from fully living and growing. Being unforgiving takes up too much space in our lives. If left alone, the damage spreads like an aggressive cancer and eats everything in sight—our dreams, our hopes, our relationships, our energy, our health. If we are bent on getting revenge, we might as well dig two graves: One for the object of our revenge and one for ourselves, the victim.

It may seem counterintuitive, but forgiveness starts with ourselves.

People wonder, *What is she saying? Why do I have to be forgiven? I'm the one who was wronged!* But very often, when we are hurt by the words or actions of another, there is a deep part of ourselves that gets into self-blame and self-righteousness. We can flip-flop between blaming ourselves and blaming others, but it is the same. We begin to wonder what we did to deserve such awful treatment. A big part of the sting of an insult or betrayal is our fear that we aren't good enough. We feel diminished, ashamed, and unlovable. The process of healing involves learning to recover our sense of self-worth. As long as we see ourselves through the eyes of our offender, we can't heal. Even when we take responsibility for the part we played in a situation that caused us pain and are willing to be held accountable for it, mistreatment is never acceptable or excusable.

Healing our pain isn't about establishing who is right and who is wrong. Our pain needs to be explored so that we can gain understanding of the situation that created it. When we are stuck in unforgiveness, it is even more difficult to learn the lesson of the experience—why we made the choice that got us into trouble. Until we understand that lesson, we will re-create the painful experience over and over—perhaps with a different cast, but leading to the same hurtful result. I encouraged Linda to explore her experience to figure out why she allowed her husband to have so much brutalizing control over her. And, as always, it didn't begin with him. It began in the cradle, in the nursery, on the playground, in the schoolyard. It began with people judging, criticizing, shaming, blaming until it became the default message.

The most important benefit of forgiveness is that it gives us freedom. When we can't forgive, we allow the offender to control whether we're happy or miserable, a success or a failure, peaceful or angry, beaten down or lifted up. We're trapped by the injury. It begins to define us as a victim. Forgiveness is a difficult choice, and so is failing to forgive. When we choose not to forgive, we're making the choice to harbor anger and resentment—in essence, to die. Forgiveness restores our power to feel, to dream, to have needs, to make choices, and to remain open to life and to love.

The biggest misunderstanding people have about forgiveness is that it becomes a gift to the offender—a "get out of jail free" card. It's easy to be swept up into a sense of righteous anger, to think it would be wrong to let the other person off the hook. I wrote about the tough journey of forgiveness in *Inspirational Vitamins*. I knew how tender a topic forgiveness was when I wrote: "You may be thinking, 'Dr. Robin, if you only knew how horribly this person treated me, you wouldn't have the nerve to talk about forgiveness.' Yes, I would, because our freedom depends on it."

Remember, forgiveness isn't something you *give* to another person. It is really a gift to ourselves—a way of releasing our hurt and resentment and attending to our legitimate hunger. It's a way of taking ourselves seriously.

## HEALING THE WOUNDED SELF

Healing is a process. It's a series of tender and brave steps. It invites us to acknowledge and own the hurts and injuries that we carry—our own, and those we have caused others on the journey of healing the wounded self. I've had more conversations than I can count about the fact that if we are living, we are wounded. There is no way to be alive and not carry wounds and injuries . . .

they come with the territory of being human. Being wounded is part of the package deal. Healing is not a linear process, nor is it well mapped out. For better or for worse, it is never-ending; always evolving and changing. Over my 40-some-odd years, I have discovered that how I heal from one wound or injury isn't necessarily how it will work out the next time . . . darn it! I had hoped for a formula, as did the thousands of people I've worked with and learned from over these many years as a therapist, minister, executive leadership coach, television and radio personality, and whatever other hats I have worn.

The work of facing into ourselves and our truth is unavoidable if we are to walk the road of forgiveness and healing. What worked for someone else—or even for you on your last go-around—will not necessarily work this time. You have to find your own way to heal, be it a broken heart, the death of a parent or spouse, losing a job unfairly, staying with someone you hate, struggles with your in-laws who feel more like "outlaws," a friend who let you down or whom you abandoned when they needed you, parenting and feeling like you never get it right, taking care of loved ones, losing your health, your hair, your youth, your dreams, your *fight,* or your passion. All of these things require a lifetime of understanding and commitment to stay awake to what hurts and heals us, to be compassionate as we hold ourselves and others accountable, and to be forgiving and kind regarding the various routes our hunger has taken. Here are some steps that will help you as you navigate, negotiate, and find your way back *home* to your truest self.

**Step 1: Gently take care of the injury.** Thoughts of revenge only bind us to the one who wounded us. They keep our pain alive. When an experience triggers us and stirs up uncomfortable and painful feelings, consider stepping back, taking a deep breath to see if we can engage with our feelings in a new way that does not re-create our painful experience. What we focus on grows. So if we focus on the situation where we were hurt and injured, we are continuing to give life and fuel to it. We must feed the thoughts and actions that empower our lives and starve those that harm us. Once we have given ourselves the time to grieve it, to wonder and ask questions about it, to be angry and rage about it, then it can be helpful to put some limits on how much we talk about it. Remember, we want to take our power and passion back. Never talking about an injury—or talking about it too much—can both be debilitating. We must find the balance between silence and obsessive focus. It does not mean that we will never speak of our pain; it just means that over time we will not speak of it as if it happened yesterday when it has been years.

Often when people have been hurt, they want to dwell on it. I have talked to people who are obsessed with a lover who betrayed them 20 years ago, or a parent who didn't give them what they needed as a child. In the past, I myself was caught in the life-draining web of replaying deep hurts and rejections that after a point did nothing but suck my life force dry. It is normal to get stuck on a traumatic event. But that doesn't mean it's good for us. As long as we hold on to our hurt, it will throb and grow—and it will hold on to us. Abandoning our hurt before we've attended to it is just as dangerous. To become aware and notice when we begin to be triggered is important to minimize obsessing. Is our goal to be free to live our lives with passion, purpose, and power as we attend to our hunger, or to enshrine the past and let it suck our lives away?

Enlisting trusted friends and loved ones to help us keep this important healing promise to ourselves is a necessary part of the equation. Forgiveness is a journey, not a destination, and it is something that our trusted loved ones can support us in.

**Step 2: Withdraw or engage—or do some of both.** When we've been injured, we have a choice: to flee, fight, or freeze—to get away from our offender, to stand up to him or her, or to do nothing. Each course of action is an option, but we want to understand and choose the action that most empowers us at any given moment.

Sometimes it is necessary to physically separate ourselves from the one who has wounded us. Only we can decide if this is the case. But if we are with someone who is repeatedly unfaithful, or who continues to lie to us, or who makes demeaning comments on a regular basis, we are setting ourselves up for having our wound reopened again and again. We need to affirm our right to be respected and whole. If the relationship is important to us and we want to see if it is salvageable, then we can begin to set limits and notice if that changes the offensive behavior. If it is not worth saving or simply can't be saved, then we're faced with what is often a very difficult decision of whether or not to close the door and begin the work of repair and healing. Pay attention to your hunger. It doesn't lie, and its message will lead you to the sanctuary of the real you.

In other circumstances, engaging the offender may ease the path to healing. I'm not talking about having a big dramatic confrontation. The goal is not to give our offender a taste of his or her own medicine. It's to restore honesty and equality to a relationship we hope to continue, or simply to reclaim our dignity. Telling the person in a calm and respectful manner, concretely and as directly as possible, how his or her words or actions affected you is a brave beginning. For example: "When you made that joke about my weight, I was so embarrassed. You know how sensitive I am about putting on a few pounds." This is a moment of truth in the relationship. If the other person cares about us, understands the importance of respect and safety in all healthy relationships, and values the relationship, he or she will be genuinely apologetic. But even if we don't get the response we want, we can still feel good that we tried a new way of relating. Doing it for ourselves, not for the other person, is what's important.

**Step 3: Ritualize your freedom.** We all need rituals when doors open—and when they close. A ritual is the making and marking of a moment. It signifies the passing of a life-altering moment or event. Sometimes a ritual is a more formal procedure or ceremony, but often it is a sacrament found in the gathering of loved ones and friends around a particularly important life event.

Ritual is important for healing as we try to make sense of difficult and challenging circumstances. Rituals can help ground us when everything around us feels uncertain and unsettled. They create a safe and sometimes even sacred place to rest on our journey.

Finding which rituals work for you is key. Some people write in their journals; others find support in therapy. There are those who talk to someone trustworthy and share their hearts, and others who go to yoga. Some meditate or pray, while still others take walks in nature hoping to find peace. Some people go on retreats, take a trip, or treat themselves to a spa experience. All are rituals that symbolize the rites of passage into a new way of living. This may be something we do only once, or it may become a regular part of our lives. We might even throw a bash to mark the beginning or end of an important part of our journey. My mentor reminds me that "Life at its longest is short." As I watch time swiftly moving, wasting time is something I really try not to do.

**Step 4: Free yourself from shame.** When another person hurts us—especially if it is someone we trust and look up to—shame and doubt are two of the deepest cuts. We may mask them with anger or thoughts of revenge, but the hurt itself is based on a feeling that we are not good enough to be treated well. One way to free ourselves from this shame is to engage fully in life as best we can and to acknowledge our divine birthright to be hungry and fully human.

Look at what happened to you. Examine the evidence. Identify errors, blind spots, failures, limitations, or the other variables that led to the crisis. This is not about beating ourselves up, but about growing from the lessons of life—and in the process, becoming stronger and more secure in our choices.

## THE MYTH OF CLOSURE

Our desire to have things cleanly resolved and sealed away, never to surface again, sets us up for great disappointment and pain. Over the course of our lives, the objective isn't to silence or stuff down the contents in Pandora's box, but to make room to safely feel and explore our hunger, which continually needs attention and expression. Closure is a tricky thing. Death doesn't necessarily deliver it. Actually, it might stir the pot of emotion more. Ending a relationship, moving to a new city, or starting a new job doesn't necessarily bring closure, either. The definition of closure that most of us ascribe to is more of a fantasy than a reality. Real closure happens each day, as you make peace with what is, even when it's not okay. This is no easy task; it's a lifelong process.

We needn't feel forced or pushed to move on before we're ready. Letting go of the way we hoped things would be is not an easy or overnight task. We will need to be patient with ourselves and throw out any timetable we had for how or when the grief would be complete.

*Closure* is a word that I seldom, if ever, use anymore. Instead, I like to call it "doing the best with what is placed, dropped, or thrown on our plates and hearts." Recently, I appeared on a daytime talk show and the topic was suicide. I was grateful and humbled to be there with the families, as well as the host—all of whom were survivors of a loved one's suicide.

One of my main points that day was that the word *closure* in many ways is insulting and unrealistic when referring to the loss of a loved one. When we spiritualize important words like *closure, forgiveness,* and *love,* we do a terrible disservice. We set ourselves up with unrealistic expectations, which only lead to deeper depression and despair. Losing a loved one to suicide is an experience that will never truly be "closed." The result of using this term is that truth is no longer the cornerstone of our lives, relationships, or existence.

There are many dangling, untied, and unfinished parts of life that each of us is forced to live with—and, at times, *blessed* to live with. Overall, the best we can do is to breathe into the many parts of our lives that we *can't* change; the many places that have left us with much more sorrow than joy.

I understand our attraction to the fantasy of closure, but it's painful to run after something that escapes most of us most of the time. I have found it more peaceful to accept that much of life will remain an open door. At times it will swing shut, only to open again. Closure is a nice concept, but it's not a phantom I want to waste my time chasing. I'd rather live with truth; be in the world and in direct connection with God, myself, and others.

## Get Out of the Ring

Fighting with reality is the biggest waste of time. It took me a long time to learn this. One day I was talking to my dear and trusted friend, who is also my interior designer. He creates amazing beauty in homes—both in little spaces, and in castlelike properties. Over lunch we were talking with our other dear friend and I mentioned I had been reading a book that really spoke to me. I looked at them squarely and said, I heard the phrase *get out of the ring*. They asked, "What do you mean?" I replied, "I am so tired of fighting with reality, I now realize that it's always going to win and I don't want to fight any more losing battles."

Now, most of the time, I'm out of the ring. Life is so much better on this side of the rope. Getting out of the ring was the kindest and most gentle gift I could give myself. I'm so glad to be out of the ring—it was dangerous and brutal in there.

# CHAPTER 20

# EMBRACE BEING FULL

————•————

*"The time will come*
*when, with elation*
*you will greet yourself arriving*
*at your own door, in your own mirror*
*and each will smile at the other's welcome,*

*and say, sit here. Eat.*
*You will love again the stranger who was your self.*
*Give wine. Give bread. Give back your heart*
*to itself, to the stranger who has loved you*

*all your life, whom you ignored*
*for another, who knows you by heart.*
*Take down the love letters from the bookshelf,*

*the photographs, the desperate notes,*
*peel your own image from the mirror.*
*Sit. Feast on your life."*

DEREK WALCOTT

Can we learn to trust again? Can we trust God or the Universe or ourselves and begin to feel secure in the world? Considering that we're human, the idea that we have to be perfect—and our circumstances have to be perfect—in order for us to be full and satisfied is a setup for failure. I once interviewed Lee Woodruff for my radio show. She had an amazing story. Lee really seemed to have it all—a wonderful marriage, beautiful children, and her husband, Bob, had just been named co-anchor of the ABC evening news. Then a phone call in the night changed everything. On assignment to Iraq, Bob had been riding in a convoy that was attacked by an explosive device. He suffered a massive brain injury and for weeks was on the verge of death. His recovery was long and labored. Amazingly, Bob is back on the air at ABC and his recovery continues. But the life Lee had before the incident was gone.

The husband Lee had before the traumatic incident was vibrant, smart, warm, successful, and outgoing. After the trauma, surviving daily activities became a great achievement. While the manicured way they had previously lived had been cruelly taken from her, Lee came to know what really mattered in life. The incident taught her that when the floor of her life fell out and all felt dark and terrifying around her, God was present. He did not punish her when she asked, "Where the heck is this 'God' when we need Him?" Her faith was tested and her relationship with God deepened. She realized that even when they weren't on speaking terms, God was interested in listening to her silence.

The rich life she shared with Bob and her children—as well as the village that supported them during this horrific nightmare—became sweeter, in spite of its dents, scratches, and scars. I believe that Lee became more whole, as we are all invited to do through our brokenness. She told me that she learned many lessons, and one was that she must give up the idea that she—or her life—was supposed to be perfect. Her book, *Perfectly Imperfect: A Life in Progress*, captures that.

Perfection is elusive—actually, it's impossible. Striving for perfection is a waste of glorious living. Being full does not mean being perfect. It means embracing your hunger and the beating heart of your identity, flaws and all, and rejoicing in this tremendous gift of life.

## The Eight Qualities of a Full Life

As we partake of each day's feast, and fill our hunger, be sure to eat from these nourishing dishes.

### 1. Wakefulness

In early 2007, I was honored to be one of the guests invited to celebrate the opening of the Oprah Winfrey Leadership Academy for Girls in South Africa. As I watched the faces of the young girls who were embarking on this great moment in their lives, I was struck by the beauty of their awakening; they were like tiny, bright flowers beginning to blossom. Their excitement was infectious. They didn't want to miss a single moment, nor did anyone else there. A large photo of one of these bright faces greets me every day when I walk into my office. The sight never fails to lift my spirits.

Watching those beautiful girls, so full of hope, I was struck by how many of us live large portions of our days in some form of hibernation—not quite present to the moments that are passing us by. People often share with me their regret at having missed out on so many of the simple, routine pleasures of life. They had intended to wake up before it was too late, to make a change, to get up and get going, but somehow the opportunities just passed them by. Life moves quickly; there are not always second chances. If we get another chance, it behooves us to take it. That's what I'm doing now—taking advantage of my second chance to build a real life with a real self, honoring my hunger and humanity.

We need to check in and see if we're on automatic pilot as we go through our days. Are we so busy going through the motions of life that we no longer consider what might bring a smile to our face, passion to our unions, joy to our journey, or peace to a painful situation? Is our life like driving our car and realizing that we've arrived at our destination but can't remember the trip?

Are we the walking dead? Are we living but not really alive? Are we breathing but not using our breath to create a life that we want to live? If our answer to any of these questions is "yes," then today we can begin to end this slow and inevitable death. Today you can choose life!

Many of us are so focused on looking good and measuring up that we rob ourselves of the precious gift of life that was given to us. But it's never too late to start living.

As we begin to see ourselves, accept ourselves, forgive ourselves, celebrate ourselves, embrace ourselves, understand ourselves, and smile at ourselves, the people who value us will begin to follow our lead. We have to be the ones to show them what it looks like to see us, treasure us, and hear us. While not everyone will be on board, we might be surprised at who will show up when *we* show up in our own life—making ourselves the priority that we want others to make us. We teach people how to treat us by how we treat ourselves; by what we accept from them. As we get comfortable with who looks back at us in the mirror, and never again look through ourselves as if we're invisible, our light will shine brightly.

## Questions to Ask:

- Was there a time I felt awakened?

- Did I see, think, or feel something new?

- What was it? Who helped me?

- Have I ever helped someone awaken to new information, ideas, and realizations? Who was it? Would I do it the same way again?

- Do I know anyone who refuses to awaken? Who is it? What is it like for me to be in a relationship with them? What does it cost me?

- If there was someone I could trust with my life that could safely and gently awaken a part of me that is still sleeping, what part would it be? What do I need to be reassured of before I can awaken?

## 2. COURAGE

Being courageous does not mean that you don't sometimes feel afraid. In fact, feeling afraid is a central part of taking care of ourselves. When I was three years old, I learned to swim—and I loved the water. The swimming teacher told my mother, "Robin is a natural, but you need to watch her carefully because she doesn't have a healthy sense of fear." Having a healthy sense of fear can help protect us from making destructive choices. Courage is different. Maybe we're quaking in our boots, maybe we're bathed in cold sweat, but we can still have courage. What gives us courage is not a lack of fear. What gives us courage is the choice to not let fear get in the way of honoring our genuine hunger. To not let fear keep us from reaching for more of what enriches and empowers our lives. Befriending our fear and getting to know it can be helpful.

## Questions to Ask:

- Where is fear hiding in my life?
- Who are the people that make me feel afraid?
- Can I remember a time when I transcended my fear and acted courageously in a situation? How did it feel?

- Are there people around me who are living in fear?
  What do I notice about them?

### 3. HOPE

Hope is a warming concept. We often say it to each other: "I hope you're feeling better." "I hope you win." "I hope you get what you want." If it weren't for hope, the wind would go out of our sails. The shine would leave our eyes. Hope is not an empty idea; nor is it a wish that things will change. Hope is action. There is a popular myth right now that if you wish for something enough, the Universe will give it to you. But the Universe has requirements. It asks you to act like a person who hopes. Having hope without determination and hard work often leads to just the opposite.

Mark Twain spoke of the doom of a hope tree that had lost the ability to sprout blossoms. Those blossoms are the fruit of nurturing. To keep hope, you must nurture the tree.

## Questions to Ask:

- What three hopes are closest to my heart?
- What specific actions will nurture each of those hopes?
- Can I recall a time when I was feeling hopeless and took action to change my situation?
- What person or persons has inspired me to make my hopes come true by modeling effective action?

### 4. STILLNESS

As I shared earlier, my house was robbed. Among other things, the thief took my jewelry—including heirloom pieces with great sentimental value—and Kalle's precious cremation ashes. He stole what he wanted, including a pillowcase, leaving only an empty small blue velvet ring box and a footprint on my bed. It was a horrible violation, as anyone who has been robbed knows. Burglary quickly becomes about something more profound than the loss of stuff—even beloved possessions.

The trauma of the burglary, Kalle's death, and my car accident imposed a sort of forced silence that uncovered what I was truly hungry for. It quieted many of the storms that raged in my mind about people, places, and things. I gradually began to realize these issues were not the root problem. I had finally gotten to the heart of the matter. My mother needed open-heart surgery twice for an aortic valve replacement. I needed a different form of open-heart surgery—the emotional and spiritual kind. One that was equally necessary and dangerous, and without which I wouldn't be able to truly live. When I started taking my life—and all the suffering and deprivation—as seriously as I had wanted others to take theirs, my heart condition was addressed. As was much of my ache and misery.

I often go to the cemetery to plant flowers at my father's grave early Father's Day morning, when it's quiet and private. (What an interesting thought, to want privacy at the cemetery!) When Kalle was alive, I used to take her with me. She would hop out of the car, check out our surroundings, and then hop back into the air-conditioned vehicle as I did the hard labor and heavy lifting of planting. She was really all about eating and relaxing and supporting me with her love as I worked.

The silence at the cemetery is blissful, golden, and cherished. I often call my mother saying, "Mommy, I don't feel like Daddy is here, he's free, but this is a space and place that holds one of the many markers of his rich life, legacy, and journey."

This past Father's Day, however, I decided to do my planting on another day. I felt drawn to attend a Quaker Meeting at my old school. It's not far from where I live, and I just felt like I needed the structured arena of collective stillness and silence. My mind needed it, my heart needed it, my relationship needed it, and even my body needed it. As I entered the space where I had spent much time growing up, I felt the comfort of the familiar. As a student I was required to attend Meeting weekly. For many of us when we were young, being still and silent for a full class period felt like too much to ask. But the older I got, the more I hungered for a period of stillness, silence, and reflection. While I'm not a Quaker, Meeting continues to be a place to lay my burdens down and have my heart held.

I seldom go to Meeting—I attend a Baptist church—but that Sunday morning I was full of anxiety, terror, aloneness, and fear. I was starving to death—dying to be me and hungry to be free. This most recent Father's Day, as I sat in the Meeting, I became aware that I am *still* hungry. I'm hungry because I'm *human*. No longer feeling anxious, something inside of me felt still. Over the last several years I've chucked the emotional junk food. Now I settle for nothing less than that which is worthy and deserving of me.

As I sat in stillness that morning, the familiar walls and cushions, the comforting smell of old wood, all the old memories, old isolations, old joys, and old comforts—everything was newly mine. All of it new, in this grand moment of stillness and warm silence. I sat there, breathing, and said to myself, "It's good to be home."

## Questions to Ask:

- Do I even know how to be still?
- Am I afraid to be still?
- Is stillness a value I want to embrace and encourage in my family and children?

## 5. RESILIENCE

The first time I watched Spike Lee's devastating documentary about Hurricane Katrina, *When the Levees Broke*, I found it so raw and heartbreaking that I wanted to turn away from the stark images of pain and devastation. My reaction mirrors the way many people feel when they encounter suffering. How many times have the levees broken in our own lives, and we've run away? Resilience will help us to face the raw moments in our lives, and provide us with the ability to pay attention to the things that require resources and effort to fix. Resilience gives us the means to pull ourselves back up when we've been knocked down; to repair as much of the damage as we can, and try to move on.

Once, when I was outlining all of my challenges to a friend, she said cheerfully, "Oh, Robin, don't worry. You always bounce back." I smiled, thinking that this was true of most of the women I know. We're like rubber bands. We stretch ourselves around most obstacles and situations, and then rediscover our shape with added strength. At least, most of the time. I have found that rebounding from hurt, shock, misfortune, and unfairness actually builds resilience muscles, although it often feels like it's going to kill us. Resilience is not just about recovering from hardship. It's about jumping wholeheartedly into life with all our passion, power, and vitality. Resilience is saying, "I survived" and "I'm determined to try and thrive."

## Questions to Ask:

- Where have I observed examples of resilience in my own life?

- Who are the models I use for resilience?

- Can I name a time when I experienced failure and bounced back?

## 6. TRUST

If we've lived in the shadows, if we've worn a mask, it's hard to know how to start trusting ourselves or others. Trust is not about someone else. Trust emanates from within. Trust is built, trust is earned, and trust is a sacred gift. When trust has been broken and violated in a relationship, we need to understand what real issues led to the trust being broken. If we don't get to the root cause as to why something happened, it is likely to happen again and again, only making us more fearful and distrusting. To rebuild trust, we must have honesty—truthful conversations about the real issues. Sometimes we avoid the very conversations we need to have to get to the bottom line and see if a relationship is worth saving and is worthy of our heart, time, effort, body, and soul.

We will need to trust ourselves to listen for the whole truth and nothing but the truth within our own heart and soul. As we trust ourselves more fully and freely, we will begin to know who is a keeper and who no longer gets to travel with us on this journey of life.

I witnessed a moving example of trust several years ago, following the collapse of the bridge in Minneapolis. As death is perhaps the greatest human fear, the specter of a loved one dying in a violent situation is unspeakably horrifying. Shortly after the collapse, while they were still searching for the living and the dead, a man was interviewed by a television station while he was looking for his wife. His face was sunken with grief and fear, and he told the reporter that he still had hope that his wife would be found alive. And then he added, "But either way she's okay, because God is with her." I was tremendously moved by this man's heartfelt expression of trust that his wife would be okay, either way. It was humbling to watch his enormous grief and a faith that was equally as big. I sensed that he, too, would be *okay*.

## Questions to Ask:

- What are the wounds that have made me say, "I'll never trust again"?
- Do I trust myself?
- Can I trust my feelings and instincts?

- Am I trustworthy?

- Do I trust my higher power?

- Have I felt like God abandoned me, let me down, or didn't protect me?

## 7. SPIRIT

Stevie Wonder is a part of my extended family. He's been in my life all of my life. Way back when, he was little Stevie Wonder and I was just a baby. Now we are both "grown folk"! Wow, how time flies when you're living life. Stevie has taught me a lot about living in abundance. He is blind, but can clearly *see*. There is a brilliant light that beams from deep within him, and has always shone brightly. Stevie has never considered himself to be handicapped. This gifted genius has lived his life to the fullest. When he sings *"You are the sunshine of my life . . ."* you sense that he has lived every word of his music and lyrics. Stevie Wonder has created sunshine for millions of people worldwide, with his incredible talents, his powerful presence, and his commitment to love and justice.

You may say, "Yes, but he's *Stevie Wonder!*" That's true, but remember, Stevie wasn't always the great success he is today. There was a time when he was little Stevland Morris. He *became* Stevie Wonder because he had spirit and embraced the abundance in his life.

As we look at our own circumstances, we may see things that are missing. Rather than letting those elements drain our energy and consume us, it's important to understand that our spirit is alive.

A young woman I know has been diagnosed with a serious form of cancer. The odds are against her. She said to me, "It's like I am a different person." I have been inspired by her refusal to give up, her optimism in the face of continued bad news, her ability to keep striving, even in the darkest times. That is the quality that we call spirit—the indomitable force of our own beings. Spirit allows us to keep putting one foot in front of the other even when it doesn't seem possible to move forward. Spirit allows us to face despair in times of loss, sickness, or failure. Spirit is a powerful force, making it hard for it to be diluted, dissipated, or vanquished.

## Questions to Ask:

- What makes me feel connected to Spirit?
- What gives me access to Spirit?
- What blocks my access to Spirit?

## 8. WISDOM

Wisdom is derived in many ways. It can come from older generations, younger generations, or even our peers. Wisdom can come from cultivating our spiritual life and practice; from truly being attuned to God, the Universe, and Truth. Of course nature, in all of its beauty, splendor, power, and mystery, is a primary holder of wisdom. Yet we can glean wisdom from something we've read or heard on the radio. I often pick up a piece or two of wisdom when I'm at the grocery store! I stumble upon a stranger who seems to understand the exact lesson I'm in need of in that moment. Recently I saw a father whose son had spilled grape juice all over his nice white sweat suit. Instead of screaming and chastising his child for the mess, he just swooped his son up and said, "Oops, Daddy's boy just got juice everywhere. It's okay, we'll clean it up together and then go get your animal crackers." What he was really saying was, "Don't sweat the small stuff." It was a lesson I needed that day.

Wisdom is a deep knowing—not of data and information, but of what the soul delights and sorrows in. Wisdom has its finger on the beating pulse of life. It is the inner voice from which all truth emanates. Joys, sorrows, and every experience we encounter has hidden within some budding piece of wisdom. I recently came across an old picture of myself. I began reminiscing about what had been going on at that point in my life. When I compared the old picture with one taken more recently, I realized how much the two pictures told me about myself. It was like looking through a window into my journey through the years.

In the first picture, I saw a young woman struggling with grief after her father's death. She looked lost and fragile, diminished. The second, more recent picture showed a mature woman, 15 years later, successful and thriving. How did I get from there to here? I remember the journey well. I got here by stumbling and standing back up. I fell down again, and once more, I pulled myself back up. I made some really great decisions, and I made some poor ones. Each time I fell down, I eventually picked myself back up.

These pictures help me remember that a journey may be slow and painful, but growth is always possible. Wisdom teaches us that everyone stumbles—that's part of the human condition—but with time and patience, we can gain the wisdom to heal ourselves and grow wiser.

## Questions to Ask:

- What is wisdom to me?
- How does wisdom show up as I integrate many pieces of my life?
- What has wisdom taught me?

### REJOICE AND BE FULL!

Feeding our hunger is a personal journey. It is specific to each life and soul. What feeds, fills, and satisfies one person will leave the next dying of emotional starvation. After many years of going hungry, I've finally discovered my own formula. I offer it here, in hopes it might help you, too.

1. Acknowledging with honesty
2. Owning with compassion
3. Nurturing with patience
4. Feeding with living and giving substances

Remember, this is my individualized assessment and plan. Becoming full is not a clinical journey. It's a personal look at, and awareness of, what each of us needs and longs for. What will authentically fill our soul and spirit. There is no "one-stop shopping" that will quench our hunger. Fullness is a journey, lifelong, that changes and reshapes itself as we live, change, and grow.

Now that I am full, I can live with being unimportant, marginally important, or seasonally important to most people. And I can celebrate being genuinely important to a few treasured souls. I am no longer owned by my childhood cravings to be chosen, remembered, or valued. My hunger is not running the show or directing my life. It will always be with me, just as sacred memories are, and I know that there will be events in life that will fill my pot with the muddy stuff that doesn't nourish. However, when those times come, I will just take the spoon out, strain the contents in the pot, keep the vital nutrients, and throw the rest down the drain.

I can make healthier relationship choices now because my hunger is no longer the driving force of my life. I can sit at the table, partake of the feast, and joyfully consume all life has to offer. I can wear my own smile, rejoice in my flaws, and even have a sense of humor about my struggles. I can speak with my own voice, ask for more when I want it, and not be ashamed.

I am free. I am full.

# CHAPTER 21

# JUST B STILL

*"Be still and know that I am God."*

PSALM 46:10

As I mentioned earlier, it was after my house was robbed that I found myself in my closet looking in a small white shopping bag that had been sitting untouched for two years. In this bag was a gift I'd been given after giving a keynote for VIP guests at a casino. I had looked at the gift briefly at the time, but hadn't opened the bag since.

For reasons I cannot know, that day I lifted the crystal bracelet out of its soft white linen pouch and put it on. I wore it regularly from that time forward. People admired it everywhere I went— and they still do. At the supermarket, the cleaners, church, a party, a keynote speech—people often comment on my crystal bracelet with its red heart in the center. As people admire it, they have no clue that they are looking at one of the major instructions that I received to address my hunger and give me my life back.

About three months after I started wearing the bracelet, I had a doctor's appointment related to my car accident. I was in terrible pain. As I was signing in, the receptionist noticed my bracelet and said, "Your bracelet is beautiful." I thanked her and she asked if she could see it a little closer. She was looking at it like a gemologist would study a precious stone. I was in so much pain that I wasn't really focused on her. She started moving the bracelet and began what seemed like she was reciting letters from the alphabet.

She said "J," then she followed with "U," as she moved the bracelet a bit to her left to call her next letter, I heard "S." As she read the confusion on my face, she said, "Dr. Smith, you didn't know that your bracelet had letters on it?" In shock and surprise, I replied, "No, I had no idea." By this point, I was wondering what kind of divine "setup" this was. What message in a bottle had I been walking around with on my arm—and living within my closet for two years—that God allowed to marinate and simmer until the time was *right*? Until my heart could fully receive the message? I was in total disbelief.

Now that she knew that I was on board, she started from the beginning so we could play this out as a team. She called out the letters "J-U-S-T-B-S-T." By this time, I was more than curious, I was anxious to know what it said. She finished the last three letters, which were "I-L-L." I had forgotten where I was. Was I in the doctor's office? Maybe I was in Hollywood as a contestant on *Wheel of Fortune,* trying to solve the puzzle, playing for the big bucks.

"JUST B STILL." Could it be that my hunger pains and needs were being addressed at the orthopedic surgeon's office? Could it be that I needed spiritual open-heart surgery—and it was taking place right then and there with no anesthesia? I almost passed out from the power and love of this moment.

It blew my mind, blew my cover, and blew my heart wide open. My eyes filled with buckets of tears as I heard the words and repeated them aloud . . . JUST B STILL. There was no "E" in the B, which somehow seemed to make it even more powerful.

Honestly, there had been many signs that sent me this exact message, but I think God knew it had to be broken down to what a preschooler could comprehend. "Robin, you want to know what to do? JUST B STILL." It was as if God were saying, "Sit your butt down and do the practice and action of STILLNESS." It took me time to learn what this meant for my everyday life, but I knew it was exactly what I needed to go the distance. The receptionist had no idea why I was crying. I told her that although I'd *thought* my reason for coming in that cold November day was to see the doctor, clearly I had been sent there to get my instructions for life. I think she might have thought I was a little kooky, but I didn't mind.

This all happened at a time when confusion and despair were running rampant in my life and mind, and I didn't have a clue what to do. I did see the doctor that day, and he was helpful—but nothing like the help I received from what I was wearing on my wrist.

When I got outside, I wept—feeling relieved that, even though I felt abandoned, God was there loving me and waiting for me to slow down and JUST B STILL.

This experience taught me that we all walk around with messages coming at us, talking to us, walking with us, singing to us, nudging us and, at times, yelling to get our attention. But we often can't, don't, or won't see the message, hear the word, receive the voice. It is at those times we need someone to point out that our instructions and next steps are ever present, always around us, and available at all times. I continue to learn that listening and leaning into clues and cues, subtle and blatant, will point me in the direction of my truest self and path . . . the only real direction there is. Our soul will always point us away from a fake, airbrushed, and photoshopped life and toward the only life we can live wholeheartedly: our own.

I wear the bracelet every day, whether it matches or not, whether I'm in jeans and a T-shirt or an elegant gown. I cherish the life-saving and simple reminder—the reminder that became a huge part of giving me a life that was worth saving: "JUST B STILL."

## Forbidden Drive

Jogging or walking on Forbidden Drive in the Wissahickon woods in Philadelphia is one of my favorite things to do. At times it has been emotionally painful—such as during my "walk for the cure"—and sadly it remains physically grueling due to my accident. Yet I do it anyway, because it is one of my favorite places to be.

I never know what or who I am going to stumble on during the walk. It might be horse manure, dog poop, the warm and welcoming smile of a stranger, dogs running with their owners on the trail, birds flying high and low throughout the thick wooded oasis, or a quick and unexpected glance from an old love. I celebrate that no matter who or what I see on the path, I am no longer on Forbidden Drive in search of *me*. There are no more ghosts or goblins waiting around the bend to jump out and scare me or to say, "I knew you when." It doesn't matter if the weather is cold—which is still far from my preference—or sunny and warm, which I adore. The frostbite I suffered from my own search-and-rescue effort, as I searched high and looked low for my voice and truest self, is over. I run with *me*, I jog with *me*, I walk with *me*, I hike with *me*, I limp with *me*. Mission accomplished!

I'm so grateful that I took the "road less traveled." It's where I found myself and my real, raw, and authentic voice. My long journey *home* back to myself on Forbidden Drive taught me that all things "forbidden" aren't bad (for me).

# CHAPTER 22

# A Child Shall Lead Them

*"It's easier to build strong children than to repair broken men."*
FREDERICK DOUGLASS

Zion was bright in every way. The room lit up when she walked in; she had a strength and tenderness that just made people love her. Like a lioness and a lamb, Zion was both strong and gentle, innocent and wise beyond her years. She was a warrior for all causes that are good for the earth and creation.

We didn't get to spend much time together because her schedule was busy as was mine, but when we did hang out, we always talked about the real stuff of life. Zion was wise and yet still very untouched by some of the harshness of life. Yes, she had suffered and struggled to live life on her own terms, but even at a young age, there was a fierceness about how she lived her life. It was important not to take her sweetness for weakness; she was anything but weak when the chips were down.

Zion was really excited about a new academic opportunity. It was a dream come true, something she had worked hard for during her years in high school. And now, when the opportunity presented itself at her doorstep, she was ready for this challenge. We talked about all of her excitement and her nervousness about being 3,000 miles away from her loving home. In the big picture, Zion was ready for this next phase and challenge in her life: Her bags were packed and her heart was pointed toward the sun. She was oh-so-ready for the warmth of a new climate, as well as an adventure into a world that was rich with promise, excellence, and more access to all of the things she loved most. So all of us were surprised when that dream turned into a painful and disappointing nightmare—and the magic carpet she seemed to be riding lost its power.

When Zion looked up, all of her hopes were shattering right before her. Her eyes, once alive with promise, had begun to lose their vibrancy. When she took that long flight across country to begin living her dreams, she could never have imagined that the floodgates of disappointment would overtake her college life and make her doubt everything that had felt so certain only months before. At first it didn't make sense to anyone that things could have gone so wrong; the match had seemed destined to work. But everyone was wrong except Zion. She trusted her inner voice. Even though everyone at school loved her, she felt like a perfect misfit. She had all the same "branding" that her classmates had—she was warm and well liked—but the shoe just didn't fit.

Being from a vibrant thriving city in the South, she assumed she would just organically fit in her new metropolitan home. The truth was very different. In a politically correct way, kids and even a few teachers made fun of her Southern drawl. Others saw her values as unsophisticated and her morals as too conservative. She was crushed. She naturally doubted herself—and the clarity that had been unshakeable only months before.

We've been special to each other for many years, since she was a little girl. We trust each other to say and tell the truth. During this tumultuous season in her life, Zion called and filled me in on what was going on. I listened as she painted a picture that left nothing to my imagination. Zion has a way with words. Both her writing and speaking make it almost impossible to miss her point even if you want to. Maybe the problem, she said, was that she should try harder to make things work at her oasis—the oasis which now felt like a tomb where she was buried alive. I was quiet, just breathing with my young friend; feeling her pain and remembering my own at her age. My pain looked different, but it was from the same pot of *knowing what I didn't want to know*. My words and question to Zion were simple as they flowed from my mouth.

"Zion, you have tried," I said. "You have given this three-thousand-mile pilgrimage your absolute best. You have poured all of you and then some into this adventure. What more do you feel you need to do in order to trust yourself? To trust your pain and your inner voice? To know that it's just not working for you?" I could hear her crying on the other end of the line. Her tears were so telling—so full of truth, questions, fear, pain, and courage.

I was humbled. It was a privilege to witness Zion's gut-wrenching pain. I believed that something life-changing was being birthed for this teenage "girl wonder," although she felt like anything but a caped superhero. Zion was in the throes of labor and the baby she was carrying was her own authentic and sacred voice. All the trappings of her current environment—which from the outside looked picture perfect—were suffocating her life force. She didn't want to die, she wanted to live! And unlike most of us, she wanted to live *her* life, not someone else's. Zion struggled as we all do, wondering whether it was her . . . whether she'd done something wrong . . . whether she could have tried harder and longer and had it all work out. It's what we all do when we run from the ache of knowing and feeling what and who fits and who and what doesn't. It's scary when life isn't what we planned for, saved for, or anticipated; when life is simply what it *is*. Zion had the help of a loving and understanding family. Her closest friends supported her doing whatever she needed to do to follow her truth; to feed the hunger pains that wouldn't let her settle for living a life that was not her own. People who "got" her knew that if this happy-go-lucky person had lost her skip and joy that something wasn't wrong with her, something was wrong *for* her—in the environment she was trying to force herself to peacefully live in.

I remembered all the times in my own life when I *knew* something that I forced myself to *not* know. I did it to tolerate relationships and situations that were intolerable; unfit for my growth and habitation. I shared with Zion that unfortunately—and fortunately—at this young and tender age, she was being presented an opportunity to honor her truth. The other option was to ignore, dismiss, betray, and deny herself.

"Yes, Zion, it sucks to be scared," I said. "I hate being scared. And it sucks to listen to your suffering. Now, if you were to choose otherwise—to jump ship on yourself and stay in a situation that isn't making you happy—I would understand. So would any awake and honest person. More people than not abandon themselves at this very point out of fear; jumping ship midstream and leaving the boat of their lives drifting in the middle of the ocean unattended and forgotten. But you have an unusual opportunity. You don't have to wait until you're in your 20s, 30s, or—like me—your 40s to pay close attention to your own longing, hunger, and cravings. You don't have to live like most women and be voiceless; you can stake a claim for your real voice, your real life, and your real smile *now*. You can avoid the trap of telling yourself, '*One day when I am older, I will do what I really want to do. I will have time later in life to listen to my heart and my heartache. Right now, this isn't so bad, I'm sure I will be fine.*'"

There is a story that I am often reminded of when someone I know is suffering—grappling with the unpredictable certainty that comes with most pain. A big dog, Hank, lay on the porch of a small-town general store, growling as people walked in and out. Hank's owner was an older man named Bill, who had previously owned the store. Now his daughter and son-in-law ran it, and Bill spent his days rocking in his chair on the porch, warmly greeting customers.

One day a regular at this quaint general store stopped and asked, "Mr. Bill, why does Hank always growl? Hank seems as angry as you are nice." Bill smiled and beckoned Hank to get up. Hank pulled his big body from the porch slowly and walked over to Bill to receive a treat. When he did, Bill pointed to where he'd been lying down. Shocked, the customer saw there was a nail sticking out of the porch where Hank had been lying. Once the dog received his treat and drank water, he returned to that exact spot.

"Why would Hank go back and lay on the nail?" the customer asked.

Bill replied, "Because it just don't hurt that bad."

Many of us live just like Hank, volunteering to lie down on a "nail" in our lives because we have been told, "It just don't hurt that bad." Zion had a chance early in life to pay attention to her "nail" and to ask for something better. To reject the idea that it would be okay; that it's not so bad to suffer.

With great courage, Zion did what she had to do. She stayed with herself despite the fear and inner turmoil. She didn't abandon herself or the ship of her life; she didn't cry "woman overboard." What she did was harness the wisdom and power of her inner voice. At first it felt faint and weak, but over time, her true voice grew stronger.

As the years have been ushered in and out, as wars have raged within the self and soul—as well as between political parties and nations—I think about Zion's courage. Without knowing it, she made me hunger even more deeply to live my own life, full time. Through her example, I recommitted myself to never allowing anything or anyone to silence the truth of my voice—myself most of all. Zion's journey was a powerful and painful reminder of how identity theft begins in the cradle and haunts us to the grave. It reminded me of the plea made in Elie Wiesel's book *The Town Beyond the Wall*, "God of my childhood, show me the way that leads to myself." This has become my own prayer.

The misleading messages begin early in life. Some children are given meaningful names, a parent's attempt to direct their child's steps from the very beginning. Others receive T-shirts from an Ivy League school, or that say NEXT PRESIDENT—early pressure to fulfill the dreams and unmet fantasies of parents, grandparents, or even a whole race of people. It's up to us to put the stake in the ground of our *own* being. To demand to live the life that we were born to live. Otherwise, we will miss the blessing and benefits of the African tribal blessing that encourages children to *become who you are.*

## OK2BU

I had the great honor and privilege to speak with an amazing group of people at The Attic, a sacred refuge in Philadelphia for LGBTQ (Lesbian, Gay, Bisexual, Transgendered, and Questioning) youth. It was a treasured night that I will never forget. The room was packed with many young people and some adult staff members. They shared their stories of trial and triumph, pain and rejection, brilliance and resilience, faith and fear, heartache and heartbreak. These young people were surviving and thriving despite suffering great isolation, injustice, humiliation, judgment, demonization, prejudice, and marginalization. I was humbled to witness their courage and vulnerability, and to be accepted by them—a stranger in their midst. By the end of the night, I was renewed and reminded that we are all children of God and deserving of dignity.

At the end of the night I was given a gift bag with their striking motto, "OK2BU!" To me, that said it all. It is every human being's divine birthright and what we are all hungry for—to be ourselves.

# CHAPTER 23

# IT ONLY
# TAKES TWO

———————•———————

*"In your own Law it is written that the testimony of
two men is valid. I am one who testifies for myself;
my other witness is the Father who sent me."*

JOHN 8:17–18

There is a passage in the New Testament, John 8:12–30, where Jesus is questioned about his identity. I like to think of it as the self-esteem passage. When Jesus is questioned by the scholars and the who's who of the temple, he doesn't get into a debate about whether or not he is the son of God. In the face of their skepticism and insults, he merely states the facts: According to Jewish law, only two were needed to validate a person's identity. He was one witness, he said, and the Father was the other. With that, he validated himself. He knew who he was; his true identity.

What Jesus did is what we are all hungry for. He validated himself after accepting and trusting the validation of the

Creator. Nobody else. While we might want the whole world to affirm us, we only need God and ourselves. This is an amazing example of true and authentic fullness, of what it means to love the skin we're in, and to unapologetically recognize and attend to our hunger by reclaiming the power of an unconquered identity. Each of us have been challenged with being Hungry because life veered us away from who we were born to be, who we truly are, making it our lifelong task and holy mission to reclaim and hold on to our true identity. Therefore, let the winds of truth and courage sing a new song in your heart and soul as you make the inward journey in search of your authentic self. This is a trip that matters! You will find that the force within you is far greater than all the forces bombarding you from without. That which has tried to steal your fullness has been caught and rendered powerless.

A new invitation has been sent. No RSVP is required. You are simply invited to attend the glorious *HUNGRY* banquet where each place card reads ***Okay To Be You***—Welcome Home!

Remember this: *It only takes two.*

# BLESSING AND BENEDICTION

---

*"The Lord bless you*
*and keep you;*
*The Lord make his face shine on you*
*and be gracious to you;*
*The Lord turn his face toward you*
*and give you peace"*

NUMBERS 6:24–26

# ACKNOWLEDGMENTS

If I thought that writing this section for *Lies at the Altar* was humbling, I had no idea how much bigger and richer the pie of humility could become. I wrote this section last because I couldn't imagine how I would ever be able to thank all the hands and hearts, the minds and mouths, the prayers and chants, and the meals on wheels that miraculously showed up to make the writing and publishing of this book possible. There was an invisible roundtable of spirits, souls, and bodies that stood with, and, at times, for me in solidarity and support. There remained a great cloud of witnesses who reminded me that the sea was parted so that desperate people could cross safely to dry land, that when the odds were stacked against me God still had a plan for my life, "to prosper me and not harm me, to give me hope and a future." I learned that God's arithmetic is based on an eternal lesson plan revealing that one mistake or any other blunder doesn't stop His divine plan for the Universe; and for this I am eternally grateful! I know that I am blessed, because what could have been a final grade of "F" ended up being a glorious "A" when I changed lanes in the middle of my heavily trafficked life and removed the CD that had me playing the song "Part-Time Lover." When I showed up fully for active duty in my life, so did all of the players who were assigned to my *case*.

Kenneth L. Browning, Esq., my attorney, deal maker, rainmaker, and dear and trusted friend. *Hungry* found its literary home at Hay House because of you, and so did I. You believed in me from the beginning and during those days that turned into weeks, months, and years when there was a drought in my professional and personal life. With a solid and unwavering belief in my gifts and talents, you quietly and strategically kept my eyes on the prize. I will never be able to thank you for your unending guidance, seasoned expertise, and your special friendship.

To my new Hay House family, home really is where the heart is. When I was homeless, Reid Tracy, you spoke with me and after listening deeply to my words and my spirit, you told me that *Hungry* was a powerful idea for a book that "no one has written about or talked about in this way . . . " You *got* me and the soul of *Hungry* from the very beginning.

To Patty Gift, whose warmth and deep understanding of soulful work nurtured this book from conception to delivery. The skilled eyes and tender hearts of Sally Mason, Kelly Notaras, and Quressa Robinson allowed the editing of *Hungry* to feel seamless. You were so kind and gracious as the book shaped and reshaped itself and made room for me to organically fill in the blanks. Thank you to those at Hay House who honored, and were loyal to, the core essence of this book and its mission in the world. Christy Salinas, thank you for working with me on the photo shoot for the book cover. You were patient, allowing the process and all the players to take their place; thank you for trusting me.

Earl A. Clairmont, Jr., CPA, you have not only been my accountant for over a quarter of a century, you have been a wise advisor and a treasured friend. You have been with me through thick and thin, through lean and leaner, and through mean winter seasons in my life that refused to be chased away. Your words were always close: "Robin, finish writing *Hungry* and do what you are meant to do in the world. If you need to worry, I'll let you know when that time comes. For now, go and finish the book."

To Catherine Whitney, thank you for your contribution and expertise in helping me get this book off the ground, and for your understanding as my steps were ordered to take *Hungry* in the only direction it could go, real, raw, and resilient, making the journey from holes to wholeness.

My two fathers in ministry and my beloved mentors and friends, the Rev. Dr. J. Alfred Smith, Sr., and the Rev. Dr. Otis Moss, Jr. (and Sister Edwina Moss), without you I would not be living, breathing, growing, and thriving. You each have sowed life and unapologetic love into my heart and challenged my thoughts, mind, and ministry with a holy fire that burns eternal. Thank you for affirming my *call* long before I was ordained.

Reverend Ernest R. Flores and the Second Baptist Church of Germantown, my local church family, you are the home I needed in times of good and plenty, as well as when my life seemed to get stuck on drought alert. You loved me and prayed for me, you missed me when I was traveling and on the road working, and you remembered me when I was on bed rest from life beating me up and down. You honored me when my hands were open and full of generosity and when those same hands were empty, barren, and in need.

Christopher Canty, my hair stylist, hair doctor, the creator of all things exceptional regarding hair, and my beloved and trusted friend. We have traveled the country together. You have done my hair at big and small venues. You were with me when the sky was the limit and when the sky fell in on me. In my darkest hours, when all seemed lost, your steady spirit and voice reminded me of who I was, with or without *success,* or my long and glorious hair. The cover for this book says it all, you not only created the look for my fresh and healthy hair, but you helped pick out my clothing and supervised, along with Sandra, the shoot knowing what was at stake, the birth of my new life and the real me. No one can do my hair like you. My hair has never looked better or more alive. I love you and will be grateful to you for the rest of my life.

Stella Mikhail (Mommy to Erica and Faith), make-up artist extraordinaire. You have always been there for me with your warm and loving spirit, creating organic beauty where I look fresh, natural, fully alive, and real. No one can do my make-up and get the amazing and spectacular results you achieve. You, Christopher, and I are the A-Team along with Kelly Hurliman, whom we missed at the *Hungry* photo shoot because she was on "baby watch" pushing out new life. Thank you for weighing in from behind the scenes. We have shared many magical and sacred moments together . . . and I trust the best is yet to come for us all!

Daniel DuVerney, a photographer for all seasons. Your highly trained eyes and warm and intuitive spirit captured my journey with *Hungry* and brought to life all the pieces found on the cover of this book. You captured a radiating light within for the world to experience and taste. Working with you was an amazing blessing.

Gudrun Frank, my web designer/engineer and consultant. Without you, the world would not know "I'm Back." Thank you for jumping into the deep end of my rebirth and working until the job was done—Bravo!

Mr. Vernon E. Jordan, Jr., a special friend who helped me in the challenging process of identifying and *changing lanes* as I learned to take my life, my heart, my dreams, my gifts, my time, and myself seriously. You will never know how much you've seeded into my authentic life. I am forever grateful.

Dr. John Vinciguerra, Kalle's amazing doctor who took care of her, Mommy, and me and literally journeyed with us through Kalle's life and "the valley of the shadow of death" when it was her time to transition. I carry you in my heart.

Dr. Lillian Aronson, Kalle's surgeon, the best in the world. Meeting you not only gave Kalle several extra years of a high quality life, but it gave me the gift of meeting an amazing woman, mother, surgeon, and human being with a heart bigger than those you save. Your humility was a gift as we literally watched you move from a high-level expert and surgeon to a humble, gracious, and willing "servant." You are an amazing example that people at the top of their game can still be kind, generous, and humble.

To Kudussan Haile who I adore and who Kalle trusted and treasured. You loved Kalle and me (and Mommy, too) with such pure loyalty and devotion, and you taught me life lessons that sing to me in the darkest and brightest moments of my journey. I hear you in my spirit and heart saying, "Dr. Smith, step-by-step . . . everything will all be fine . . . just go step-by-step . . ." Thank you, Kudussan, I love you!

Jennifer Lavelle, you know that Kalle, Mommy, and I simply could not have made it without you. You are not only the best groomer, but when we needed you to be much more, to walk with us through Kalle's delicate life and impending death, you were there, loving, steady, and a gentle rock that we could lean on; and for the rest of my life I will be grateful to you with a heart full of love.

Debbie G. Levin and Kelli Domizio, who believed in me during financially difficult and challenging times and offered me the support I needed as I was rebuilding my life. My heart and life are grateful to both of you.

David L. Hyman, Esq., a friend who in the 11th hour came through for me and helped me with a *stay of execution*. You know and I know that without you, I was up the creek without a paddle.

To Mary Beth H. Gray, Esq., for reviewing contracts and offering your seasoned wisdom and expertise and whose gentle and expert counsel over the years has encouraged me when I was *Hungry* to live life in *my lane.*

To Joel D. Feldman, Esq., for caring about the tragic events of my life and doing all that was possible to help me in a terrible time of need.

Colby Tyner, thank you for honoring my gifts and your long-held desire to put me back on radio doing what I am here to do, helping people make meaning of their lives as they *keep it real*, learn to embrace self-compassion, and live fully their "one life to live."

To Sunny Shulkin, forever your wise words and teachings will be with me. Thank you for helping me find the stranger who was my *Self* and for making room in the early days for me to ponder what it meant for me to be *Hungry*.

Dr. Howard C. Stevenson, Jr., my brother in the struggle and friend who always affirmed my voice. I honor our special connection and the magic we make in the classroom.

I offer my sincerest gratitude to all of you whom I have met on my journey that have impacted my life through conversations, well wishes, prayers, or encouraging greetings—whether in the supermarket, at church, walking through the community, at a speaking engagement, or through countless e-mails. You have no idea how much your love, encouragement, and support means to me. Thank you for asking, "Dr. Robin, when will your next book be out?" and for patiently waiting for its arrival.

I am grateful to my strong, healthy, solid, and vibrant family and friendship circles, my "village" that is there for me through all seasons. There are too many to list, but it is essential to call a few names. To Sandra and Thelma for facilitating, hosting, and being at "The Table" where God always met us and gave us life more abundantly. For the comfort found in honest connection, the revelation regarding our many questions, the aches and pains we held with and for each other, and the peace we found that passes all understanding. Selena, my *alma*, your soul has kept me company throughout many life seasons, you taught me that true love is never measured by distance or miles. And you, my sisters, Rosaria and Marilyn, and E. Lou (who has transitioned but still walks with me . . . and Simone who followed E. Lou and left too soon), I treasure your love and support. Faithful Aurelia and Arthur, who were there in the best and worst of times and held me when life collapsed right before my eyes, forever, we are connected. Dr. Pam, my sister of the heart and spirit, where safety, trust, and joy abide. And dear Philip, who brings beauty and elegance to homes, hearts, and lives, and whose wisdom and friendship are a treasured companion. Barbara (Barbs), a true friend whose soft tenderness has kept me company in some of the coldest hours of my life. And Viviane (Shorty), who welcomed and celebrated my "drumming to a different beat" and who has been dancing and singing with me since we were young children in Sunday school. To Tracey, my beloved and trusted friend, our daddies are watching over us. Melanie, you are not only a singer, songwriter, and musician, but you are a fellow artist who, even when giving up would have seemed much easier, your *call* and passion just wouldn't let you. Thank you for being an example of what it means to stay in the game of life and live your calling no matter the cost. Patrice and Gary, your love and commitment to each other is a humbling and sobering inspiration. Johnny, Scott, Mikki, and Sandy, thank you for being family of the sweetest kind. To Dudley, a friend who helped one very special dream come true, and Johnny who made everything bloom with simple elegance and color for Mommy, Kalle, and me—thank you. Steve, Mary, and Duncan, you are more than good neighbors, you are true friends. There are others who have been with me in the sandbox praying for me, playing with me, and holding me close . . . I carry you in my heart.

Charlene, Char, my own Lena Horne, what can I say for all the filming for TV and radio you've done for me so that others could embrace what you believed the world was *Hungry* for, what lived in me. Thank you for the editing, cutting, and pasting you offered that helped me with my thoughts, feelings, beliefs, and pain. Thank you for chanting when it seemed that your words were hitting the wall of my hard head and for laughing with me until we were both joyfully in tears. We are both so funny. I love you.

Eris (Kim Barnum), my faithful, personal, trusted, and brilliant assistant. We all know you are so much more. You are my wise big cousin. You are the keeper of my big dreams that only you fully see. You are the arc and the umbrella that protects me and my *calling* when the winds of adversity have dared to blow my house and life down. You were there from the beginning and without a doubt we will swim again together into the deep waters of liberation, abundance, and freedom. I honor and love you with my whole heart and I owe you big time!

Sandra E. Scott-Waller (aka, Lizzy), in the 11th and a half hour, when I was in the longest labor, but not yet ready to deliver, you single-handedly provided the physical and emotional refuge and sanctuary for this book and even bigger, for my real self to be birthed. You were the doctor, nurse, midwife, and coach for this book and for my new and real life. Seven-twenty-eight is where so much of the magic, mystery, miracle, and ministry unfolded line by line, precept upon precept. Without you, not only would this book not be the rich, healthy, living organism that it is, but I would not be alive and thriving. I owe you more than I can ever repay you.

To Grandmommy, Addie Belle Spencer (my maternal grandmother), you hung out here on the planet until you were 107½ years old, and almost all of those years with excellent physical and mental health. In the end, when those areas of health were failing, your spiritual health remained resilient, was intact, and was clearly the unshakable foundation of your life and that of our family. To Granddaddy, Samuel Spencer, and my paternal grandparents, Alfred and Irene Smith, all who died many years ago, but left a legacy of excellence, a value for education and hard work, a love for family, and a deep appreciation for the importance of having a personal relationship with The Loving God of the Universe. And to my ancestors, those who were born free and those who were kidnapped, made to live as slaves, and suffer, but whose spirits could not be captured, owned, or slaughtered. I know that I stand not only on your shoulders, but on the holy ground of your shed blood and indomitable spirits. I will not let you down!

Mommy and Daddy, Rosa Lee Smith and Warren E. Smith, M.D. Daddy, you stayed around lovingly instilling in me, by your compassionate and dignified example, all the greatness that was possible for my life until you knew I could run my own leg of the race. Mommy, at 90, you really came through for me big time when I needed you most. To be both my Mommy and the wise *Good Mother* in my 40s, in my season of deep crisis. You helped me to find my way *out*, into the marvelous light of self-love, dignity, and respect—with my whole heart and being. I Thank You and Love You More! I am so grateful that we figured out our love and connection in a way that is rich, real, and vibrant for both of us.

Damian and Joy, my big brother and sister, who love, care for, support, and believe in me when the chips are up, down, or gone, and who always have my back . . . I love you beyond measure and you both have taught me so many life-affirming lessons. To my nieces, nephews, and great-nieces, you are my reasons to want to do all things well. I know you are all watching Auntie Robin. And to my extended family, my aunts (especially Aunt Essie and Aunt Gisela), uncles, cousins, and relatives who have my *back* and are cheering me on as I run, walk, and at times, limp through this leg of my race—with all my heart, thank you.

The Deer—two big bucks, who lived on my land for two months making my manicured gardens an unrecognizable, barren beauty as you guarded, guided, and taught me life lessons about peace, gentleness, grace, partnership, trust, ease, simplicity, and clarity. Thank you for giving up your summer roaming in the wondrous wild to *move in* with me until your tutoring assignment was complete.

Kalle, my daughter-dog, you blessed and changed my life. Our love set the bar back where it belonged. Thank you for passing my way and for staying longer than maybe you had planned until you were sure that I had really gotten the message that "Love doesn't hurt!" I got it, promise. I miss you like crazy but can live more fully and freely because of the healing that took place in your heart and mine. Mommy loves you forever and always!

And, yes, I saved the very best for last—God! You are *everything* to me! Yes, You are, and always have been. You are the Lifter of my head, the Lover of my soul, my Rock and Refuge, my Light and my Salvation, my Warmth when it's cold and a Breeze when it's hot. You are my Provider, Protector, and Comforter. You are my example of all things loving, alive, peaceful, dignified, brave, truthful, and free. Thank you for reminding me that "Thy gentleness has made me great" and that You are pleased that I heard and said "Yes" to Your call to share this book with a *Hungry* and hurting world. Being your mouthpiece is my highest privilege and honor. I Love You and I know that You love me more . . . *and that You loved me first!*

# ABOUT THE AUTHOR

Dr. Robin L. Smith is a national television personality, best-selling author, ordained minister, keynote speaker, and licensed psychologist. Dr. Smith's relationship book, *Lies at the Altar*, published in 14 different languages, has been a #1 national bestseller on the lists of the *New York Times, Wall Street Journal, USA Today, Publisher's Weekly, Entertainment Weekly,* and many other publications. Dr. Smith's first book, *Inspirational Vitamins,* has been received with great enthusiasm and acclaim. Her media appearances include *The Oprah Winfrey Show, Anderson Live, Larry King Live,* the *Today* show, *Good Morning America, The Early Show,* MSNBC, the Fox News Channel, and many other news and talk-show formats, including her own five-day-a-week call-in Dr. Robin Show on XM Radio. She can be heard on the *Tom Joyner Morning Show* and *The Michael Baisden Show,* sharing pearls of inspiration, empowerment, and wisdom. In addition to Dr. Robin's busy media and speaking schedule, she develops seminars and workshops for corporations and organizations nationwide. Dr. Smith earned her Ph.D. in counseling psychology from Temple University and a master's degree from Eastern Baptist Theological Seminary.

Website: http://www.drrobinsmith.com/

We hope you enjoyed this Hay House book. If you'd like
to receive our online catalog featuring additional information
on Hay House books and products, or if you'd like to find
out more about the Hay Foundation, please contact:

Hay House, Inc., P.O. Box 5100, Carlsbad, CA 92018-5100
(760) 431-7695 or (800) 654-5126
(760) 431-6948 (fax) or (800) 650-5115 (fax)
**www.hayhouse.com®** • **www.hayfoundation.org**

■ ■

*Published and distributed in Australia by:* Hay House Australia Pty. Ltd.,
18/36 Ralph St., Alexandria NSW 2015 • *Phone:* 612-9669-4299
*Fax:* 612-9669-4144 • www.hayhouse.com.au

*Published and distributed in the United Kingdom by:* Hay House UK, Ltd.,
Astley House, 33 Notting Hill Gate, London W11 3JQ
*Phone:* 44-20-3675-2450 • *Fax:* 44-20-3675-2451 • www.hayhouse.co.uk

*Published and distributed in the Republic of South Africa by:*
Hay House SA (Pty), Ltd., P.O. Box 990, Witkoppen 2068
*Phone/Fax:* 27-11-467-8904 • www.hayhouse.co.za

*Published in India by:* Hay House Publishers India, Muskaan Complex,
Plot No. 3, B-2, Vasant Kunj, New Delhi 110 070 • *Phone:* 91-11-4176-1620
*Fax:* 91-11-4176-1630 • www.hayhouse.co.in

*Distributed in Canada by:* Raincoast, 9050 Shaughnessy St.,
Vancouver, B.C. V6P 6E5 • *Phone:* (604) 323-7100 • *Fax:* (604) 323-2600
www.raincoast.com

■ ■

## Take Your Soul on a Vacation

Visit **www.HealYourLife.com®** to regroup, recharge,
and reconnect with your own magnificence.
Featuring blogs, mind-body-spirit news, and life-changing
wisdom from Louise Hay and friends.

Visit **www.HealYourLife.com** today!

# Free e-newsletters
# from Hay House, the Ultimate
# Resource for Inspiration

**Be the first to know about Hay House's dollar deals, free downloads, special offers, affirmation cards, giveaways, contests, and more!**

 Get exclusive excerpts from our latest releases and videos from *Hay House Present Moments*.

 Enjoy uplifting personal stories, how-to articles, and healing advice, along with videos and empowering quotes, within *Heal Your Life*.

 Have an inspirational story to tell and a passion for writing? Sharpen your writing skills with insider tips from *Your Writing Life*.

## Sign Up Now!

*Get inspired, educate yourself, get a complimentary gift, and share the wisdom!*

http://www.hayhouse.com/newsletters.php

**Visit www.hayhouse.com to sign up today!**

 HAY HOUSE

HAYHOUSE RADIO
*radio for your soul*

HealYourLife.com